WHEN *Life* CRIED OUT

*One Woman's Spiritual Quest
to Be Fully Alive*

Paddy Fievet, Ph.D.

When Life Cried Out: One Woman's Spiritual Quest to Be Fully Alive

Published by Cloverhurst Publications
PO Box 5546, High Point, NC, 27262

Publisher's Cataloging-in-Publication
(Provided by Quality Books, Inc.)
 Fievet, Paddy.
  When life cried out : one woman's spiritual quest to
 be fully alive / by Paddy Fievet, PhD.
  pages cm
  LCCN 2014951162
  ISBN 978-0-9906706-0-5 (paperback)
  ISBN 978-0-9906706-2-9 (ebook)

  1. Fievet, Paddy. 2. Mystics--United States--
 Biography. 3. Mysticism. 4. Spiritual biography.
 I. Title.

 BL625.F5389 2014   204'.092
        QBI14-1867

Printed in the United States of America

ISBN: 978-0-9906706-0-5 (paperback)
ISBN: 978-0-9906706-3-6 (e-book)

Contents

A Note from
the Author

WHEN I FIRST began to write about the profound seven-year span of change in my life, I had no idea it would become a memoir. At first, what I truly wanted to accomplish with my writing was more along the lines of forgetting the troublesome times I'd had just before and after my divorce. By not exploring my own problems, I fully intended to mask those times by focusing on my current relationship. Instead of writing about the reflective spiritual lessons found in my travels, I wanted to recreate myself as a brave adventurer. Most of all, I wanted the embarrassment I felt during the panic attacks, the agoraphobic moments, and the profound loss of self to simply disappear between the lines of my writing as I hoped to recreate my history. That first draft had nothing to do with authenticity, healing, or even self-discovery. I wrote a fairy tale.

After I keyed in the last page, I put the manuscript aside for several months thinking I was finished. When I revisited it later, that driving spiritual force that guides me intuitively kicked me into realizing I truly needed to write about the perceptive trips to Egypt. I felt the need to revisit a mystical experience in Ireland on the pages of my memoir. The anger I experienced in Malta needed to be put into words on paper. I even had a dream one night that I opened a book with blank pages and "This should have been your sacred story" was written in the middle of one of the pages. At the time I had not completely realized the full impact of thinking of personal problems, as well as personal wisdom, as part of a sacred story. The chaos I had experienced seemed to have nothing to do with holiness, God, or sacred love, at least not until I had objectively processed my own awakening through pen and paper.

Even though I truly did not wish to write at any vulnerable, personal depths, an inner Muse just would not leave me alone. This annoying little Muse wished to express faithfully as me, to play on the pages authentically, and to understand herself and all her troubles as part of a sacred whole. The Muse danced through my sleep, she entered my thoughts randomly, and she showed up synchronistically in many articles, television programs, and conversations mentioning the importance of writing down the profound stories of life. After the Muse asserted herself into my life frequently in many different ways, I could do nothing else but write about the mystical experiences at a depth I was terrified of showing to the world.

For most of my life I had done everything I knew possible to act in ways unnatural to my authentically-created being because I felt it safer to do so. Instead of accepting my high levels of intuition, I wanted to hide them because they didn't match what others seemed to perceive. Instead of owning the panic attacks and seeking their cause, I wished to mask them into oblivion. In the place of a personal spirituality—the realization of an inner connection to God—I wanted to reinvent my experiences into a form acceptable to the established rules and directives of America's Southern Bible Belt in order to gain support from an exterior source instead of an intrinsic, interior state of being. It never occurred to me that the rich and orderly process of being so confused by my situation in life was included within an innate wholeness, part of a soul's journey. Evidently there was something else about my story I had not learned thus far needing to reveal itself through my writing.

As I rewrote the book to include my intuitive, spiritual adventures, I began to comprehend deeply how God had guided me during those years of healing. I realized that during this painfully honest, gloriously spiritual, and wonderfully mystical adventure of following Spirit's guidance, places of silence and dysfunction inside my psyche had cried out, found solace, and gleaned wisdom so profound that it can only be understood as Divine Love. In its authenticity, my story had become an example of a living manifestation of Jesus' explanation to the officials who asked him to silence the people shouting and praising him as he rode into Jerusalem that last time, as quoted in Luke 19:40: "...if these were silent, the very stones would cry out." My own life cried out to be understood fully; authenticity would not be stilled any longer.

As I wrote, I began to realize at deeper levels how I had been amazingly assisted by a very strong spiritual dynamic immediately after I became determined to discover the sacred in my life as a way of feeling whole. This same spiritual dynamic carried me from the broken pieces of psychological dysfunction to what psychologists call "self-actualization." This ability to not only know my full potential, but to live it, prodded at me intermittently the entire time I wrote. When I could neither get answers for myself nor figure out where my own chaos began and ended, insight began to cry out to me through those intuitive whispers of Spirit. Between the lines of my writing, wisps of intuitive whispers asserted themselves into my consciousness— What are you afraid to say? What does that experience mean? What wisdom did you glean?

As the book took form, tiny epiphanies began to explode into my consciousness, relating not only to my specific experiences in life, but also my life as it entwined with others. It was just as Soren Kierkegaard wrote: "Life can only be understood backwards; but it must be lived forward." Slowly, I knew that regardless of what anyone has done or been, or the choices—optimal or not so optimal—

made in life, when recognition that the loving authenticity which has always been sought is a Holy Essence within expressing itself as you, you then feel not only fulfilled, but whole. Life then presents itself as an expression of love in the highest form, an awakening to your own life as a sacred story. A sacred story is not about what you do, what you have done, or what you own, but who you are—a specific expression of God in physical form, a direct manifestation of Holy Love. When this is realized, you become fully alive.

Beginning to understand my story more deeply as an awakening journey—a sacred experience—I became determined to write it yet again from the beginning, in more depth and with complete honesty. I rewrote the book in its entirety a third time, adding specific experiences I had never wanted to share with anyone to existing chapters, such as my experience in Birkenau and my paralyzing agoraphobic moments. I also added more depth to the intuitive experiences I had always held back from others. Because I wrote with an opened consciousness, I realized more and more the profundity of the insight presented as a form of Divine guidance. Many rewrites and edits later, these parts of my story are completed and onto the pages of a book. The memoir became a written account of my own spiritual awakening. This is a sacred story of one woman who finally became fully alive.

This is the major reason I recommend memoir writing. Objectively seeing your own story in front of you on the printed page moves your experiences from the trauma center of the brain into areas more suited for analyzing, understanding, and processing. When you claim your own life's history with your heart, you lovingly accept it as a divine journey, one with recognizable spiritual power. First comes the being, the recognition, and the acceptance of your I AM nature. Afterwards, everything else in life just becomes an intuitive flow of Spirit.

I have included some examples of the spiritual messages I received in meditation as they apply to specific situations. Also, the intuitive experiences mentioned are pertinent to my own understanding as I learned from them. Yet, like the spiritual messages, I did not include all, but chose just to mention the experiences that were the most reflective. I also have used many names for God throughout this book, my choice determined by my own processing and understanding of the particular aspect of God at the time. To separate these names of God from ordinary words, I have always capitalized them. Because there are so many intuitive instances and spiritual dreams in this book, I have taken the liberty of putting those in italics. For me, often spiritual insight comes as a Divine whisper as if I feel a sacred thought. Honoring intuitive insight in this way separates them from ordinary thought, dialogue, and text. By italicizing, I believe I have made them simpler to read and have also made it easier to discern their meaning.

From the beginning, my intent has been to treat others mentioned in this memoir with respect, honor, and grace. Therefore, the names of all people have been changed. Also, conversations are based only upon my memory, and therefore some may be approximate, not always exact. However, these changes do not alter the actual events important to the memoir or their significance. The story is true.

I'm convinced the entire Universe eagerly waits to help each of us with our own spiritual growth. The fervency, influence, and frequency of this help exist in direct proportion to the intent of the person wanting or undergoing the spiritual awakening. Dreams, intuitions, and synchronicities become the norm in these circumstances, though they will be tailored to the ability, understanding, and particular sacred journey of the individual.

Since I am a lucid dreamer, my dreams were quite profound just before my divorce and for the many years I spent traveling the world. Even though my intuition has been strong since childhood, during this profound time in my life it occasionally soared beyond my own understanding. For this reason, I often had to seek help; it always came just as I needed it. I would not be where I am today without the profound help of some very spiritually-connected people.

First, I thank the Director of Turning Point Healing Center, Dr. Susan Russell, LMSW, LAC, PhD, ThD, for all her knowledge, faith, and intuitive connections. Her wisdom still astounds me, yet her innate healing ability still pushes me into new understanding as to what is possible with Divine help.

I also thank Dr. Rob Ciaphone of Essential Healing Chiropractic, Inc. His knowledge of applied kinesiology, the issues-in-the-tissues phenomena, gently guided me into new realms of body-mind healing.

I bless the eight pages from the New York editor who wrote that my first draft was lacking any personal substance. I thank her for being so brutally honest. Without that first painfully honest feedback, I never would have understood my own experiences at the depths I do now.

Christina Brandt is a brilliant life coach. She has the talent to be able to listen with love and then ask the questions that truly matter. I am indebted to her expertise.

I appreciate the work of Donna Burick, life coach and energetic healer. Her expertise was profoundly synchronistic as I glided through the emotional transition from memoir writing to memoir publishing.

I also am indebted to Wayne South Smith for his editorial feedback as he gently prodded me into writing what justly needed to be written. Although he knows full well the process of content and copy editing, I appreciate him most for understanding how hard it was for me to write about my own intuitive experiences. I bless him for helping me realize it was safe to do so.

I also thank the men who have been in my life, whose identities are protected in this memoir, for allowing me to discover my real story; they were great teachers.

Most importantly, I bless the man who showed up in my dreams toward this journey's close. At this time we've been married over three years, the happiest of my life. I honor your love and support throughout this entire memoir process.

Honestly, I don't think of my own story as unusual. After all, each of us already lives a sacred story even during the most ordinary moments. Most of us, though, spend our lifetimes trying to remember our storyline, substituting relationships for our authenticity, and bonding to materialism instead of self-worth. This book is simply my story explained the best way I know how. I treasure those who read it, hoping one day we all can look deeply into the eyes of each other, loving the spiritual depths of individual souls.

Bless you all. I really mean it, with love.

Paddy Fievet, PhD

Prologue

LOVE PROPELLED ME beyond everything I knew, beyond everything I'd experienced, and far beyond any rationalization. It felt like part of me, yet much more than me. Had I been in physical form, tears would have flowed endlessly due to overwhelming adoration. "Forever Divine" became a simple exhalation just outside of time. More than anything, this love felt like home.

As if awakening into a magnificent dream, five formless beings appeared before me, suspended between our respective dimensions. Flickers of light emanated white-like purity that glowed not only through them, but also around them and past them. Their loving passion was palpable. Spiritual radiance not only affected everything in their presence, but also far beyond.

Recognizing them as Seraphim, I became an energetic sponge absorbing everything they offered. Intuitively I knew if I were to continue, if I were to become a thriving, functioning human again, I had to carry this Holy Love with me. Without integrating it into my being, I could not be what my spirit longed to experience. Therefore, it was imperative that I become love—imperative that I remember.

With grace, the Seraphim merged together, individuals uniting as one. Swirls of blue, purple, and green mingled within intense fields of white light before settling into a somewhat steady appearance. Slowly, the Seraph on the left incorporated golden rose hues of sunrise that leisurely eddied through each of them as if it were engulfing the evening sky. By the time the colors twirled into the last Seraph on the right, the sunset glow all but dissipated. Somehow I knew this color sustained communication between our respective dimensions, yet I don't know how I knew.

With all of my being, I yearned to be one with them in order to have the colors swirling through me also. Their intensity felt warmly penetrating—not hot exactly, but filled with glory, with divinity, and with passion. Most assuredly, I would have allowed myself to dissipate into their loving energy fields completely, forever.

Nevertheless, that was not to be. The Seraphim would not allow me to do that; I had other passages yet unfulfilled. More than anything in the world, I ardently craved this concentrated, powerful level of love. It felt more real to me than anything I encountered on Earth. I knew this loving essence supplied the foundation of my being. Actually, it supplied the foundation of all beings, on Earth and beyond.

How could I remember this? How could I take it with me in order to pull it forth when I needed it? How could I bridge the contrast between my future and this loving existence? I longed to feel this loving intensity forever.

"Look to the blue in the sky," the Seraphim transmitted. "Absorb the blue sky when you need to know this love. Hold in your heart the color of nature's green, and you will feel God's love surge through you. Be still and know purple mysticism is your own birthright; you will have the ability to remember each numinous moment. Feel the intensity of the sun on your skin, be one with the starry twinkles at night, and emotionally bond to the changing cycles of the moon. You will not be alone. Earth will help you remember. Instead of seeking love, this time be love."

As I turned to absorb the blueness of sky all around me, I felt myself grow large enough to be one with the Seraphim, the cosmos, with everything. God's love swirled through me, as me, and beyond me. I could be there forever. For a moment outside of time, I became loving infinity. I was forever.

Abruptly, immensity sucked me back into physicality as I morphed into third-dimensional reality. Infinity suddenly became dark, cramped, and dreadfully uncomfortable. My vastness was swallowed yet again into human form. The watery comfort of mother's womb pushed at me, engulfed me, and nurtured me back into life one more time.

"Where are the colors?" I implored. "Where are the Seraphim? Why is mother's body squeezing me like this? I want to float, to flow, to expand, not be shoved or squeezed. Infinite love will not fit inside this little body! I'm too small. Much too small!"

Mother's voice became still; her painful screams quieted. Cold metal clamps grabbed my body, shocking it out of womb's safety into glaring artificial lights. These lights were not affectionate and twinkly like the Seraphim. Instead they glowered around me, hurt my closed eyes, and shocked me fearfully. Everyone hurried about trying to take care of my exhausted mother. The soft cloths swaddling me in that metal and plastic container did nothing to provide comfort.

"Someone hold me, please," my newborn self cried. "I'm scared. All I want is that level of Holy Love I remembered. Where is it?" Exhausted, I fell into that soft sleep of newborns, feeling confused and far removed from what I desperately needed to remember.

PART I

The

Simple Period

"Faith is the strength by which a shattered world shall emerge into the light."

HELEN KELLER

"Countless numbers are deceived in multiplying prayers. I would rather say five words devoutly with my heart than five thousand which my soul does not relish with affection and understanding."

ST. EDMUND THE MARTYR

◆

CHAPTER ONE

The One Sentence Prayer

COLD SHEETS OF rain pounded over the roofline just outside the basement office. To me it felt like another barricade forcing me to be penned inside a tight cocoon. Lightning electrified the entire backyard only to be climaxed by screaming levels of thunder, and yet the real storm raged inside my soul.

For the last hour I had sought refuge at an ostentatious mahogany desk in the corner of a windowless office of my Georgia home. The main section of the desk loomed in front of me, sandwiching the computer between the desk base and its towering hutch. Unopened mail and old spiral-bound notebooks filled with heartfelt meanderings lay in chaotic piles behind the glass doors of that hutch. The lower desk wrapped to my right side and then, just behind me, enclosed me like a protective fortress. This part of our home had become the only place I felt free enough to write myself whole again.

From the other side of my basement world, I heard the heavy rain pounding on the cement walkway as it cascaded off the metal stairway just outside the double French doors. To my right, a yellow legal pad lay opened to a blank page in the middle section, while old pages with copious notes folded over the top and back under—used, perused, and discarded. Quickly, I dropped my pen as the glow from a flash of lightning shot through the door panes into the corner of my basement hideaway. Thunderous claps jolted every cell in my body. Emotional tingles surged from my heart down my backbone and back up again.

"Oh, God," I whispered, knowing no one could hear me. "Something's not right."

Usually my writing, albeit just words earnestly expressed on paper, nurtured me back into some form of life. Tonight I could not retreat from the world; the storm pulled me into its fury. Instead of safe and comforting, the office felt confining, compressive, and frightening. With the palm of my hand, I touched the cement wall to the left side of my desk, making sure it remained in place. Indeed, the wall felt secure, yet more than ever I felt like I had been trapped in a coffin of my own doing. I did not know why.

Panic was a reprehensible enemy to manage on a daily basis. Sometimes it hid quietly in the catacombs of my psyche, never making a sound. At other times it screamed forth like a monster from hell, wrapping its dastardly fears of annihilation around my soul while threatening my very existence. Breathing would become a series of shallow, fitful gasps filling desperate tissues with much-needed air. My heart would race an eclectic beat of its own accord while my hands tingled and my vision tunneled to the point that nothing looked normal. In those moments, I knew I would never stay alive. Eventually the monster slithered back into the netherworld of my psyche, amused anyone could be so powerless. I did survive, but that was all I was able to do. Thriving dissipated into an unobtainable dream.

During my five decades of life, I had slowly become a simple period at the end of everyone's sentences. Instead of the profound intensity of an exclamation point or the beautiful seeker's quality found in one who questions in order to glean wisdom, my period lifestyle consisted of not only doing what everyone in my life expected me to do, but also being what they needed me to be.

This is how I survived.

◆ ◆ ◆ ◆ ◆

Regardless of the situation, dutiful southern daughters of the 1950s and early 1960s learned at their grandmothers' knees to be nice above all else. Even when speaking up in defense or setting a much-needed personal boundary, any words spoken should be dripping with sugar and wrapped with ancient Victorian lace. After all, it was not good manners to push the male-dominated status quo. Weren't women made to serve men, attract men, and be sheltered by men? What would polite society think of a brash woman who dared to live her own truth?

Like other women who warp, mutilate, and compress their spirit into pious submissiveness, I also girdled my feminine worth into a charming, docile daughter and wife. Whereas the exclamation point shouts, cheers, and stands grounded in non-altering truth, and while the question mark forever strives to become wiser, as a period I usually waited to see how others reacted before I managed to participate, if indeed I ever did manage to contribute. Over and over, I sat on the outside seat in the back row of life ready to run, observing, but not quite participating. Living as a period became learned behavior for me beginning not long after my birth. By the time I was five years old I was already becoming an expert.

As a young child, I had an innate fascination with all sorts of nature. I thrived walking on the granite and marble stones lining my grandmother's driveway. I loved the way my feet felt when they touched their solidness. I loved their unique shapes and the way they fit or did not fit together like pieces of the earth's puzzle. Literally, I could discern with eyes closed the energetic difference of the rocks upon which I stood; like me, they cried out to be understood.

The sandstone felt as if I were going to sink right into the center of each stone. The granite felt very solid as I stood on them, like stepping into something quite heavy. But the quartz stone on the shelf of my grandmother's living room held my fascination the most. The spiraling energetic flow mimicked a merry-go-round at the county fair. Not only could I see those invisible spirals with my mind's eye, I could feel them, like effervescent bubbles popping off the top of a soda can when I opened it. Quartz stones were my favorites. Holding one felt as if I held tangible evidence that life held many delightful secrets far beyond words.

I loved the way the green leaves of summer contrasted with the soothing blue sky as they waved gently in the South Georgia breezes like many hands applauding life. Standing on the shore at Fernandina Beach, Florida, I imagined infinity ahead of me as the unfathomable ocean and endless sky merged together as if both were just expansive expressions of a holy version of "wonderful." I felt as I were part of everything. Best of all, with awe I watched the stars moving through the sky at night. I longed to be home with them in that special place filled with overwhelming love, nestled far beyond the firmaments. Nature called to me beyond ordinary everyday events. I could feel it clearly in my soul.

How does a child tell the adults in her family she understands love discovered in the beauty of the soil? In the energetic diversity of rocks? How does a young child explain she not only sees the green leaves in trees and the blue of the sky, but also feels deeply connected to nature through part of her spirit? In my own innate way, incidents beyond ordinary human perception were the norm for me. My common sense resided within the realms of mysticism instead of anything remotely having to do with the reality of my five physical senses. To me, mystical moments felt like loving bursts of home while ordinary perception seemed quite devoid of all logic.

In the southern culture that nurtured me through childhood, the male not only dominated the household decisions, but also imposed his ideals upon the female. Like June Cleaver, our role was to get the homemade cake baked and look good doing it—and for heaven's sake, not to get the flour on our shirtwaist dresses or high heels. A large part of a woman's life had to do with presentation. It never dawned on me that I had the opportunity to have a career, that I could actually choose what I wanted to do when I grew up, or that having ideas of my own could be quite acceptable. Instead, I was told the best thing I could do for myself was to marry well, which meant to marry wealth, status, and, above all, someone who was from a good family, whatever that was. Were it not for modern conveniences, I could have been raised during the time of Paul's letter to Timothy, with the same results. "Let a woman learn quietly with all submissiveness. I do not permit a woman to teach or to exercise authority over a man; rather, she is to remain quiet." (1 Timothy 2:11-12). Actually, I did silence very well; unfortunately, it was quite natural.

Many decades later I discovered I was born an INFJ which, according to the Myers-Briggs psychological assessment, means I am introverted, intuitive, feeling, and judging. In simple terms, instead of being talkative, gregarious, and assertive, my natural tendencies lead me into deep thoughts, non-assertiveness, and not particularly having the need to always express myself vocally. I have always been a keen observer of life, simultaneously processing information on many levels. Sensitive beyond the ordinary, I realized from the beginning that, regardless of what people were saying, an essence residing just on the other side of their eyes often did not match their expressions. In other words, I always felt like truth was far beyond the obvious, lurking in the quiet spaces of a soul, within the energetic fields of nature, and in the beautiful energetic expressions of stones.

I knew intuitively the mood of my father before he walked into the house after work each night; I felt it in every cell of my body. When he had a good day, I felt like I had been immersed inside a garden filled with beautiful daisies. If his day had been harsh, I felt like dark, nasty cigarette smoke had invaded my body with the intent of choking me to death. I knew just before my mother got angry; I could see her aura turn to what looked like shadowy porcupine quills. I also could see her aura twinkle delightfully when she laughed or swirl with many colors when she'd used her creativity. While this seemed so natural to me, I thought of it as love. My quiet tendency to observe and withdraw confused people who did not understand this level of perceptiveness.

"Don't be so sensitive," my father would demand when something would upset me. "Get your feelings off of your sleeves."

However, my feelings weren't on my sleeves. They resided inside my heart, tucked away as often as possible in order to protect myself emotionally. Although he thought he was helping me deal with my sensitivity, my father might as well have told me that being authentic was totally unacceptable.

Just like many other intuitive children who don't have worldly validation for their experiences, eventually I put my gifts aside in a closed box of my own making. For instance, I remember vividly perceiving what I now call "others" come to the foot of my bed at night, silent souls caught between this life and the beyond. Daddy usually would come in, answering my childhood petitions for help; at my young age, I had yet to realize what I was intuiting. The formless essences frightened me as they moved in and out just at the foot of my bed, yet my experiences would not be validated because his personal gifts did not include witnessing souls who simply wished to communicate before moving onward. Trying to help, he told me what I saw did not exist. Validation is paramount to a child's healthy sense of self.

Oh, the decision to abandon my intuition never became conscious, but slowly, one experience after another, I ended up being what others expected me to be, what others wanted me to be, and what culture and tradition dictated, all the while seeking an intense love from the people in my life. Time after time, year after year, I bent myself into an unauthentic pretzel shape, craving a profound love from those who were unable to give it. *If I just try harder to do what my friends and family wish me to do and be what they want me to be,* I convinced myself, *they will love me more. Then everything will be right.* Instead of living authentically, my experience became a mirror of others as I desperately sought loving self-validation. A simple period at the end of someone else's sentence became all of life I could manage.

Once, when I was in my mid-30s, I was standing in my closet getting ready for a Junior League Sustainer luncheon, and I wanted to choose something suitable in order to blend in with the fashionably-attired ladies at this society function. When I held my choice up to me in front of the mirror, the petite flowers in the print matched my blue eyes perfectly. Yet, when I looked into my eyes, I saw nothing there—no excitement, no inner sparkle, no joy. The dress was appropriate, however, for this luncheon; high society would approve. Unbuttoning it, I slipped it over my head, expecting to feel comfortably put together in some way. That moment, though, I did not feel contented, I did not feel pretty, and I did not feel safe. Instead, I felt like a trained dog going to the circus.

Usually, I would have been nurtured by the thought of pleasing others by wearing this particular dress. That day, however, it felt confining, scratchy, and generally inappropriate. Crossing my arms in front of me, I pulled the dress off as quickly as I could, threw it to the floor, and then stepped over it as I entered the closet to make another choice.

The next outfit I chose was one I had sewn from a pattern design I created. If I wore my padded, push-up bra, the olive green material draping across my breast teased minimal cleavage to peek just above the folded cowl neck. The skirt hugged my hips before falling in soft layers around my legs. As I approached the mirror, I felt like death warmed over. Olive never was my color. It made me look like I felt—sallow and completely washed out. Why then did I put it on? In fact, why did I even make it if I didn't like the way it made me look?

I had made this particular dress so I would look enticing.

When I took this dress off, I didn't bother to hang it back up either. Instead, it landed next to the blue flowered dress wilting on my bathroom floor. The red dress with the ruffled sleeves fell to the floor next because the ruffles made me feel too frilly. The seersucker suit I had worn the past Easter made me feel like I should be sitting next to Andy Griffith in his Matlock television series. One by one, I tried on every dress I owned.

The pile of clothes on the bathroom floor covered the area from the toilet to the edge of the shower. Like a soccer player trying to score a goal, I kicked at the pile with all my might, yet the pile remained solid. I slid precariously on the fluffy bathroom mat whose rubber backing had seen better days. Lurching to the right, I fell into the side of the oversized garden tub, catching myself on the shiny gold faucet handles to keep from falling completely inside. With my head in my hands, I just sat there on the tub's bottom step, willing myself to feel good about something. Anything would have sufficed.

Absolutely nothing in my closet felt like my clothes. That day they felt like something my family would expect me to wear or something society expected me to adorn myself with in order to fit in at a Junior League luncheon. I hated every unauthentic minute of this little charade.

What was it *I* liked to wear? Did I like dresses at all, or did I prefer pants? Did I like soft knits, or did I like starched perfection? Why did I always tug at my neck when I wore turtlenecks? What was that all about?

"Oh God," I implored to no one (except perhaps the Divine). "I don't have a clue. Really, I don't have a clue."

After a good cry, I walked across the bathroom floor into my closet yet again, determined to find something left in my closet that felt like me. Eventually, I pulled on an old, faded sweatshirt covered with stains. It felt good, like a mature friend that had been through a lot, scarred yet nurturing. Liking my choice, I then put on a pair of sweatpants that had had the pants legs whacked off indiscriminately. One leg reached just above my ankle while the other leg barely covered my knee. I did not care. To complete the outfit, I slipped on earth mother shoes, comfortable and molded to my feet. Oh, I would not have won any awards for the best dressed, but I felt like myself in these clothes. It felt very good.

I never went to the luncheon that day. Instead, I stayed home to work in the garden. Just outside my basement, across a large expanse of grass, silver and golden koi played hide and seek underneath the leaves of water lilies floating in an oversized pond. On each side of the pond, the loving essence of impatiens graced the woodland setting with profusions of hot pinks, intense oranges, and pristine whites. The coreopsis that naturalized on the edge of the woodland setting sang to me, welcoming their yellowness into my soul. Reaching down, I touched one, feeling the goodness of its nature warm my hand just as if I had stroked the family cat lying in the sun. The pansies growing nearby had funny faces as if they knew I needed good cheer. I relished this area of my backyard, not because of the obvious beauty, but because of how I felt when I entered this fairyland world: cherished, loved, and part of something wonderfully intimate.

Digging in the earth felt nurturing, almost as if I belonged in nature. I knew about these plants from childhood. I knew how they grew, knew how they bloomed, and knew what they required to live. Still, I missed knowing those things about myself.

Not knowing my talents, not owning my own authority, and not claiming my own self-worth disconnected me from life. More so, it robbed me of the beautiful connection to my feminine soul. My spirit floundered like the petals of a flower drooping because of lack of life-giving water. Living for others disconnected me in many ways from those whose life I hoped to fulfill.

In the day-to-day routine of people pleasing, I learned what happens to a period. Eventually it becomes so familiar that people become conditioned to having it there, remaining in place, and just doing what it always does. No one really needs to see it, react to it, or love it. Instead, they just need it to remain as it is. They are also threatened when it is no longer there and most often react accordingly. Without self-validation, the period eventually becomes so insignificant it doesn't even recognize itself. Life, love, and laughter shrivel in gloomy despair.

Toward the latter part of my marriage, other than the normal trips to the grocery store, outings with friends, or church, I rarely felt it safe to venture into new experiences by myself. Usually, I remained home. Occasionally, the need to go somewhere different presented itself relentlessly through dreams or a strong inner nudge. (I usually felt it had to do with God's angels or something holy I simply called

Spirit guiding me into new adventures when I could not do so alone.) Eventually, though, even that was not enough. My life felt like the interior of a coffin, a small confining space that threatened to bury me alive.

Underneath the front seat of my husband's Ford pickup, he always carried a handgun tucked away in a leather pouch. Although I had no idea of the make or model, I knew how to insert the clip, knew he kept the bullets in the hidden compartment of a chest of drawers in our bedroom, and knew the clip inside the handle of his gun was always loaded. The coffin feeling had become far too familiar.

One night I decided to make sure the gun was still there. After my husband finally finished his late-night calls, he went to his bedroom to watch The Tonight Show with Johnny Carson. Although the television was still blaring at 3:00 AM, I knew he was fast asleep; I heard his overbearing snoring. Silently, like a mouse creeping across the floor to grab a leftover crumb, I gingerly eased myself across the hardwood floor of our den toward the front hallway. I paused momentarily, listening for the uneven sound of my husband's nasal passages as air rushed in and out at irregular bursts. I was hardly breathing. Feeling sure I was still unnoticed, I continued across the oriental carpet on the hall floor, opened the front door, and moved out into the cold winter night.

Just before me, across an expanse of front porch flanked by massive, traditional columns fashioned in old plantation style, was a short walkway to his pickup truck. Knowing the doors wouldn't be locked, I opened the driver's side door, feeling very much like a thief in the night. I held onto the steering wheel with my right hand while my left arm bent under my torso to reach underneath the driver's seat. I pulled the gun out.

It did not take much effort to unzip the black leather pouch. The black shiny metal felt cold in my hand as if it had been inside the refrigerator. In contrast, my hands felt clammy and warm in the silent, frigid winter air. I checked the clip just as I had been taught, discovering enough bullets there to end it all quite nicely if I could find the courage.

Holding the bitter metal next to my cheek, I then looked into the barrel, angling it to use the light of the moon in the obscure night. The tiny hole seemed to get narrower from my point of view, yet this tunnel had no light at its end. "So cold," I mused to absolutely no one. "Where's the light? God, where's *my* light?" Quickly zipping the gun into its pouch, I stuffed it back onto the floorboard of the truck before going back inside.

"What's wrong with me?" I whispered, straddling the contrast between wanting someone to give me an answer and hoping no one would hear the question. Silently, I walked up the three steps toward the front door I had left ajar into the empty space of my home filled with antiques, trinkets, and furniture, none of which meant one thing to me anymore.

My plan was to go back outside one night and remove the gun from his truck while he was sleeping. I then would hide it under my bedroom pillow, wait until morning, and then drive to a wooded section nearby our house. The field road into the woods was long and curvy enough for my car to be tucked away out of sight. I would leave a note on the floor of the hallway in plain view so whoever walked into the house next would be able to find my body. Yet something happened before my plans could be finalized.

God interceded.

As unlikely as it sounds, my intuition, formerly as silent and cold as gunmetal, kicked into high gear; I felt like something was physically wrong with the skin on my back. The feeling was so strong, it was impossible for me to ignore. For some unknown reason I felt like I had to see a physician—a dermatologist. The contrast between going to a dermatologist because I felt like something was unhealthy with the skin on my back and my desire to end my life made no sense to me at all. Nevertheless, the third dermatologist I saw within ten days ended up discovering a stage one melanoma dead center on my back, just behind my heart chakra. Perhaps I wouldn't need the gun after all; all I had to do was let the thing grow. I would be out of this life naturally in about 6 months or so.

I'm convinced this stage one melanoma was a gift from God to awaken me as to my true intentions. It wasn't death that I wanted, but life! I wanted to live fully, to laugh, to hug and be hugged, something I had not experienced for years. I wanted to know Love intimately, not love in a relationship, but self-love—God's Love. And I wasn't experiencing these things because I not only did not know how, but also I was afraid it might entail making life choices other than what others wanted of me. Yet, I decided to choose life. The decision was conscious, open, and permanent. After five operations, the melanoma became history. Somehow, I intended to discover what my life was meant to be. I had no idea how that would happen; I just trusted it would with God's help.

It did not take long after this initial realization of what I truly needed in life for my intuition to kick me in the gut once more, this time causing me to venture to a Dr. Carolyn Myss lecture in Atlanta. Frankly, I hadn't ever read one of her books, but after reading about her forthcoming visit in the Atlanta newspaper, I just knew beyond a shadow of doubt I had to go hear her. Because I was not able to sit by myself in a tremendous room filled with over a thousand people, I asked a young massage therapist friend, Samuel, if I could sit with him. He encouraged me to do so since he had another client attending with him. The group seemed quite friendly and safe.

Just before the lunch break, the inside of the massive auditorium shifted into a tight, minuscule box enclosing me forever. For a moment I stared at the three-story ceiling, attempting to reassure myself of its distance. The walls felt close and confining even though they stretched out far beyond me. I felt as though I was going to be pressed into oblivion.

Like my other panic attacks, the feeling slowly started with a profound sense of anxiety that would not abate. Native drums pounded a syncopated beat inside my upper chest. After a while, my fingers began to tingle, I had trouble catching a breath, and when I did, the air sucked right out of my lungs. My vision blurred and tunneled as if it were shutting down. I felt like a wild animal caught in the snapping, razor-sharp jaws of a trapper's snare. I ran outside into the open, thinking I was going to die.

Engulfed in complete panic, I ran down the street to the left of the auditorium, trying to find air. Within less than a quarter of a block, I spotted a small, two-lane cement bridge over a railroad track. Without any forethought, I ran to the cement wall of the bridge and hung over it from my waist up, gasping for air. Looking down, I noticed the earth seemed at least several stories below me. Curiously, I also noticed small pieces of granite gravel lying between the tracks. I leaned a little further, wanting to touch those stones, wanting to feel solid and in control again. As I reached out my hand toward the gravel stones far below, I felt a hand on my left shoulder.

Immediately I straightened up and turned left to face Samuel, who had come out during the break to walk to a fast food restaurant.

"The train hasn't come yet," I muttered incoherently. "How long will it be before the train comes?"

I was totally out of my senses. Meaning did nothing but ramble through my words incomprehensively. However, Samuel understood the situation.

"Paddy," Samuel implored. "Come back into the auditorium right now. Take a deep breath first, and come with me." Samuel knew about my panic attacks from reactions I had during massages when I would be touched anywhere near my throat. It wasn't his words that felt comforting to me, but his tone of voice. I trusted his authoritative demeanor.

When I got back to my seat inside the building, the woman next to me said, "You are having a panic attack. Turn your back to me and I can help." Out of sheer desperation I turned my back to this unknown woman. With minimal effort, she tapped some acupressure points on either side of my backbone, up and down. In about forty-five seconds, the panic was totally gone. I came back to myself, safe and sound.

"This is unbelievable!" I blurted out. "What did you just do?" I was incredulous; the shift from what I felt before to what I felt now was as though I had stepped into someone else's calm.

"I am an intuitive," she explained. "You were having a panic attack because you're allergic to the perfume of the woman sitting in front of you. It changed your brain chemicals. By using a specific system of breathing techniques and acupressure points to counteract the offending allergens, I can help you." The woman to my right was Maria, one of the most intuitive women I have ever known—an answer to an unstated prayer.

According to her, having fears so profound they manifested in many ways—including allergies—was the most common thing in the world. In contrast, according to my experiences, her help was a synchronistic gift sent from heaven. No wonder I felt God's strong internal urge to hear Dr. Carolyn Myss. It was not just to experience Myss' intuitive wisdom, which is astounding. My higher purpose in being led to attend was to find help for the panic that was so debilitating.

After I had been successfully receiving treatments from Maria for several months, she asked me to attend a seminar at her house. At the time she was studying energy medicine with Dr. Carolyn Myss and Dr. Norman Shealy in order to earn a doctorate degree. Because the seminar was about using your intuition to receive information from God, I hesitated to accept the invitation. I thought only devoted, pious prophets could receive words from the loving stillness of God; for certain, I did not qualify.

Later she told me that she felt I needed to open up intuitively. She recognized that I, like other very intuitive children, had closed off the intuitive part of myself years ago for lack of validation. She was right.

"Please come, Paddy," Maria requested.

"I don't know, Maria," I said, insecurity dripping from every word. "I'm not sure I'll fit in with those ladies attending."

"That doesn't matter," Maria answered in her most reassuring voice. "Just come and give it a try. I need at least twelve people to come before the class can be held. Right now, I only have eleven."

I hesitated before speaking. "I'm not sure...." However, my softened tone alerted Maria to try one more time.

"Tell you what—I'll give you a couple of free healing sessions if you come that weekend. I know of a motel nearby that has been remodeled. It's quite safe."

Maria would not take no for an answer. I decided to go.

The seminar was filled with eleven of the most psychic women I had ever met. They talked like it was the most normal thing in the world. To me it felt fearful, not because of intuition itself, which felt like a breath of fresh air into my soul straight from the heart of God, but because I was terrified of what others would say, think, or especially do to me if I displayed my own intuition. Safety, therefore, consisted of hiding it away in the dusty catacombs of the airtight box of my own psyche.

Throughout the two-day seminar, each woman participated in the exercises with great triumph. My own successful participation shocked me, because it contrasted with an overwhelming lack of confidence. Not only was it not difficult, it seemed quite natural and peaceful. Additionally, in some way I felt filled with grace, like I was doing what was meant to be. Gradually, my comfort level increased right up until the last exercise.

"Write a question at the top of your paper," our instructor Tina suggested. "Make it something you really wish to know, something only God can answer. Then go into a quiet corner of the house somewhere, and with pen in hand, receive the answer through your writing. Don't think about it. Just remain open to receive."

Eagerly, everyone left to take part. I sat there dumbfounded, doing my best imitation of a period.

God answered questions? Personal questions? Questions of my longing heart?

That was not what I had learned in church, not at all. Somehow I had ingrained a version of a "get it right and I will love you" or "get it wrong and I will punish you" religion that did nothing to comfort my soul or ease my fears.

Once in a childhood Sunday school class, my teacher showed us, her young students, a very graphic picture of people eternally burning in hell. She shoved the picture in front of each of us in turn, making sure we had a thorough experience of the tortures of hell. "This is what happens to bad little girls and boys when they don't do what God wants them to do," she taught.

In my best five-year-old voice I announced, "I am going to believe in Santa Claus then, instead of God. At least he gives you presents when you're good." After all, who always gets it right, whatever this means? Not even the saints achieved this level of spiritual competency. However, my teacher's horror at my response caused her to banish me from Sunday school class that day.

Tina's voice was soft and reassuring, like a loving mother coaxing a child into her arms as she said, "Paddy, it's quite okay if you don't get the answer right away. At least go to a quiet corner and try. Ask your question, stay open, and trust."

Reluctantly, I nestled myself in a corner of Maria's guest room. I sat on the floor in cross-legged fashion, mimicking an experienced, meditating Sufi mystic who knew exactly what she was doing even though I did not.

I wrote my question at the top of the page: *Why is it that I never feel good enough?* In all honesty, I expected the words to boom out of the sky, "BECAUSE YOU ARE NOT GOOD ENOUGH!"

This never happened.

Instead, I slipped into an altered state of consciousness, a dream-like state of minimal participation. My hand took on a life of its own, writing the first sentence at the top of the page. At the time, I was so detached from the result that I didn't even know what I was writing. Phrases felt like they were coming from outside of me, through my heart right into my hand. The process felt very right, like coming home to settle down in a worn, comfortable lounge chair after a long, arduous journey. After the first sentence, I wrote something at the bottom of the page. Then I moved to the middle, alternately filling in the spaces with more phrases. The sentences just flowed without my having to recognize any of them. Eventually the entire page was filled. When the paragraph was finished, I knew the received answer was profound. I could feel a higher vibration surge through my entire body.

Carry not with you inappropriate ideas ingrained
about your self-worth. The journey you've traveled is

filled with castles of silver and gold shimmering with all their opulence, outshining each other, each one stating its worthiness by out-glimmering and overwhelming all. With these castles, only the resplendence of their being, that which blinds the observer taking away his light, will even be considered. Beloved one, have you ever seen the details of these castles, found their true substance? I am here to tell you an ordinary wind could smash these castles into unworthy debris. Their power derives from your weakness. It is not how much you glitter and shine in life that is important. Still the old voices. Listen to your authentic truth. Our Creator has made you complete; you have not been born without. Your eyes have only been blinded by what you perceive as a better castle. You are your own castle, and it houses your spiritual soul. You know that this is the precious part of God that thrives when the earth journey is over. Live in your own castle and feel its importance. If it is good enough for God to house part of Himself, is it not good enough for you? Blossom with your time on this earth, for a lotus will not bloom in an area pressed by judgmental stones. Leave the stones where they fall and breathe your journey with trust and patience. Your own castle shines.

When I didn't return to the group at the appointed time, Tina came to look for me. Tears formed lakes in my eyes before they dripped onto the paper I handed her, on which the answer to my question had been written.

"I did it," I blubbered. "Or someone or something did it. I got an answer."

When I read it, it was for the first time. I was completely unaware of what I had written. In that moment, I knew the kiss of Spirit had lovingly given me one of the most spiritual answers of my life.

"It's your message, intended just for you," Tina answered. "Trust me on this one. Find the courage now to read it aloud, feeling its truth with each word." She confidently handed the paper back to me.

After I calmed down, Tina and I went back to the group. I read my answer out loud again, primarily because Tina asked me to read it. For a moment, I thought the words would choke inside my throat. Because my hands were shaking, the paper quivered between them. Trying to focus harder on my handwriting, I squinted my eyes and then blinked a couple of times to clear the forming tears. Then, as I took a deep breath, calmness overtook me. The voice I used came from an unfamiliar place of depth located somewhere between my heart and stomach. The message I heard myself read sounded spiritual, loving, and quite reassuring. For the first time in my life, I realized Spirit was connected to me quite beyond my own forced shallows.

Something profound happened to me that weekend, stretching my own consciousness beyond its stoic reality. At the time, I had no idea how this shift would affect me. What I did know was that I had to readjust my own personal values about what evidently could be possible through spiritual guidance. The help I needed evidently would not come because of something I did, someone I contacted, or anything I perceived. Instead, it would come directly to me from the Divine through surrender, faith, and trust. Unfortunately, it did not come with directions. My job would be to listen, discern, and follow. The week after I attended the conference at Maria's house, Guidance again caught me by surprise by awakening me to my inner confusion at a deeper level.

I had been sleeping in the guest room for almost ten years, long enough to call it my bedroom. The pink roses on the soft green wallpaper felt loving to me. I wanted to touch their soft petals, to hold them close to my heart, to feel their love. Moreover, I wanted my own love to come alive. I wanted to look into the mirror and see the woman there smiling back at me, accepting me, and loving me. I wanted to create my own fun-loving life where I could live my own sentences instead of just being a period at the end of everyone else's sentences. The flowers remained two-dimensional, however, plastered on the walls of unfilled dreams.

One particular night, while sleeping in the guest room, the first in a series of eagle dreams occurred.

> *A young eagle found herself misplaced in a barnyard filled with chickens. She tried to act like the chickens, to be like the chickens. Yet, she did not cluck, she did not have white feathers, and she did not lay chicken eggs. While the chickens seemed to be content waddling in the barnyard, she wanted to sail, to soar, to be free, whatever that meant. The eagle was miserable.*

The dream did not awaken me. Instead, I was awakened by dampness on my pillow, wet from tears.

The eagle dream should have alerted me to the reasons behind my own inner turmoil. Even though I related profoundly to the eagle's inner pain and emotional confusion at feeling out of place, my own chaos so confused me I could not even identify all of it. Soaring into my own life would be too foreign and way too fearful for me to even fathom at this point. I could only move through each moment at a time. The contrast between what I wanted out of life and what I experienced seemed like the opposite sides of a great sea no bridge could cross.

Over the next couple of years, I delighted in going into my basement office to write my questions and listen for the answers, a process I began to call "spiritual messages." Though windowless, the office always seemed to be filled with light streaming into my soul as I wrote. At first, I would utilize the method Tina taught me, writing a question in longhand and then going into meditation to receive the answer. After a couple of sessions, I tried typing the answers as they came. This only worked if I covered the computer screen. My internal, infernal editor tended to change the words around, add to them, or rephrase, taking power and love out of what had been written. To me, this process felt like a prayer in motion through questions and answers. Together, God and I mystically listened to each other's hearts through written words.

These sessions became my private, spiritual time. They were also my prayer time, for I never ever attempted this type of writing without stating a prayer of intention, asking that the messages come from a holy place filled with God's grace and love. No endeavor at this type of writing would ever have been attempted—not by me at least—without this type of directive. I treasured these moments day by day.

This time in my life was characterized by profound opposites. On one hand, I was living in vastness and openness, writing questions and answers. Yet to the rest of the world, I functioned like a recluse. Oh, I would go to see Maria, get gas, and do whatever it took to perform as a dutiful wife. I visited my grown children as they established themselves in their careers. On occasion I would go by myself to the movies, provided there was something playing that made me feel good for having seen it. Mostly, I felt safer inside the house or in my own yard. Still, I had no idea why.

After a while, I realized that my spiritual writing was not supported or understood by friends or family. When a creative person starts writing, most people think it is to be published. Writing for self-gratification, or even for spiritual direction, personal understanding, and increased wisdom seems too foreign for most people to appreciate. For the most part, this type of writing is intended to nourish the writer's spirit. Also, it is deeply felt at soul level. Divine moments do not lend themselves to ordinary sentences. When one writes about spiritual matters, the process involves utilizing words specific and limited in meaning while describing the numinous and unlimited. It does not always fit into ordinary perceptions. Nonetheless, I kept writing mainly because it was quite impossible to stop. It called to me out of the depths of my own fearful dysfunction like soothing waters poured on burning coals. Slowly, something began to happen during these writing sessions that lurked just beyond consciousness. I began to feel an uncomfortable surge of impending change.

◆ ◆ ◆ ◆ ◆

While darkness crept into the evening through threatening clouds masquerading as fingers of death, my spiritual messages got lost in the storm. As I sat at the basement desk, lightning and thunder climaxed simultaneously like two armies in the explosion of battle. I felt trapped, confined, and totally depleted. Smokey, the grey German short-haired cat that always cuddled in the red, overstuffed lounge chair when I wrote, squealed suddenly as if her life were in danger. The squeal frightened me; overwhelmed, I all but levitated out of the office chair.

I wanted to know why the office space that previously soothed my soul suddenly felt meaningless and empty, like a tomb of incarceration. The lights flickered several times. My computer belched, rebooted, and lit up the page upon which I typed my immediate thought to God: *This room feels confining to me instead of nurturing.* I closed my eyes and poised my hands over the computer keyboard waiting for inspiration to come through me as usual.

Nothing happened.

Rationalizing that the storm outside may have been preventing me from intuiting what always presented itself in quiet moments of stillness, I opened my eyes before uncovering the computer screen in order to stare at it while the thunder abated. The blank page glared back at me with emptiness, threatening to swallow me whole. Thinking perhaps the statement I wrote did not lend itself readily to answers, I added a question to the statement. *Why does everything in my life feel like a trapper's snare?*

Again, nothing happened. I shifted from side to side in the squeaky office chair, stretched my legs out under the computer table, and then drew them into my chest, a sitting version of fetal position. Even though I closed my eyes again in order to block out the room around me, I knew the familiar red recliner to my right still had the worn places covered with cat fur. I heard the raindrops pelting down in sheets over the roofline onto the metal steps going to our first floor. On the walls to my left and to my right, bookshelves contained volumes about intuition, stories of those who went against the norm in order to discover God and self, and books about psychology, topics that filled my soul. Everything in the room remained the same, except me. Unlike every previous spiritual message experience, my fingers were not moving. Loving whispers of God's thoughts did not fill the blank page in front of me. Wisps of my life were being sucked into a black hole of despair. A more powerful inquiry was needed.

Dear God, I typed. *I want to be me! Help me be free!*

There it was. The truth boomed before me on the computer screen, oozing out of the depths of my psyche, out of the fear that captured me like a prisoner of life and tortured me when I compared my limited existence to others. The daily routine of submission to others' needs while ignoring my own weighed me down like heavy stones in a journeyman's backpack. In fact, for three months the previous summer, I had spent most of the days inside my home. At my physician's direction, I was taking a medication for depression, which was not helping at all. Like bulbs retreating back into the bowels of the earth after a spring's bloom, I had also retreated.

It wasn't the world that frightened me, but my lack of knowing what my power as a functioning, happy human felt like. What I did know was the expectations of others for my life. When I did not fulfill those expectations, I did not feel safe. Most importantly, I did not feel loved. Inevitably, when those rare opportunities came when I enjoyed myself in some form or other in gardening, art museums, or painting, the dreaded monster took pleasure in leaping forth unexpectedly from the smelly bowels of fear, causing me to recoil to the safety of the car, house, or even the office retreat. Because I never knew when it would happen, fear-induced anxiety became a constant companion.

Late this stormy November evening, I cut off the computer before sitting for a moment in the quiet confines of the basement office. Even though the computer screen was dark and unlit, that last truth lingered with me, shouting from the gloomy catacombs of my being—I wanted to be free. I wanted to laugh. I wanted to be outside in the world, doing whatever it was that I was supposed to do, being whoever I was created to be, whatever that meant. No longer would I be able to endure life inside the confines of a basement office.

I walked over to the sturdy double French doors, which were bolted shut to keep the storm outside. Tears flowed from my eyes and down my cheeks, forming a wet puddle just over my heart on my new white cotton blouse. Whatever I lacked knowing about myself, I knew that very moment I never would find it in my current role as a wife. It could not be found in my family's ideals, my religion's directives, or society's expectations for me. I also would never find it in fearful reclusion. Through the windows of the doors I could see the fall chrysanthemums I had planted in late October lying on the soggy ground, petals pounded into the earth. All that remained were yellow remnants drowning in muddy puddles.

Somewhere inside my dysfunction, there had to be a spark of yellow. Somewhere in the chaos of not knowing who I was, of not feeling like I could be loved if I were myself, of not owning my authenticity, there had to be something left, some Light of Divinity shining brightly through the storm like a lighthouse beckoning to sailors on a troubled sea. That had to be my beginning, the key to self-awareness. I not only wanted to recognize this personal divinity, I wanted to live it, to treasure it, and to understand it as my loving, sacred story. Most of all, I was determined to feel this Loving Light as me. Nothing else would suffice.

Again, lightning and thunder electrified the silence. I stared at my feet firmly planted upon the green industrial carpeting on the cement floor of our basement. I looked at the comfortable old red recliner our cat mistook as her bed. I scanned the office retreat that had made me feel safe for so many years. Instead of feeling warmed and comforted like a cozy fire in mid-winter, I felt coldly detached from everything I saw. Nothing mattered to me anymore, at least not anything in my current surroundings or personal relationships. Discovering my own sacred story, actualizing my own divinity, was the only thing that mattered.

Suddenly, as lightning flashed down from the heavens to Earth, an electric awareness streaked through my entire body. Radiating from that special, long-silenced place within my heart, it surged upward to my head, then down my backbone, as a new awakening gushed into each cell of my body and soul. With every fiber of my being I knew I truly did not belong in the life I was living. If I were to find freedom to express my life authentically, I had to discover a passage through the center of my own storm before I could find peacefulness and loving fulfillment only God could provide; I could not heal without Divine help.

Out of desperation, I dropped to my knees, consumed in the holiness of earnest despair. Increased sobbing caused my shoulders to shudder chaotically. Reaching my hands upward to God, to heavenly freedom, I prayed with all the intensity I have ever mustered. Instead of lingering in consecrated stillness, this time petition raged through my own bawling, rasping breath.

"Whatever is standing in the way of living the way I was created to be," I cried out in complete earnestness from the depths of my unfilled heart, "may it fall from me."

I did not know what was ahead of me. I only knew what I no longer could endure. Out of sheer desperation to find everything, I was ready to lose it all.

> *"Hope has two beautiful daughters:*
> *their names are anger and courage. Anger*
> *that things are the way they are. Courage to*
> *make them the way they ought to be."*

SAINT AUGUSTINE

◆

CHAPTER TWO

Leaning Off Center

AS I GLANCED out the railroad car window to my left, I noticed that the trees—not only those standing like tired old soldiers guarding open fields, but also those lining roads and driveways—all leaned profoundly in one direction as if they had decided in unison to experience life in a non-ordinary way. I leaned my head slightly to one side and then to the other, establishing that the trees indeed leaned slightly off center. Not realizing that Belgium had strong prevailing winds causing the trees to slant in one direction as they grew, I determined that both the trees and I were slightly tilted, each for our own unique reasons.

According to the mystic philosopher Kabir, "The only woman awake is the woman who has heard the flute." Although I could not actually hear the flute of divine feminine life playing sweet notes from the depths of my soul, I did hope it existed somewhere, sandwiched between my intense anger that things had been as they were and the thread of courage it would take to make my life worthwhile. Actually, my choices within the last year made it imperative that the melodious notes of the flute did actually exist. My entire world had turned upside down to allow me to search for this level of sacred love.

A psychologist once explained to me how a marriage will go one of two ways when one of the partners has a spiritual awakening. Either both parties awaken to their own unique spirituality, supporting each other emotionally as their marriage reconfigures, or the marriage detonates with an explosion that brings down two worlds. Ours detonated. The fallout inundated me with paralyzing fear due to the loss of home, friends, and all that was familiar.

Turning from the window, I glanced at the people sitting nearby on the train. Three young women whispered to each other; their giggles seemed to connect them in ways I had not experienced in years. Two men sat across the aisle from me, not talking yet nodding to each other in a friendly fashion as one crossed over the other to reach up to grab his computer case positioned on the tubular, stainless steel shelf overhead. Every seat nearby had two people sharing it, getting along famously as if all were meant to be just as it was. The entire passenger car seemed to be filled with all types of connections between people, some obvious and some not so obvious.

On the other hand, I sat by myself, willing to share my seat space but unable to attract anyone to do so. Just like the lyrics to the song sung by Arthur Godfrey on the radio more than half a century ago, I indeed did feel like a "lonely petunia in an onion patch." I quickly wiped the forming tears, hoping no one would see, even if they were looking in my direction. Not only did I not have anyone on the crowded passenger car sit near me, I also heard no English spoken. I wondered if my being American in a foreign country had anything to do with the emptiness I felt.

Nonetheless, I had never felt so alone or misplaced in my entire life. Reaching down to the computer case lying between my left foot and the car's exterior siding, I opened it, booted the computer, and then I typed the only question I needed to know at that time: Am I really so alone? After I closed my teary eyes to go into deep meditation, the answer came readily.

> *When despair overwhelms your space, causing forward movement to be riddled with depressed stillness, and darkness surrounds your very breath, remember, you are not alone. When functioning throughout everyday events seems as though you are literally moving through blackness—an unavailable thickness penetrating the air around you—remember, my child, that you have support. You are traveling in the company of angels, and they will not let you be alone. Reach out from your troubled position for their hands of guidance to empower you. They will lead the way forward. The angels will help you find the pinpoint of light ever-present within the veil of your despair. And as you move toward this lighted portal, what seemed like a hopeless distance will decrease in size. Although the journey may seem difficult—plagued with sadness, with tears, with life's challenges—the movement within the Light is so sure. When you are going through troubled times, keep moving forward in the direction of hope's delight. Examine the Light from within to see the illuminated power of God shining brightly through the other side of depression. Feel the beauty of His grace flood your entirety with love, with support, with guidance. The Light overwhelms the darkness; you simply must move your intentions to it. And as you travel, never will your journey be singular. Angels are with you. You are never alone.*

I turned off the computer in order to allow a small thread of trust to flood through every cell in my body. My life would be changing in ways I had never expected. And I would not be alone in my journey, only in my growth. That idea quickly felt like a warm teddy bear snuggled up to my vulnerable skin, soft and cuddly but swiftly fleeting. I put the computer back into its case before placing it on the seat beside me to my right where a seating companion could have been. It seemed to be the only link I had to ending the loneliness I felt.

As the train moved through community after community, Catholic churches dotted the Belgian countryside, steeples reaching upward while bells intermittently pealed ancient tones of religiosity. I wondered if the women in those churches had been led to pious silent submissiveness as I had. Perhaps the subservient role infested all feminine life. Perhaps not. When the train passed a small church in the center of the next community, I saw just outside the door a weather-beaten statue of Jesus suffering on the cross, reminding the parishioners to behave themselves and conform. Guilt surged right along with my blood; I had walked away from marriage, church, and community, challenging the status quo with my choice to seek personal freedom. When lifestyles are challenged, usually there are consequences. My experience was no different.

About four months into the heated battle of horrid divorce, I decided to go back to church for the first time since the divorce had been initiated. Actually that choice wasn't something I thought about at great length—instead, I just had an intuitive feeling that I would make some sort of discovery if I went back. More specifically, I sensed that some sort of attitude had shifted that would affect me. My great-great-grandfather and great-grandfather both had been pastors of this particular church, so I felt like I belonged if for no other reason than genealogical connection. Before the first organ note tolled, I learned otherwise.

"Sinner, why have you come back to this church?!" a former Sunday school classmate extolled, his words spitting out like sparks from the fires of hell. "Women who leave their husbands have no business in this church." He was the initial sinless rumormonger to throw the first stone.

Not wishing this to happen again, I slid down to the middle of the pew, hoping to shield myself from more target practice. Unfortunately, it did not work.

A rather large woman jiggled enormous girth over three people as she maneuvered her way just behind me on the next pew. "Well, I didn't think you'd ever have the nerve to be here again," she spouted, shoving my shoulder. Her nose turned up like she had just gotten doused by skunk spray.

Startled, I moved to the other end of the pew and then walked down the aisle toward the front of the church. I had no idea what to do at this point other than to try to protect myself by being right under the minister's nose. This didn't work either.

As I waited for the service to begin, another woman in my Sunday school class turned suddenly toward me as she walked down the aisle. "Matthew 19. Read Matthew 19. We never expect to see you here again. This is your husband's church now!"

Evidently she had decided I had no business in her religious establishment. Until that moment, I had thought she was my friend. Obviously the entire Sunday school class had taken sides. Because I had not expected any of this, my legs, arms, and fingers began to tremble. Tears puddled inside my broken heart, overflowing and spilling out like a small farm pond overwhelmed by a monsoon. Pulling myself up by the pew in front of me as I balanced on legs that preferred to crumble rather than move, I left the building vowing never to go back.

I never have.

I turned back to the window of my train, noticing yet another small Catholic Church as the train moved onward. Established religion evidently had nothing to do with the spirituality I so desperately sought. I knew the events of that day in my ancestors' church profoundly pointed me into a new direction. For this reason, I bless those who threw the first stones changing my path forever. No longer could I merge into rooms full of judgmental people filled with exaggerated versions of right and wrong, or a religion with rules of sin and condemnation totally lacking in love. Somewhere out there, beyond my old familiar, I knew Love awaited me. Not love from one soul to another, but Love found in divinity. Like Rumi wrote, I needed to be the drop in a sea of God. Most of all, I had to feel it deep within my soul.

Like the goddess Inanna, I felt naked, raw, and vulnerable, pinned to the walls of Hades in complete despair. If I were to keep going, I had to not just believe, but know in the depths of my own being that something wonderful lay waiting for me at the end of this passage through barrenness. Only this level of faith would sustain me.

I looked around me again at the other passengers on the train, realizing that not only did I not know any of them, but that I also could not communicate with any of them. Personal security for me at this time presented itself through anonymity. Until I could feel my own spirit flooding through every cell in my body, I had determined to find a place on this earth totally different from southern culture and religion, far away from Georgia. In this way I could follow the yearning of my soul as it cried out for self-expression, dignity, and grace through the minute everyday tasks of learning what I liked to eat, wear, or do in total obscurity, without the need to justify myself to a single living person.

Instead of hiding in the basement, I would hide somewhere out there in the world seeking my own feminine soul. The pull to live in ways unlike anything I had previously experienced became a private mantra, a battle cry for freedom. Like the family church, I gifted my hometown to my ex-husband and his new wife.

Although the unknown terrified me, remaining in the thralls of my limited life terrorized me much more. One night about thirty days after the final decree, while sitting in the office space I had created out of the extra bedroom in my new rental house, I made the flummoxed decision to find another culture in a land far away from my home state—a desire for personal freedom urged me onward. Accepting the challenge was not hard, for I could do nothing else. I contacted about five people on an Internet message board for very intuitive people asking each if he or she would help me find a place overseas to live for a month. Frankly, I did not care about the location at all, as long as it was different from what I had already experienced. I just knew that if I were to heal, I had to leave the area that felt so constricting. My desire for personal freedom was manifesting more strongly than the fear I would have to overcome in order to find it.

Within several hours, I received two offers for help. Both Peter and Thomas lived in Belgium, although neither one knew the other. (Although I didn't know Thomas except through sharing a couple of online posts about specific types of intuition, Peter and I had already had several Internet conversations about a phenomenon called street light interference, which is the ability to have street lights go out when one is near or walks under them. Our conversations began about the time I first saw the divorce lawyer. They were always hovering around the esoteric, as well as how hard it was to be so psychically sensitive you were hyper-aware of so much more than those around you who only knew the world through the experience of their five senses. For the first time, I was introduced to the power of myths, wonderfully ancient stories with deep wisdom. We also talked about spirituality and how knowing God in a personal manner differs from religiosity.) Without hesitation, I accepted their generosity to help me get established temporarily. Within twenty-four hours after my first email request, I had a round trip ticket from Atlanta to Belgium.

This urge to experience life differently presented itself in synchronistic, out-of-the-ordinary ways as I yearned for spiritual self-recognition. For instance, about six months before this Belgium trip, I first heard about the beach resort called Topsail, North Carolina, at a writer's group. One of the ladies had planned a family vacation there for the upcoming summer; the essay she read to the class reflected her anticipation. On the way home from the meeting, I noticed a billboard I had never seen before advertising Topsail. That surprised me, since I lived in North Georgia far away from any North Carolina beach, and North Carolina beaches were not usually advertised in Georgia. The next day, an email mentioned Topsail. After about five such occurrences during the next week, I asked Maria what she thought it could mean.

"They want you to go to Topsail," she said in her most matter-of-fact voice, as if anyone should have recognized this fact for themselves. Her hand gestured toward what looked to me like an empty corner of the room.

"Who wants me to go?" I asked, not having a clue what she meant.

"Your support team." After she noticed my puzzled expression, she then added, "You know, angels and guides. *God.*" She raised both hands to her side as if to illustrate the common sense of this thought.

Until that moment, I had not been asking angels and guides to help me on a daily basis. Oh, I had taken a course in angel therapy from Doreen Virtue, in which I learned we all have angels to help us—but lately, because I had been so discombobulated by the humans in my life, I had not consciously turned to the angels for help each day in my spiritual development. Perhaps it was time I listened to their advice. After all, I had nothing planned the next week. If Maria was correct, then I certainly would welcome help for my healing, if not from humans then definitely from The Divine in whatever form it came. Maybe that would even be better than human help. Accordingly, I went to Topsail.

On the third day I noticed my one-room beachside efficiency had more than one hundred lighthouses decorating it; I counted every one of them. The bedspread and towels were decorated with lighthouses. The pictures on the walls were of lighthouses. The shower curtain, the throw rug, and literally everything else, including light switches, had lighthouses on them. It was not only unusual; it was phenomenal to the point of being overwhelming. Still, it took me three days to notice.

"Tell me about the decorations in my room," I asked the young motel clerk the next day. "Are all the rooms decorated with lighthouses like mine is?"

"No, only yours," she explained rather nonchalantly. "When you came in to register, I knew that you were to be in the lighthouse room. It was just meant to be."

"Well, why?" I asked her as if she had inside information to spiritual matters kept secret until now.

"That is for you to discover. Only you will know the answer." She then went about her task of filing paperwork in the cabinet at the back of the room as if the experience was completely commonplace.

It took me three more days to realize that the meaning of the lighthouse room involved recognition of the Light within each of us. Romans 8:9 states "...you are in the Spirit, since the Spirit of God dwells in you." Just like the lighthouses, we each have a Light of Spirit within our being. It is always turned on. Yet, unlike the lighthouses, we must recognize this Light before we can feel the illuminating spirit of God's Grace and Love. It is not something that shines upon us occasionally, but is a gift innate to our being shining within. I think of it as our true essence, a little beacon of Spirit shining as each of us individually.

After I finally understood the message of the lighthouse room, I knew it was time to leave Topsail. No wonder those angels and guides Maria mentioned wanted me to visit Topsail. The message was extremely important, although it would be several more years before I incorporated this message into my heart. Until then, my only job was to keep moving forward in whatever direction I felt led.

As I turned my gaze from the Belgian countryside back to the interior of the train, I felt the engine gearing down. Perhaps the passenger train had finally arrived at my destination, Bruges. I tucked my knitted purse into my stomach, holding it securely with both arms like a shield of protection to keep what little courage I had from leaking out.

Moving forward was my only option if I wanted to survive. Regardless of the way life presents itself, the best way to get out of hell is to keep going, keep moving, keep taking those baby steps forward, even if you have no idea where forward leads. To stay in a place that has no future for growth, peace, or spiritual and personal safety is tantamount to death by being trapped.

Intermittently during the past hour I had been watching the monitor at the front of the train car while frantically trying to match the flashing yellow Flemish words I did not understand to the Belgian destination I had hastily scribbled onto an index card. The Flemish and French versions of "welcome," "arrived," and "next stop" meant absolutely nothing to me. The flashing sign could have been announcing terrorist attacks, and I would not have known the difference or have been more frightened.

When a signaled word finally matched the letters on my index card, I hoped I was where I needed to be when the train eased to a stop. As I hastily moved my possessions toward the door, I noticed a sign that indeed indicated the Bruges station hanging from the wooden shelter situated in the center of the arrival platform just to the side of the train. When the train doors opened, I tentatively stepped out of the familiar into what could possibly be the perilous brand-new.

Fear of being alone in a foreign place for the first time in my fifty-two years clawed at me like a mother bear on the kill. The intense fear of being trapped was ever-present, fueled by my own insecurities. Though it did not visit on the airplane to Europe because I felt safety in the fact that I was flying far above my traumatic past, it visited while on the train to Bruges. This feeling was shifty, like a masked burglar jumping at me from a darkened corner near the garbage cans in a suspicious alley of my mind. I never knew when it would happen. I was scared to death of it taking over more of my life.

During my divorce battle, I met many brave women who were each in their own way overcoming life choices that had robbed them of their personal depths and emotional widths, leaving each to flounder in the narrowness of their forced shallows. One had to walk in open areas of nature a lot. She climbed to the tops of mountains, visited the western plains area of the United States, and wandered for hours at a time on the seacoast. She eventually took up skydiving because she loved the idea of being off of the earth, floating far above her past.

Another woman created a home that contained no interior walls. She chose an existing metal building with steel beams and support poles to make her home, adding interior partitions to divide room areas.

A childhood friend of mine felt absolutely trapped if she was in a place for more than several months at a time. She not only would move at the end of her six month apartment lease, but actually sold all her furniture each time she moved in order to experience the freedom of a new place and new things. For her, movement was safety.

As for me, I had to get out of Georgia, far away from my past experiences to feel safe. Freedom is a precious commodity. To find it for ourselves, often we push into the unknown, especially when freedom screams within us like a banshee warrior charging into closed-hearted familiarity demanding to have its way. I was no different.

As a period at the end of everyone's sentence, my power had dwindled to a minuscule point as I came to believe in my own vulnerability. Like a bobble-head dog sitting atop the back seat of a car, I not only nodded in agreement to almost anything anyone said, but also said only those things that would make others nod appreciatively in my direction. Any new incident in life, any new situation, or any new experience of any sort that caused me to feel trapped or helpless sent invisible chains into action, grinding me to a standoff battle with the monster called "Panic." Most of the time, I felt like it won each battle. However, I had to win the war.

What were those chains made of? What was the profound fear all about?

Several years after this first Belgium trip, I was at our local supermarket near my home in Roswell, Georgia, getting something for dinner. Fear of supermarkets had waned several years previously, probably because I kept prodding myself to visit them out of necessity. During this particular visit, a table for book sales had been set up near the register. Interesting books always call to me, even in the grocery store. Yet, when I paused by the table, only one book remained: *It Ain't All About the Cookin'* by Paula Deen. After a brief pause, I picked the autobiography up, thumbed through the pages, and then put it down again. I had many other books at home waiting for me to read.

Even though that book remained at the store, it did not get out of my mind easily. After I arrived home and put my groceries in the pantry and refrigerator, the book still called out to me. I tried watching something on television, yet I could not get the book out of my mind. My friend Ann and I had an extended phone conversation about the upcoming holidays, but still the book called. I ate dinner, yet the book beckoned. Finally, out of a need for peace more than anything else, I drove back to the grocery store, walked inside, and purchased that last volume, leaving the table empty. That night I curled up to read it in bed, for when something calls to me that strongly, I have to listen.

Approximately a third of the way into the book, Deen began to describe the havoc in her earlier life. Like the women I mentioned above, she left a relationship that had not been beneficial to her. She had two sons in her care but had trouble with an overwhelming fear that would appear suddenly without obvious reason. Like me, she never knew when this problem would surface. Nor did she realize what it was about. While I called it monster, chains, and the panic enemy, her term was It. After watching a Phil Donohue show about agoraphobia, she recognized her It for what it was, the fear of not being able to escape. Reading that brave lady's account of her agoraphobia gifted me with the blessing of recognizing a piece of my own puzzle. Because I had disconnected from my personal power, I was afraid of being trapped.

Once a problem is recognized, then it can be dealt with successfully. When I was on my own right after the divorce, I did not recognize this problem by name. Even though I had sessions with a counselor, minister, psychologist, and even two sessions with a psychiatrist, none of the professionals I saw recognized agoraphobia because I had no idea how to present it to them.

The major problem with agoraphobia is the unrelenting anxiety that comes when escape doesn't seem possible. It develops in response to anxiety-provoking events, mainly in women ages twenty to forty who have been taught avoidance behavior as a way of coping with difficult situations. Agoraphobia does not mean you will become panicked by all crowded places. Instead, it may happen in one of those places and not in another. Triggers buried deep within the psyche activate the panic usually at the most inopportune times.

No wonder I had panic attacks out of the blue. No wonder I felt trapped in situations that actually should not have been fearful, like buses, auditoriums, or intensely crowded places. No wonder I had trouble in places that were new to me, places without readily discernible exits, or unusual situations. No wonder I felt absolutely paralyzed if I became lost or disoriented. Most of all, no wonder I had not left a dysfunctional marriage sooner. Even though that situation was stifling in the greatest way, the unknown abyss out there in the world was also frightening because of the relentless fear I could not escape.

My anxiety about being alone in a foreign place where I couldn't even read the signs for direction reached epic proportions. That dastardly enemy consumed me again. It wasn't that I felt safe on the train, but I got used to it after an hour's ride by concentrating on the scenery passing just outside my window. As I looked around the station to see which way to walk, the feeling of being trapped was fueled by the unfamiliarity of the station platform.

My vision began to blur. Panic's familiar tingling started in the tips of my fingers, moving into my hands and then my arms as if I had stuck wet fingers in life's most profound electric socket. My legs shook like two straws balancing a heavy container of assorted fears. With paralyzing uncertainty, I tried to reassure myself that there was indeed oxygen in the air. My lungs were laboring to find it, though. Small airy gusts wandered briefly into their dark confines like weary coal miners exasperating into blackened nothingness. If I could speak, I would have shouted to these bursts of oxygen to return, to bring their buddies, and to bring me some help. (For that matter, bring me some Xanax!) Never in my entire life had I felt this alone, this unloved, or this confused.

Moving with the crowd, I silently blessed the creator of suitcases with wheels as I jostled mine down the first few steps of the cement platform. Weighted with a month's worth of clothing, it bounced off the last step before flipping over with wheels mimicking a dying bug as I struggled to pull it along unaware.

Breathe, I reminded myself silently. *In, two, three, four. Hold, two, three, four. Out, two, three, four.* The Yogic breathing technique I had learned kept me from absolutely passing out during my panic attacks. Currently, this was all I had going for me in the way of help. That and prayer. Intense, heartfelt prayer.

Dear God, I implored with honesty so silent it lingered between spoken word and thought. *What the hell am I doing? For that matter, what in the name of sanity have I done coming to this place? I'm scared. Send me some help, please.* My prayers these days were more pleading for safety and clarity than they were for pious religiosity. After all, if indeed I were following some kind of mission to assemble my fragmented pieces, I had a profound need *to know* help was there, even on the spiritual plane. Looking back, I realize that I did have angelic help as well as heavenly guides. Yet, at that particular moment, I felt nothing but paralyzing trepidation.

Not having one clue where I needed to be next, I followed the crowd. Belgians, for the most part, keep to themselves. At least it seemed that way to me, for I saw not one soul talking to another. In that regard, I felt like one of the Belgian masses, for it would have been impossible to carry on a conversation; counting breaths and staying upright was taking most of my focus. On the crowd moved as if each person had some exciting destiny to follow. The only thing I had to follow was my index card of directions creased so deeply by my automatic folding and unfolding during the train ride that I could hardly read the faded pencil marks on it. Even though I clutched it tightly, by this time it seemed grossly inadequate.

Destiny seemed too far in the future, really uncertain, and felt to me like an alligator-filled moat of bad dreams. I truly wanted some magic pill to make the panic subside. Perhaps the only destiny I would be able to fulfill right now involved staying conscious, breathing, and taking those tiny, fearful steps forward into my own future.

By the time I reached the hallway to the station exit, I righted my suitcase. "Almost there," I said not so reassuringly to myself. "Almost there, whatever that means."

Just before I reached the door of the station leading out into the summer sun, I leaned against the whitewashed cement wall hoping to calm my body down before the next part of my journey. While navigating the unknown corridors of the train station felt like being trapped by strange paths leading into unfamiliar destinations, the open air was another version of being trapped. Oh, I was going to go outside. That was certain; I had to keep moving forward through this fear if I were to survive. I needed a moment, however, before I could venture outside to face a different type of fear.

"Excuseer mij," an older woman said. *"Kan ik je helpen?"* Although the look on her face was one of concern, the unexpected suddenness of her voice startled me into the present moment.

"I don't speak Flemish," I said in my shakiest southern drawl. Although her words were not familiar, her tone resonated reassurance for some reason. For all I knew she could have been the proverbial devil in disguise asking me for the rights to my soul. However, the soothing sounds I was hearing felt to me like an angelic whisper in answer to my inner pleading to survive.

"Ah, that is okay," she said in English, without much accent at all. "I noticed you watching the train monitor for directions. I do not wish to be rude or to intrude, but perhaps you would like some directions now?"

"Oh, yes," I blurted out, the tears forming in my eyes. Hastily, I reached into my purse for sunglasses as if masking my eyes would keep her from realizing how frightened I was or how hard I was fighting to not turn into a teary puddle because she was helping me. "I truly do. I need directions. Thank you."

Reaching into her open canvas bag, she pulled out a map of Bruges that she unfolded before handing it to me. "These are free. I picked one up just over by the ticket counter," she indicated with a nod of her head to the wall over to our left. "I think this will help. Often having a map in hand feels reassuring."

With a grateful heart, I accepted the little map of Bruges, clinging to it like it was my own personal treasure map to the Holy Grail. In some ways, perhaps it was. After thanking this kind woman, I thought of how many times I had not listened to my heart in order to assist someone who obviously needed help. I could have tipped the baggage handler at the Hartsfield Atlanta International Airport more than I did. Instead of hoarding my granola bar on the plane, I could have offered it to the gentleman sitting next to me. Most importantly, I should have listened more lovingly while the ladies in my writing group read their own passages instead of focusing on how I was going to get back into the safety of my own personal space. "Do not neglect to show hospitality to strangers, for by doing that some have entertained angels without knowing it" (Hebrews 13:2). Angels, it seems, come in unique forms, all answers to spoken prayer.

This very human angel was right on all accounts. Having the map in my hands gave me courage. Oh, I could not read one word on it, yet there were lines for streets, blocks, and a curving blue line indicating the meandering river just across the station courtyard. Surely I could get to that river; being in nature would help calm me. After all, it was little more than one block away.

After a deep breath, I slung my shoulder purse over my head in order to free my right hand to clutch the map and laptop case, leaving my left hand free to drag fifty pounds of clothes into the unknown. As I stepped into the sunlight, instead of peacefulness, I felt like I had just dived into the depths of a bottomless pit.

"Almost there, whatever that means." Taking one step at a time across carefully-placed squares of concrete, I slowly walked across the area in front of the station with my suitcase thumping along behind me. When I neared the street, I noticed a plethora of hanging blooms in shades of white, purple, and pink draped over what looked like two suspended rowboats made of wire and moss hanging from four poles about fifteen feet apart.

"Aren't they beautiful?" I remarked to myself. How odd it seemed to me that people around me were in such a hurry they did not seem to feel the fragrance of those gorgeous flowers clear inside their souls. I don't know how long I stood under them, for time seemed irrelevant. I felt nurtured by the shadows of those rainbow colors dangling just overhead. As I held my arms out to my sides, those purple, pink, and white rays danced with my fingers. An empty sponge could not have soaked up that beauty one bit more than I did. My hands stopped tingling, my eyes were free to focus, and my body began to relax somewhat. Panic had come and gone yet again.

As I crossed the street in order to walk beside the river just ahead, I realized that my plea for help while leaning against the wall of the station had been answered. I had tangible evidence right there in my hand: the map. Stopping momentarily to discern where I was in relation to the train station marked on the map, it would have been most helpful to have one of those little marks showing location: "You are here." For that matter, it also would have been helpful to have another little mark with words that showed me the future: "You will be there" and "You will be just fine." My future was nothing less than a foggy mist masking that yet to come. Turning the map first to the left and then to the right, I finally turned it upside down so that I could hold it parallel to the ground matching my forward movement.

As I walked onward, I breathed into welcoming daylight. I took my first steps into what I hoped was a new understanding of freedom. Over and over I dueled with panic, losing an occasional battle while maintaining the confidence that I would eventually win this war. No counting necessary at this time, for I had the paper map answer to my need for help. I knew I could pray again and again to receive help each time in whatever form God felt best. The row of benches next to the river's edge was just ahead of me. One faithful step at a time was all that was needed.

Just one.

> *"It takes courage to grow up*
> *and become who you really are."*
>
> E.E. CUMMINGS

───────────────◆───────────────

CHAPTER THREE

On a Bench in Bruges

THE CEMENT PARK bench with bumpy, splintering wooden slats felt nurturing to me, a solid place of refuge for an emotionally weary traveler. The river flowed gently, so still it could have meandered out of a storybook of dreams. Ancient trees dipped their large branches toward the water's edge, bowing humbly to the calming peacefulness. Wood ducks and strange birds resembling odd black water chickens swam toward me, eagerly anticipating morsels of nourishment. Three swans kept their distance in the middle of the watery stillness. I gazed past them to the far edge of the pond, the canalized lake called the Minnewater, which means the "lake of love."

The Flemish sign read *Niet Kasteels*. Not Castles. Because I didn't recognize the English translation, I missed an important spiritual clue. Letters at least two feet tall in screaming, bright red truth were plastered on an old rock wall just on the other side of the Minnewater,

43

which had been formed from a canal that meandered aimlessly through Bruges. Even though my attention intuitively hovered over those letters like a mother watching a child at play, I did not relate the meaning to my first spiritual message session at Maria's house when I learned from God that there would be no false castles in my journey but only increased self-worth and authenticity. Instead, I simply stared straight ahead. Personal insight floundered like the shallow shores of a misty moor. At this point, I had no idea what anything meant any longer. Instead of answers, all I seemed to find were more questions.

The experience of meeting someone is naturally preceded by your expectations of what that meeting will bring forth. Was this going to be the stupidest thing I had ever done? Or was it going to be the grandest? Even if I was brave enough to have come all this way to renew myself, would I be courageous enough to be able to protect myself if the need arose? Could I trust Peter to help me get established during the month in Ghent, Belgium?

How in the world do you "live the questions," as Rainer Maria Rilke wrote in *Letters to a Young Poet*, if you aren't even able to recognize them? In my mind a million monkeys were chattering away while swinging back and forth within the fearful tangles growing everywhere.

The deep, soothing voice just behind me whispered, "You must be Paddy. Hello. I'm Peter." Wings attached to my fearful questions flapped furiously along with the river's wood ducks that suddenly sailed from the safety of their watery habitat. The overwhelming questions I had about being lost forever in a foreign country began to ease into a more manageable hysteria. My emotions mimicked the water chickens, though, remaining hopefully at the edge of the river waiting for someone to hand them breadcrumbs to keep starvation at bay.

I needed help in the worst way, enough so that I traveled five thousand miles into the unknown in order to receive it. At first, I couldn't even answer Peter to say who I was. I must have nodded though, taking comfort in the hope that all would be in order. Like the famous mythologist Joseph Campbell wrote, my "familiar life horizon had been outgrown; the old concepts, ideals, and emotional patterns no longer fit; the time for the passing of a threshold..." was at hand. Even though I walked out of the familiar, while staring at the water's edge I wondered what manner of initiation I would experience in order to discover that golden light shining brightly as me. So far, nothing had been easy. Even though Peter's support was minimal, it was the only human support I had other than myself. I hoped it would be enough, for I intended to lean on it entirely.

Hope is an interesting experience. According to *The Merriam-Webster Dictionary,* "to hope is to cherish a desire with anticipation." If we hope for a thing to occur, whether it is an event, an entitlement, or forthcoming help, we are expecting something beyond ourselves to come into our lives and make it all better, like a mother would put a bandage on a scraped knee. This form of anticipation has nothing to do with participation other than the fact that we are wishing for something better.

However, hope changes into a very powerful attraction when it becomes a co-creating bond with Spirit. When this happens, a knowing that things will work for our highest good surrenders itself to a higher spiritual directive to make it all happen. Although we don't know the specifics, we hold tight to the fact that our own choices will intuitively lead us in the right direction. In meeting Peter, hope filled the empty places in my soul. I just wasn't sure about the definition or whether my hope had to do more with Peter's help or Spirit's guidance.

"Hello, Peter," I finally managed to reply. "I appreciate your coming to help me today."

Peter was the most unlikely-looking wise person I have ever seen. From our Internet correspondences, I had stereotyped him into a male shaman, expecting long, straight hair and perhaps something poncho-like covering a handmade cotton shirt, pressed crisp for impression. Peter, on the other hand, was dressed out of season for the hot August day, wearing a plaid, long-sleeved flannel shirt and jeans that barely reached down the entire length of his long legs. His curly brown hair was slicked back on top, waving about in exaggerated expression down the back of his neck, while a full beard dappled with grey hid most of his throat. His black horn-rimmed glasses were perched midway down his nose, giving him the look of a philosopher at odds with society.

"Let's just sit here in the shade a moment to cool off before I take you to your rental," he suggested.

At the time, Peter was my lifeline, one of the two people who had promised to help me get established for this first month's visit to Belgium and the first who had followed through. Although his accent was heavy, I could easily understand everything he said. His mannerisms reminded me of someone who would be quite at ease standing in front of a classroom. Words flowed effortlessly from this man who was definitely comfortable in new situations.

"How was your trip?"

Not wishing to go into the sordid details of how I had managed to fly across the watery fathoms to a foreign country for the first time by myself, I simply answered in a very weak voice, "I am exhausted. It's been a long day." I pushed my own wayward curls from my forehead, gathering strands between my fingers in order to fluff them back into place.

With the gentleness of a feather not sure where to land, Peter sat on the opposite end of the bench, angled not to face me directly but focused just in front of me as if to intuit something of the vast unknown between me and water's edge. Unspoken moments drifted together aimlessly with no intended purpose as we sat in pregnant silence, neither of us needing to say anything immediately. Although I knew by Peter's demeanor that his position on the bench anchored some as-yet undiscovered authority, he placed his arm on the back of the bench as if to demonstrate his openness. I wondered if this gesture expressed his sincerity, facilitated his need to cool off, or if it were to simply put me at ease. For certain, his arm did not drape across my shoulders. Two people could have been sitting between us.

The five water chickens at our feet waddled off to my right hoping for crumbs. I turned my gaze past Peter to the water's edge, looking into the unknown as if some future movie was playing out my story. I watched as the swans glided toward an ancient stone bridge to Peter's far left. Just beyond this bridge, tourists moved through an enormous gated opening of a walled compound. Because the words printed on the compound's sign were unfamiliar, curiosity nagged at me like the movements of the swans, calm on the surface, but moving furiously underneath.

"Peter," I asked. "What is a b-e-g-u-i-n-a-g-e?" I had no idea how to pronounce the word, so I simply spelled it.

"So you have an inquiring nature! Wonderful!" Throwing back his head as if to shake some odd debris out of his hair, Peter laughed heartily as a more spiritual conversation between us finally broke through. "*Beguinage,* Paddy. They existed as Roman Catholic monasteries for women in the thirteenth century. A Beguinage was the compound for the Beguines, who, unlike the other Catholic nuns, preferred to do their charity work in the communities instead of living sequestered."

Many rectangular stones lay in row after row in order to create this wall, like small individuals adhered to a greater purpose. It was an imposing edifice, and I wasn't sure whether it kept people out or kept them inside. "It looks sequestered to me, Peter."

His smile widened, but slightly twitched as if he were trying to cover a large belly laugh. As he turned toward me, his right arm left its perch on the back of our bench in order to draw more into this new conversation. Obviously he needed both hands to help him illustrate his words. Evidently Peter enjoyed the role of tourist guide.

"*De Wijngaerde,*" he said, both hands now gesturing back and forth wildly as if smearing letters on a blackboard. "This particular Beguinage is called *De Wijngaerde*. It means "the vineyard." Now it's a monastery for Benedictine sisters. But that's only been since about 1937 or so. Before that—say about the mid-thirteenth century—it was created as a home for women, and perhaps a few men, who wanted to live simply by doing Christ's work in the community. We have many of these ancient Beguinages in this area of Belgium."

Momentarily, I forgot my own story. I forgot how unfamiliar Bruges felt, how afraid I felt in traveling alone by myself for the first time. I also forgot how long I had known this male encyclopedia of historical spiritual information sitting next to me on a bench. Something about the Beguinage felt familiar. Oh, the land, the river, or the building themselves were not recognizable because of any pictures I had ever seen of the area. Instead, my heart felt like something had turned the doorknob in order to open my soul just a little, so a bit of light could crack into the darkness. I had to know more.

Looking back, I wish I'd had enough courage to actually cross that bridge that day. I wish I could have trusted Peter to watch my luggage for a moment while I peeked into the Beguinage. It wasn't just curiosity that drew me to the walled compound like swarms of buzzing yellow flies to a country picnic on a hot summer day; instead, my soul yearned to reach out, to grab something familiar in an unfamiliar area.

But what was the attraction? What about the Beguinage drew my heart into this ancient bit of feminine history?

"Do you know any more about them, Peter?" I asked. This time instead of gentle whispers, my voice enthusiastically jiggled its way out of my throat without warning.

"Of course," Peter smiled. "I know lots about the Beguines. What do you wish to know?" Peter enjoyed teasing me with just a tad of knowledge, sitting back as he waited for me to ask for more, purposefully beckoning me into his world. Later, this type of behavior would cause a reckoning. But right now, his knowledge dangled before me like a minnow hooked on a fishing line. Mimicking a hungry salmon swimming upstream, I snapped at the bait.

"Well," I said slowly, trying to put what I did not understand into words that made sense. "Why? What was the draw to cause women to become Beguines? Something about them differed from the nuns of the times. Yet, what?"

Every cell in my perceptive soul simultaneously screamed at me to find out more. *This is important,* the intuitive whispers shouted. *Something is here, and I need to know.*

"In the twelfth and thirteenth century, the Catholic church became more powerful in this area. Religion served as not only a method to control the population, but also as a way of gaining wealth. The Beguines sought a purer and simpler religious way, often embracing the mystical element of faith. Poverty, plainness, and different forms of service in the communities called to these people. Often their methods threatened the established church hierarchy." As Peter paused for emphasis, he turned his glance to the waters. Both of his arms returned to the back of the bench as if his lecture needed a pause in order to allow the wisdom of his meaning to find its flow. On the other hand, I needed a pause in facts in order to allow the flow of something stirring in the bottom of a very dry spiritual well.

Turning my glance from the Beguinage just over Peter's left shoulder, I followed the lake back to the widened area just in front of us. Although I assumed it must be coursing from one direction to another like rivers do, it seemed still as if it paused for contemplation just like me. The words *Niet Kasteels* still loomed before me without meaning. The swans paddled to the middle of the wide pond, pausing just as I was, before deciding the next course of my life. How graceful they looked when gliding across the waters. I wondered if I looked calm, if I presented myself as a woman of the world to anyone.

Instead, I felt dizzy. My stomach churned like angry waves upon the beaten shores during a storm. Clutching my purse to my stomach like I had earlier in the day, I started breathing and counting. Yet, this was not a panic attack. No tingling in my hands, no shallow breaths, no anxiety in my chest at all, but I felt drunk as a sailor on shore for the first time after an extended sea voyage. Swaying back and forth, I grabbed the edge of the bench in order to steady myself.

"Paddy, are you okay?" Peter asked. Obviously I looked as smashed as I felt.

"I feel drunk, Peter. All of a sudden I feel drunk." I chatted away aimlessly, my words dancing on the delight of incoherency. "Are there any bars around here?" *Merciful God be with me,* I thought. I don't drink alcohol, yet I felt like I had downed an entire bottle of Southern

Comfort that had not been comforting at all. Stranger still, I felt like I needed more. I angled my body to lean on the back of the bench for support.

"Well, the drunk man behind you probably wishes he hadn't been in a bar today," Peter indicated, pointing just over my right shoulder to a man who obviously had about twenty too many.

"Oh my...." I did not finish my sentence, swinging around so fast that I almost fell off of the bench. "Anything that is not mine, leave now!" I exclaimed. If the intensity and intention found in my tone of voice could have created weather changes, the winds would have whipped through the trees, the lake would have had ripples, and the feathers of the swans would have ruffled right off of their backs.

Catching myself before I splattered down upon one of the little water chickens in a dead run for his life, I pulled myself together, becoming calm as I could be.

"Will you please..." Peter began to say, but did not finish because his expression said all the words for him. His eyes pierced mine while the palms of his hands opened upward to catch whatever knowledge might be falling from the sky.

"Peter, I am a psychic empath who has absolutely no idea how to control it at this point," I blurted out. "You know, I can feel the energy of other people, levels of consciousness, and places on the earth. I learned to do this as a child in order to read the intentions of my parents. The problems come when this sneaks upon me sideways without my knowing it's happening. I've learned how to clear myself, though."

"You mean you acted like that drunk behind you because you felt how he was feeling," Peter mused more to himself than to me. I could tell by the way he paused that his thoughts came more from imagination than logic. It didn't matter, though. I could tell by his expression he fully understood. If so, he was the first person in my life other than Maria who understood this quite annoying ability of mine.

"You know," Peter pondered. "I live intuitively. Actually, I prefer to rely more on my intuition than I do most anything else. Living this way allows me to know beyond the mind." Peter slid down further on the bench; he could have been reclining in a lounge chair with just as much ease.

"As you can tell," I offered, "I'm more clairsentient. Clear feeling. But I also utilize clairaudience when I hear the thoughts I call my spiritual messages. I've had some profound experiences with other forms, though." Until now, the opportunity had never presented itself to actually have a conversation with anyone about intuition. Momentarily, I forgot my fatigue. My eyes sparkled instead of drooping like shades ready to be pulled down for a long-needed sleep. A quickened, lively spark danced on each word. I loved the way this conversation flowed, wherever it took us.

"I just know, intuitively," Peter pronounced with an air of authority that made me giggle. He smiled with me, adding, "You know, claircognizance."

This information did not surprise me at all. Peter evidently retained information quite easily. He spoke four languages fluently, had studied Latin extensively, and had a passing knowledge of Italian. From what I learned when I studied intuition, it is not uncommon for highly intelligent people to have a clear-cut sense of knowing without knowing how they know.

Again, we paused our conversation. We were both quite comfortable with the silence between us; I wondered if tourists walking by could tell if we had ever said anything to each other. My shoulders eased into a calm bend—slightly forward, but not quite slumped. My left elbow relaxed on the back of the bench while my right hand still clutched my purse tightly. I felt like a turtle just peeking out of her shell to determine if the area around provided enough safety to move freely about. Meanwhile, Peter turned to face me directly.

"You're a lucid dreamer, aren't you," he pronounced, making it more of a statement than a question. "You understand the meaning of lucid dreaming, I assume? You know, dreaming in colors, interacting with the dream? Remembering the dream in exquisite detail?"

Giggles started slowly, like fizz popping out the top of a glass of soda.

Gathering force, they burst forth like bubbles that no longer wished to adhere to one another in a bubble bath, each larger, hardier, and braver than the others. Caught up completely in the joy of having someone to talk to about my dreams, I finally laughed out loud. "Oh yes, I'm a lucid dreamer. Sometimes my dreams are more real than my life! In fact, they also reoccur; I dream the same things over and over."

"Like what?" Peter questioned. He leaned toward me ever so slightly, closing the physical distance between us by a couple of inches. I knew immediately he would understand almost any dream I had to present. Calmness radiated out of his eyes, beckoning whatever I had to say to find refuge in his comfort. I decided to jump forward.

"The one that used to repeat the most was about an eagle that had hatched in a chicken coop. Poor little fledgling kept thinking it didn't fit in with the rest of the chickens because she was so different. I dreamed this dream intermittently for several months before my divorce started."

Peter said nothing at first, although I think it may have been hard to remain quiet. He turned away from me toward the water for what felt like five minutes or so before he said anything. I wondered at first if he were going to laugh at my dream. However, that worry held no substance.

Instead, Peter turned back toward me with the most earnest voice I have ever heard and said, "Are there other dreams?"

I decided to share one more; I felt his silence revealed respect. What I desperately needed more than anything right now was a compassionate listener. I leaped right into the dream of the moment.

"Well, there is one I have had for the last two nights."

"Yes? If you're comfortable, please tell me."

I liked the way he asked instead of demanded. It felt safe enough to be me this time. It felt safe enough to share this very real dream that played in my sleep like a sad movie. Without hesitation, I began, "Because the mother of a little seven-year-old girl died, the father placed her in a compound of some sort. Many women of different ages were present. Those in charge of her seemed to be quite austere, especially about suffering for religious reasons."

Peter ran both hands through his hair, not so much to put it in place (which was quite impossible because of the way the brown curls tangled with each other at the back of his head); instead, the move felt to me like a processing of some sort. Slowly, he turned to me before asking one more question about this dream. "Do you have any recollection of what the area looked like in that dream, Paddy?"

"Oh, yes, I certainly do, Peter. I know exactly what I saw in that dream. The little girl is crying, lying in a very small room many, many centuries ago. She can see through some sort of wooden slats at the window, perhaps a window covering, or perhaps a shutter of some kind. She sees out into a yard where there are other small houses in rows, forming a U-shape. Her room is not quite warm enough, so she has bundled under the covers. It's almost time to get up; she knows she will not have choices about her daily activities. Instead, she will be following some preset schedule not of her own doing. She just wants love. She really, truly, just wants to be loved. Love is the most important thing for her now. She knows different forms of love are possible, but she's too young to understand further."

From behind those black-rimmed glasses, Peter's eyes widened as if seeing something invisible. His mouth formed an oblong shape as if he were going to sigh. Instead, he inhaled a long slow breath before blowing it out so gently it was almost indiscernible. I listened intently because I knew he had something to say. I wanted to hear it.

"Paddy, have you ever heard of Beatrice of Nazareth?" Peter asked, correctly assuming that I had no idea who he was talking about. "She lived in the first half of the thirteenth century. Because her mother died when she was seven, she was sent to live with the Beguines in the nearby town of Zoutleeuw, not far from this area. She only stayed there a year, but her interest in this form of life seemed to call to her. She became an oblate at age ten when she rejoined the Beguines."

The lids of my eyes came together, forming narrow slits in order to eliminate the sights around me yet just wide enough to maintain steady vision. As I tried to wrap my mind around the thought that perhaps I had in some way dreamed about an incident that actually could have been true around a thousand years ago, it seemed impossible at first. Yet, since I had been on my own, what Carl Jung termed "synchronicities" seemed normal.

According to *The Merriam-Webster Dictionary,* synchronicities are "the coincidental occurrence of events and especially psychic events that seem related but are not explained by conventional mechanisms of causality." After the fact, I determined the lighthouses in Topsail were quite synchronistic. The gift of a map not long after I needed help was not only synchronistic; it was an answer to a prayer. Literally. Perhaps, after all, that was the basis for synchronicity—being divinely led to evolve as your own sacred story.

Opening my eyes a little wider, I noticed one of the swans had moved away from the other two—perhaps to think, I supposed. At least that seemed logical to me. I also had some things to ponder deeply. Something about Beatrice of Nazareth drew me to her story. An inner surge welled up inside some part of my consciousness. I knew something about Beatrice without knowing how I knew. It felt important enough to ask for confirmation.

"Peter, like the other mystics of her time, Beatrice wrote, didn't she?" Really, I didn't need an answer. For some reason, I felt energetic surges of mysticism every time I thought of her.

"How did you know that, Paddy?" Peter asked before nodding. "Ah, yes. Yes, indeed." He looked at me with a knowing smile and then continued. "First she wrote a book of hymns. In her late thirties she wrote *Seven Ways of Divine Love.* Her manuscript survived, actually, and has recently been translated into English. It's quite a treatise of mystical love."

Mystical love, I mused to myself. Then out loud, I said, "Seven ways of mystical love. I find that incredible. Do you know one of the ways she describes?"

"Only the first. It's got something to do with longing for love in a state of purity and freedom. Or something similar. I'm not sure of the rest. I've given you enough information to find this for yourself. Actually, it may be online now."

My mind turned into a homeland for ten thousand important questions. Was personal freedom actually about the search for love? Had another woman actually longed for this type of spiritual love so much that she would have left family to join a group of women who did nothing but seek this love? Seek it as well as express it? Right now I had no answers. But like Rilke's letter to a young poet, I determined to "...have patience with everything unresolved in your heart and love the questions themselves as if they were locked rooms or books written in a very foreign language." I vowed right then I would pay more attention to my own dreams and visions. For sure, my life from the point of the one-sentence prayer seemed to be taking a path of its own, a spiritual quest straight into the metaphysical land of deeper meanings. From fragmented pieces of who I thought I had been, bit by bit a reassembling had begun. I just had no idea of the outcome.

"Life's a journey, not a destination," wrote Ralph Waldo Emerson. Perhaps he also had been on a quest for a deeper knowledge of self. What I realized while sitting on the bench in Bruges with this man who had such knowledge of not only history of Europe, but also the esoteric, was that I would not be alone on this journey. Oh, I still had to take each step for myself; that I knew for sure. Yet, when my steps faltered, I would get a map, I would get a dream, or I would get a guide or a friend giving me the information I needed to continue on yet again.

I glanced at Peter, who was intent on his solitude. Enough information had passed between us for this one day. Frankly, my mind felt as crammed and overstuffed as the suitcase lying at my feet. Yet, I recognized that the Beguinage, the dreams about Beatrice of Nazareth, and the other synchronicities I had experienced would eventually be understood as the stepping stones of a grand journey. Right now, I just felt filled to the brim with new information.

I don't remember how long Peter and I sat in silence. Time had nothing to do with either of us at the moment. Hours pass as moments when one dives into the regions of the soul. Deep meanings thrive on timelessness quite beyond the present. One lingers in trust while in the grips of deep mysteries, aware of nothing in the immediate area, but knowing all is in order.

I thought of Ariadne, the heroine in the Greek myth of the Minotaur. From what I remembered from reading this myth, she helped the warrior Theseus slay the half-bull, half-man monster who was shunned and confined to a labyrinth. She falls madly in love with Theseus, who takes her to the island of Naxos. Realizing he does not love her, he sails off into the sunset leaving her standing on the shore feeling betrayed, abandoned, and devastated. Theseus served as a rite of passage to Ariadne, for if she had not left the home of her father, if she had not bonded in some way with Theseus, if she had not been left on this island alone, she never would have been discovered by Dionysus who provided her the chance for happiness ever after. It took all of these events to get her to the place of her desires.

Would the man, Peter, sitting next to me on this bench in Bruges live up to his biblical name, which signifies "rock"? Would he be the rock upon which I leaned in order to find my own freedom, my own love, and the passageway to my own version of spirituality? For sure, I knew I did not need rescuing; I had done that myself by divorce. Yet, something lingered just out of consciousness—wordless feelings hidden from the conscious words. The most important question was more about me than it was Peter: How much would I allow myself to lean on this modern-day version of Theseus before I got deposited on the shore, alone and quite confused?

Right now, I was quite confused enough.

Sometimes we come into each other's lives for purposes quite beyond our initial human understanding—human bridges from life as it is known into life expanded. Relationships, after all, are teachers in the best sense of the word, whether we realize it or not. The lessons, however, only evolve into wisdom if we are aware enough to do the inner work involved.

As the morning turned to early afternoon, a profound stillness washed over me as if the moment were frozen in some sort of hyper-aware state of being. I had yet to identify the mountains that I needed to climb, the forests that I wished to explore, or the seas I knew I was going to sail. I had only taken baby steps into the unknown, hoping that I was going in the right direction, wherever my own flow was located.

Did I have Peter's help? Honest help? And how much of myself would I abdicate to his directives? Old personal patterns of behavior do not die easily. Instead, they linger, grasping at brass rings as the carousel of life spins around and around until one finally decides to disembark. Would I be grabbing at Peter's profound esoteric wisdom to find the truth for my life? And would he even let this happen?

I got my first clue when Peter stood up, stomped his right leg briefly in order to allow his pant leg to fall back down his long leg, then turned to me saying in a matter-of-fact tone, "Okay then, Paddy. Gather your belongings and follow me. The room should be ready now since it's afternoon. We have a couple of things to do before you can get settled." He then ambled off ahead of me in the direction of a stone footbridge located to our right spanning the Minnewater.

Even though we were headed outside of Bruges, I clutched my map tightly in my hands just in case I would need it. For one brief moment, I glanced back across the pond, past the water chickens, past the Beguinage, and past the rippling current easing its way into the future. *Niet Kasteels*. Indeed, whatever this experience would be, it would not be as if I were a princess in a castle filled with maids and handservants. Any benefit I was to receive on this particular journey of self-discovery would be equal to the amount of effort I put into the experience. I could accept help, but the steps in the journey had to be only mine. Would I be able to realize this?

Pulling along my suitcase, I followed the direction Peter walked. Tourists with their own guidebooks in hand passed me. Most were in small crowds of specific ethnic origin following a tour director who held signs to designate the name of their group. I had no sign to follow, at least not the paper kind. Instead, I had only my faith that the synchronicities would continue, leading me from one place to another like the bread crumbs of Hansel and Gretel.

Peter paused briefly at the foot of the bridge to allow me to catch up with him. The bridge arched slightly into the air before cascading gracefully down to another side. The many tourists blocked my view of the other side of the bridge, leaving me to wonder what lay just before me. "Paddy, are you ready?" Peter asked. "May I help you with any of your bags?"

I looked intently at him, realizing for the first time that from the beginning, as we sat on the bench in Bruges, he had continually called me by my name. Because I was so unused to hearing my name called by someone, I had not even realized it had happened until now. This made me feel very real. "Yes, I am ready!" I said in earnest.

I wasn't aware exactly what I was ready for, but I did know that I was ready for positive change in whatever way it would present itself. I had to face the future in its entirety, learn to pick myself up again and again if I should fall, and learn that I am capable, worthy, and self-reliant. Most of all, I had to learn exactly who I was created to be. Nothing else would suffice. Nothing at all.

"I'm going to do this myself, Peter," I determined. *"All by myself.* I do appreciate the offer though." The wheels of the suitcase bumped, plopped, and rolled across the ancient footbridge as I struggled to pull it along. Even though Peter walked way ahead of me at a brisk pace, I stopped at the top of the bridge and looked back to the bench that had cradled me for several hours, firmly grounded between the trees on the side of the pond. It looked empty, but sturdy, like a statue constructed in remembrance of those whose path had crossed that way. For a brief moment I felt as if it were still processing the day's experience, just like me.

I took one step forward and then hesitated once more as my foot slipped on a slight bump in the bridge. Steadying myself with the railing on the side of the bridge, I moved forward once again. In a most profound way, I also was crossing my own personal channel as I intended to move from the side of being a victim and martyr across the unknown abyss of healing into personal joy, peace, and perhaps even love. My own prayerful intentions were leading me into the greatest metaphysical adventure of my life.

PART II

Exclamation Moments

"*Men go abroad to wonder at the height of mountains, at the huge waves of the sea, at the long courses of the rivers, at the vast compass of the ocean, at the circular motion of the stars, and they pass by themselves without wondering.*"

ST. AUGUSTINE

"True humility consists in not presuming on our own strength, but in trusting to obtain all things from the Power of God."

ST. THOMAS AQUINAS

◆

CHAPTER FOUR

Finding Strength

"I CAN'T BE here anymore," the eagle realized as she looked around the chicken coop. Chickens were happily pecking the ground near her, but she just did not relate. She twisted her head one way, then another, as if to discover what lay out there beyond her current surroundings. She stretched her neck out in front, straightened her shoulders, and started walking. Whatever lay ahead of her had to be better than chickens waddling around. Somewhere, an open sky called her to freedom. On she walked into the unknown.

Once again the eagle visited my dreams. This time an inner resolve propelled her forward as she started a new chapter in her life, just like me. The clock on the floor besides my open suitcase said 6:15

a.m. Morning dawned much too early. Intense August heat streamed through the cracks between the blinds on the windows of my room making shadow patterns on my bed mimicking iron bars. Already the enclosed room was stifling. My sheets were wet from my own perspiration.

As the morning light continued to trickle in, I wondered what the day would bring forth. Although the hand crank to the blinds was located inside my room, the blinds themselves were more like louvered shutters on the outside of the window placed there not only for privacy, but for protection, or so I assumed. Streaks of light and shadow gradually moved from the bed sheets up the wall, making the mustard yellow of my bedroom look more inviting than it had with just the one lamp lit inside the room.

As it turned out, most houses in Ghent do not have air conditioning, which is considered a luxury item. Except for midsummer, the prevailing winds and changing weather usually created cooler air. This early August morning, however, it seemed hot as hell inside the room. Most of the heat came from my own body, an exterior manifestation of an emotional furnace out of control. Slowly, I cranked the blinds open. The wisps of daylight dancing over the bed sheets and up the walls linked my room and the outside world together. I was ready for my day, whatever it would bring.

Late the previous evening, when I had finally gotten to my rental for the month in an area in the northern part of Ghent, sleep had overtaken me quickly. Peter had graciously driven me to the bus station before I reached my room so I could purchase a bus pass allowing me to travel anywhere in the country for the entire month. At around 40 Euros, I thought it was a very economical deal. Additionally, he showed me the bus stop near my rental home, told me what number bus to look for in order to go to the local market for food, and the number of the bus that would take me to the city center of Ghent, Belgium, the nearest town. Then, having done his duty to help me get settled, he left me on my own. He promised to check up on me in a few days to make sure I was doing well. Frankly, I could not fathom "doing well"—my thoughts ran more along the lines of "survival."

After a breakfast of an apple and some almond butter that I had picked up at a little market in Bruges on the ride into Ghent, I ventured outside my room to find out more about my home for the month. College undergraduates who normally would have been in the various bedrooms of this student house were on summer break. Therefore, I had the rental part of the house to myself. I liked it that way.

The hallway staircase seemed steep to me as I gingerly eased myself up each step. It angled sharply to the right before coming into an upstairs hallway. Just off one side I discovered what had been described in the marketing literature as a kitchen. However, it lacked a stove or cooking surface of any sort. A grand refrigerator by European standards—at least five feet tall and half as wide—was placed in the midst of an otherwise-empty wall. Other than a table, a basket of utensils, a microwave, and a garbage can, I saw nothing else that made me think I was actually inside a kitchen. Whatever I found to eat this month would evidently have to be cold, microwavable, or eaten at a restaurant. Indeed, the month would be filled with cultural differences.

Leaving the kitchen, I stopped by the bathroom hoping to use the upstairs toilet. The entire room was tiled—floor, walls and ceiling—with a shower head and drain built into the corner. The sink was next to the shower, with a small opaque window to the right. What I did not see was a toilet. Evidently, the bathrooms in Europe are for just the purpose of bathing. The toilet has its own purpose, and it was nowhere near the bathroom.

Instead, the toilet was downstairs in the hallway just beside the front door. That was the only facility in the entire house, or so I could find. Therefore, anyone who wished to bathe had to first go into the front entrance hallway to use the toilet before going upstairs to wash. The setup reeked with inconvenience to my American way of thinking.

The first time I used the toilet I almost didn't figure out how to flush the thing. There was no handle off to the side like we have in the United States. I didn't see a chain to pull like I had seen in magazines of antique facilities. Additionally, I saw no foot pedals, nor did I discover any kind of keypad like the fancy electronic toilets made in Japan that had lids opening and closing on an invisible timer. Instead, there was a small metal button on the tank of the toilet that had to be pushed in order to flush. After several tries, I straddled the toilet bowl to face the tank. It took me two thumbs and a strong push to get this toilet to work.

The entire operation had to be done in the dark if I had to go between the hours of 10:00 p.m. and 5:00 a.m. because the overhead light was on a timer. It stayed in the off position all night. It had never occurred to me that I would need a flashlight in Belgium in order to use the toilet, so I hadn't brought one. After a month of this hassle, I couldn't help but wonder if people were using their showers as toilets all over Europe simply out of convenience—but then realized I really didn't want to know.

After a very awkward bath (with water spraying all over the room due to the lack of shower doors), I ventured outside into the little garden to the right and just behind the five-bedroom student house. Although the house seemed smaller than the marital home I had lived in for so many years, the garden was just as exquisite. Every leaf, flower, and even the dirt itself was manicured to perfection. Flowers bloomed that I had never seen before, filling the entire area with the most fragrant perfume. A little lounge chair had been placed on the grass, beckoning me to sit, read, or write. I sat in it for a long time in prayer, asking for help in order to complete the day's activities.

Somehow, I had to get to the grocery store in order to find food for the next couple of days. This seemed to be the scariest thing on the earth to have to do. Not only would it mean a long walk to the bus stop, it would involve having to catch the correct bus, figure out how to get off at the right stop, and then walk into the store. I didn't have a map for security this time. What I had was Philippians 4:13: "I can do all things through Christ who strengthens me." Surely that would be enough.

Since I had no idea about the bus schedule, I ended up waiting for at least an hour before it came. By that time, I had grand expectations of all sorts of problems I would incur on this bus trip. How was I to know when I got to the grocery store if it were located on a side street? Did the bus stop at each intersection, or would I have to notify the driver somehow? Best yet, how would I get the bus door to open?

Breathe in, one, two, three. Breathe out, one, two, three.

I hate buses more than I hate trains. When in buses, I tend to feel at the mercy of the driver, as if I am being taken somewhere against my will. I don't feel that way in trains as much because they automatically stop at each town along the tracks. (I rationalize that I can get off of a train easier than I can a bus. It's completely illogical, yet nonetheless it's very much how the experience processes for me.) Somehow, I did find the grocery store, which was located within walking distance of my rented room. I could have walked there and back by the time the bus had come. Ah, well, live and learn.

Inside the grocery store, nothing was in English. In Belgium, everything is written in French and Flemish, which did me no good whatsoever. Therefore, I had to rely on the pictures on the cans. Even that was insufficient, for if the picture was of a tomato, for instance, would the contents of the can be stewed tomatoes, tomato paste, or tomato soup? Decades ago canned lard used to have a picture of fried chicken on its label, but anyone who bought it knew that chicken is definitely not inside the can. My grocery shopping was to be a process of guesswork.

All fruit had to be placed on electronic scales first and then priced. However, not all the pictures on the machine matched what I had. Which variety of apples had I chosen? All pictures were of red-colored fruit, but which did I have in my hands? Better still, where was the button on the machine that would cause the pricing label to squirt out of the slot like a ticket at the parking lot? This particular day, I priced nothing, for I didn't yet know it was my responsibility. I soon found out differently at the checkout counter.

"Ik ben van de USA," I stammered in my best-practiced Flemish. I had no idea what the male clerk had asked me, but I thought if I identified my country of origin, perhaps I could be understood better.

Earlier I had read that it is polite to at least try to speak the language of the country you are visiting. I gave it my best effort.

"And you certainly do not speak Flemish," he answered in impeccable English with a slight hint of humor. "Welcome to Ghent." He then directed me to the counter where I had to weigh and price my vegetables. Once learned, it was simpler than buying bread or meat.

The bread wasn't packaged like it is in the United States. Instead, it was freshly baked each day before being placed inside plastic bread bins with doors that lift. I picked up the bread with bare fingers hoping no one else had touched each loaf. Then, to get it sliced, I had to carry my naked bread to the slicing machine and navigate yet another set of buttons. I've always been a theorist—one who can imagine most anything—and an intuitive. What I am not is a mechanic. This first time I tried the bread-slicing machine, my bread got pulverized because I placed it inside the slicer twice at ninety-degree angles.

Many people looked, clucked to themselves, and moved on, but no one came to help like they would have in the Southeastern United States. Indeed, I was on my own in all ways. Belgians absolutely do not interfere at all. Because so many people live in such a small area, space is excessively important to them. Even in lines people stood at least four feet from each other. Your space is honored even if you need help. I did end up with bread that day, but it was cubed instead of sliced.

The meat counter was another experience altogether. I never quite understood it the entire time I was in Belgium. Trying to purchase a chicken breast to microwave (to eat with my bread cubes), I pointed to it through the case.

The clerk asked me something, but I had no idea what she was saying. *"Ik begrijp het niet,"* she said incomprehensibly.

I answered by lifting my shoulders and shaking my head to indicate I did not understand. *"No comprende,"* I muttered, inexplicably relying on my high-school Spanish in order to communicate in Flemish.

She repeated with an attitude, *"Ik begrijp het niet."* Then, for what I assumed was good measure, she added, *"Kan ik jou helpen?"*

I pointed to the chicken again. I held up one finger. She just stood there alternating her glance between me and all the meat in her counter. No communication between us whatsoever. So what was I to do in order to get chicken?

I looked at her intently and then out of desperation started clucking. In my best chicken imitation, I completed the charade with my arms bent at the elbow flapping like a bird. I felt like the eagle of my first set of dreams, out of place and acting like a chicken. I finally got my chicken as well as stares, giggles, and head shaking from those who were waiting in line behind me.

What I did not know is that in grocery stores in Belgium one has to pay for meat at the meat counter. When I tried to walk away, security was called. At least he spoke English. I paid for the chicken properly and then tried to leave. But there was another bit of foreign manners to be dealt with, unfortunately.

"Alsjeblieft," the clerk said as she handed me the chicken the security guard had temporarily confiscated.

I had no idea what the response was so I smiled as best as I could at her.

"Alsjeblieft," she said again in a louder voice. *"Alsjeblieft! Alsjeblieft!"* She kept shoving the meat I had just purchased toward me, sliding it back toward her, and then shoving it back to me without ever releasing it from her hand. She was obviously very annoyed with me.

My stars, I had no idea what I was supposed to say. Fortunately, the security guard explained that in Belgium when a purchase is made and payment exchanged, the clerk hands the purchase and says in effect, "Please take this." It is always done with a smile. The purchaser then should say, "Thank you," and smile back. Only after this verbal exchange has happened is the purchase considered to be complete.

"Dank u wel," I said as best I could. My fake smile looked like the Joker in the old Batman series. In the United States, I can imagine the expression on the purchaser's face if the clerk said, "Please take

this," especially after it was already purchased. *Of course, I am going to take this. I just paid for it!* But I was in Belgium, not my own home. I kept my thoughts to myself.

On my walk back from the grocery store, I mused about the deeper meaning of home. If a man's home is his castle, then what is a woman's castle? Would it be the place where she cooks three meals a day, cleans the toilets, and washes the same clothes day after day? Or perhaps it is the hiding place where all her vanished dreams of moonlight walks, affectionate hugs by the warming fireplace flames, or kind words of admiration have withered away like dusty old newspaper pages rotting into oblivion? Could a woman's castle be her own loving heart? Would that literally be possible?

Within my soul, a tiny seed had started to grow unaware. Though it was unrecognizable at first, I simply honored the daily routine as best I could while giving myself space to open up to new experiences brought to me by my Belgian adventures. Unlike most writers I know now, I did not start writing by journaling. Instead, I simply wrote my questions, prayed, and knew answers would come either through automatic writing or new experiences. I never knew how, why, or in what form. Perhaps it was hope more than anything else that kept me going from day to day—hope and a desire to figure what really living actually meant.

Confidence was a devil's lair for me at this time. Yet, as human traits were being given out in that pre-birth place in the heavens, I must have stood in the willpower line twice. It was all I had to function with— that and faith that I would get through this journey somehow, perhaps meeting my soul and spirit along the way. Before that happened, I intuited I had to get into the old city section of Ghent. To do that, I would have to ride on a Belgian bus for over an hour.

God help me.

After the trip to the grocery store, I considered my day over. For the rest of the afternoon, I lounged outdoors enjoying the manicured garden. I pulled a chair to the back side of the house, angling it to face flowers, green leaves, and low-hanging branches of trees instead of the road in front of the house. The garden encircled me just like my old basement desk when I was married. I felt safe.

The next day, after a repeat of the previous early-morning routine, I donned athletic shoes, comfortable pants, and a knit shirt in order to spend the day in Ghent. Talking myself into going was not as hard as I'd thought it would be; I knew I would go crazy if I stayed inside the same room all day. Yet, summoning up the courage to get outside the safety of my room took all the willpower I could muster. This time, I didn't even have a map of Ghent to clutch. I did have my camera, and a purse slung over my shoulder that I grasped as if my life depended upon keeping it positioned close to my side. Gingerly, I opened the front door, checking for at least the umpteenth time that I had my key, the number of the bus I was to catch, and my bus ticket. Above all, I made sure I had my passport tucked away just in case I needed it. In fact, I checked it one more time just to make sure.

What I needed was confidence. Security. Inner peace. What I had was determination. And fear. Oh, yes, I had great gobs of fearful thoughts running through my head like a pack of hungry wolves.

What if I don't find Ghent? What if I take the wrong bus? What if I get lost, never to be found again? What if I never find my inner self?

Oh God, what if I never had one?

After stepping outside the house, I made it to the curb before I had to stop to breathe. As I counted breaths, I took a step with each one, mimicking a bridesmaid walking down the wedding aisle. Eventually, the initial panic of heading out into the foreign world eased somewhat. The bench beside the bus stop was not so far. After all, I had just done this same thing yesterday. The only difference was that I had to stay on the bus longer this time in order to get to St. Peter's Station. Peter told me I would know I was there when the bus engine turned off.

"Please, God," I prayed as I walked ahead, "don't let this bus turn off its engine before I get to my destination." My prayers mimicked a beggar holding out his tin cup for pennies. Yet, it was all I was able to do. Thankfully, I had the same driver this time. For some reason, it comforted me just knowing that I was in a familiar presence, even though I knew nothing about him at all other than the fact that he could indeed drive the bus. Sometimes a familiar face is all that's needed when life hurls fear your way.

While sitting in the bus early that morning as it chugged through stop after stop in an area I had never seen before (and in which I couldn't read the language of the signage), I felt like I was being led to the gallows instead of going to an ancient cobblestoned center filled with tourists.

At first, everything I saw looked interesting. Row houses tightly packed together looked manicured, yet older. They also looked crowded to me, as if they could not find enough space to live or enough air to breathe. Lace curtains seemed to adorn most windows, allowing light to filter in while maintaining privacy. The bus passed several Catholic churches, each one a center of community life. I saw no shopping malls, but instead noticed that small grocery, hardware, or clothing markets were located in narrow shops downstairs while their owners were housed upstairs. Bicycles were everywhere, with men and women of all ages moving along the narrow bike paths squeezed between the sidewalks and the street.

Eventually, it all looked the same to me, like a muddle of confusing sights, situations, and people in the midst of an unforeseen purpose. The surrealism of so much unfamiliar life taking place outside the bus windows reminded me of watching sitcoms on a television screen. Definitely, I was not part of it in any way, but was more of an observer of life flashing by. I began to feel separated from what I was seeing, as if I were falling into a dreamlike maze. Once I even placed my hand on the bus window as if touching it would somehow connect me to the world outside. Instead of connecting to Belgian life, I felt nothing but glass—slick, indistinctive glass. I returned my right hand to my lap, alternating my hand between fist and open palm before touching my hands together just to make sure I was real.

Finally, after about an hour of chugging through what I assumed was the city of Ghent, our bus pulled into a large bus station. The bus engine finally became silent. When I noticed the tracks and what looked to be a train station, I knew I was in St. Peter's Station, my destination. The chaos I heard evidently came from my ever-present fears; passengers were disembarking from our bus in total silence.

Looking back to that day, I wish I had counted the number of streets that converged upon St. Peter's Station. I know there were at least five directions from which to choose. Unfortunately, I only wanted the one that led directly to the old section of the city. Two days previously, Peter had described to me the direction I was to go in order to find what he called "the main shopping street," a street with the most up-to-date stores. Oh, I had no intention of shopping, but from what I understood from Peter's directions, that was the most direct way to the ancient cobblestone streets. I really had no particular destination in mind other than to discover some of the older parts of Ghent, preferably a bench besides a meandering river. I intuited a flowing river would be peaceful to me. Yet, the urge to get to that city center pulled at me from some unrecognized place in my soul as I longed to bond with anything familiar. Even though I did not understand this, I trusted the inner urge.

Even though Peter had explained to me that the trolleys labeled "number one" would go directly to the old part of the city, I had no intention of getting onto one of them because I was still reeling from the long bus ride. Instead, I stood for a while until one of them came by and then watched the direction in which it traveled, delighted I was not riding in it. What I truly needed to do was to walk, to breathe, and to move within my own flow. As I slowly followed the trolley tracks, I made my way through an area near the station that had more parked bicycles than I had ever seen in one place. At first, it seemed simple— at least a lot simpler than the bus because I was moving under my own power.

Crossing streets seemed easy enough to me. I simply followed the crowd. Unlike the cities I knew in the United States, pedestrians in Ghent walked out in front of cars when they needed to cross the street. The cars always stopped. Evidently pedestrians had the right of way. However, I always hesitated before crossing the street. Frankly, I had no intention of being hit by a car, even if I did have the right of way.

For several blocks I followed the trolley tracks, confident they led to the city center. Just like the second and third stanza from Psalms 23, I felt the need to be beside the still waters in order to restore my soul. Literally, it was more than a feeling; it seemed to be more of an intense inner directive. I could do nothing other than keep walking in order to find a place where a river meandered through the older part of Ghent—even though I didn't know for sure a river even went through Ghent's older section. For the life of me, I had no idea why I felt this way. However, my intuition was screaming at me to keep going.

I really had to find a bench by a river. Watercourses always have been soothing to me. After the calming effect of the little canal that twisted and turned through Bruges, I truly wished to find a tiny place apart from the hustle and bustle of city life that had a bench on which I could watch the river flow through the city. In fact, for some reason beyond my conscious thoughts, I craved it. Perhaps it had to do with recognizing a current externally, hoping I would find one internally one day. It seemed extremely important to reach a river though. Extremely important.

Sidewalks in Ghent are made of squares of cement, between one and two feet square, laid right next to the buildings, instead of poured concrete with joints every several yards like we have in the United States. These squares of cement formed many joints of concrete, making sidewalks that were very narrow on some streets and not always even. Some were so narrow it was impossible for two people to pass each other. Still, my walking shoes with the rubber soles felt comfortable to me. Made of substantial leather with arch support on flat soles, they weren't fashionable and looked more like something my grandmother's mother would have worn when she milked cows. Not only could I not have worn heels like the ladies all around me, I would not have even tried.

After about three or four city blocks, I reached an intersection where the tracks in the road forked. Either I followed the tracks straight, or I turned to the right. Because the choice to the right was a wider street, I turned to follow these tracks. Yet after one block or so, the tracks again turned abruptly to the left. This time the road was dark and narrow. Taller buildings were built really close to the street, making the sidewalk only three squares wide. To me, it felt like I would be entering an extremely tight cave if I took this road. I felt very uncomfortable just thinking about it. If I were to walk down that narrow street, I knew for certain I'd never be able to get back.

Breathe. In one, two, three. Out one, two, three.

After a very determined pause loaded with anxiety, I retraced my steps to go back to the street I had originally chosen. This section of the street was narrower than the part I had walked before, but it was not nearly as dark and foreboding as the very scant one had been. The sidewalks were four to six squares wide instead of two. Besides, there were more people on this street. It seemed safer.

As I walked, I began counting the squares in the sidewalk, hoping to overcome my walking companion, anxiety. Since I had turned back to my original path, many thoughts had begun to swarm in my mind— was I walking in the right direction? Would I ever find my way back to the bus? Why was the street so very, very narrow? Where was the light?

It was not the narrowness of the street that panicked me, but the intense fear of being trapped somehow and not finding my way through the city.

Counting was not working this time, even though I was counting as hard as I could, matching my breaths to each number. As I clutched the purse that was slung over my neck and shoulder like a warrior's belt of bullets, I felt completely disarmed. Feeling very vulnerable, I reached up with my left hand, joining it to my right while grasping the strap tightly as if to keep it from vaporizing into the close Belgian air.

What air?! I can't find any air to breathe!

Anxiety gripped my throat like a soldier's fist in hand-to-hand combat—kill the enemy before he kills you. As I looked down at my hands, I opened the fists momentarily to examine my palms, making sure they were still there. The tingling had started again, running up my arms to the elbows. My vision began to blur, as if the narrowness of the road were going to trap me under an anvil of weight. The sounds of the city began to fade because my hearing was shutting down. As my legs became weak, I knew I had to find support before I fell to the ground. Panic was winning the battle this time.

The building next to me was painted mustard yellow, an unusual color for a building in Ghent. Frankly, I did not care how unusual it was or how dirty it may have been. Turning my back to the building, I leaned against it for support, shoulders pressing against bricks hot from the August sun. My legs were angled out in front of me, giving me the appearance of a human sliding board. The street was in front of me, people were passing me by on the sidewalk, and the world seemed busy—yet all of it seemed surreal, as if I were watching it all through an old leaded window with blurs in the glass. Just as I had experienced before, part of me fragmented from the rest, a dangerous situation when totally alone in a new area. As my thoughts began to fade, I cried out with the last bit of strength I had in order to get Divine help. My words were hardly a whisper.

"I can do all things through him who strengthens me." Over and over I said it until the words of Philippians 4:13 were silent whispers of faith oozing out of the depths of my soul. The rest of me had become quite undone.

"God, I need help," I sobbed. Tears were gushing by this time, silent sobs of terror filling my every moment. It was then I heard the first answer. Usually, I was writing my questions to God and writing the answers, but this time I could not have taken the little notebook out of my purse to write if my life depended upon it. I had to get to the answer for my plea for help any way I could. That still, quiet voice of God within me needed to shout an answer inside my sensitivity in order that I hear it. By this time, I was all but deaf. Nor could I see clearly. My entire body was shaking in terror.

Turn around, the intuitive, holy voice of my soul beamed into my heart. *Turn to your right.* The words were so quiet; it was almost as if I had heard a thought. *Take three steps forward, and turn toward the building's windows. Place your back to the street.*

What else was I to do? I could not write, I could not walk onward, and I could not even breathe well. I had asked for help, and now I was receiving words of instruction. Three steps forward was about all I could manage. Even at that, I held out my right hand on the wall to steady myself watching each foot to make sure it touched the ground. If I hadn't done that, I am sure I would have melted into a puddle of human nothingness. This placed me at the middle of the yellow building's wall, directly in front of the far right side of a store window.

Eye to eye, right in front of me, printed in English, were the words "Travel Books." Literally, without knowing it, I had leaned against a bookstore specializing in travel books and maps of the world. My prayer for help had been answered; with a map, I would not feel so trapped by the uncertainty of being lost.

My breathing began to slowly turn to normal as I pressed my face to the window, cupping my hands on either side of my eyes in order to see inside the store. I straightened my legs, shifting from one foot to the other as I slowly came back to a more manageable state of hysteria. Evidently, my eyes were again able to focus, for I saw inside the store many maps, travel literature, and what looked to me to be welcoming shelves of travel books. The little travel bookshop seemed to be as peaceful as a library, a beckoning boon for confused travelers. When I glanced over my right shoulder just for a moment, I realized the street was not as narrow as I had thought after all, and the sidewalks were much wider. Rays of sunlight trickled through the clouds in waves of hope. I began to trust life again. The panic battle was over; I had survived.

"Hallo!" Evidently, the shop's proprietor decided to come outside see about the woman who was breathing vapor marks on his window. *"Kan ik je helpen?"*

His words startled me momentarily, for I had not heard nor seen the door of his shop open. Fortunately, his demeanor was pleasant, his smile seemed genuine, and best yet, his tone of voice sounded soothing. Although I did not understand Flemish, one of his words sounded like "hello" while two of his other words could have been "can" and "help." Hoping my guess was correct, I answered, "Hello. I speak only English."

"*Vanwaar ben je?*" he first said, then quickly translated in impeccable English, "Where are you from?"

"I am visiting from the United States," I answered. "From the southern part of the United States."

"Oh, I could tell that," he said. "Your accent could stop traffic!" With that, his head tilted back as he laughed heartily, thoroughly enjoying himself. Truly, the man was a jolly as one of Santa's elves. "Can I help you find something?"

"Well," I said as only a Southerner could, exaggerating the word into at least two syllables and making it last several seconds to amuse myself as well as my Flemish helper. Perhaps if I laughed, my mood would shift into something more positive. "Actually, this is the first time I have been in the city of Ghent. I have no idea which direction I need to walk." Just voicing that particular fear seemed to give it substance beyond myself, allowing me to detach more from the problem at hand instead of feeling I was going to be swallowed whole by my own dilemma.

"You are at exactly the right place at the right time for what you need!" he answered gustily. His words seemed to blow out of his mouth before moving along currents of wind like many angel feathers shaken out of a gunny sack beyond the clouds far above. "Come in. Come in!" he gestured with both arms to the inside of the shop. "We'll find exactly what you need right in here."

Before walking up several small steps into the shop, I steadied myself by standing straight while still touching the window for support. Hesitating while I established a firm footing, slowly I released my palm before lifting each finger at a time until only my first finger pointed at the books beyond the window.

"Yes, yes, you will find exactly what you need right in here. I have several maps, as well as travel books about our wonderful city. Just come on in, and I'll point you in the right direction. You can browse to your heart's content."

With that, I fairly bounded into the shop like a cat jumping upon a counter to nibble at Thanksgiving dinner. By now, I was almost purring. After a while, I found exactly what I thought would help me navigate the roads to the center of the ancient city of Ghent. I stuffed the travel guide, as well as a free map of the bus routes he gave me, inside my shoulder purse. Content with the world—or more content with knowing my location in the world—I thanked the cheerful proprietor for helping me and turned to be merrily on my way. Again, help had unexpectedly come just when it was needed.

Had I missed something in my life? Was it truly this easy to get help when you most needed it by simply asking? I wasn't sure yet. Nevertheless, I tucked these thoughts away just to the left side of my heart just in case I needed help again in an emergency.

With maps in hand, I felt comforted knowing that even though things were foreign, totally unfamiliar, and beyond anything I had ever experienced before, at least I would be able to look at the map to pinpoint my location, wherever it may be. Even though I was totally lost to myself, and had lost a home, friends, and familiar surroundings by walking out of marriage misery, in a pinch I could look at the street signs near the intersections to find where I was on the map. As strange as it may seem, one has to start somewhere in self discovery. For me, it was finding my physical self on a map, a truth I learned in Bruges. This tiny seed became my starting point in personal growth. With that map, I could walk anywhere, choosing left or right, and not get totally separated from all reality.

I was moving into my own direction one step at a time.

*"The intuitive mind is a sacred gift and
the rational mind is a faithful servant.
We have created a society that honors
the servant and forgets the gift."*

ALBERT EINSTEIN

◆

CHAPTER FIVE

That Inner Voice

DURING THAT FIRST week in Belgium, it took three attempts for me to get to the old section of Ghent called the city center. After I received the map from the shop owner, I used it not to get to the river that meandered through town, but back to Saint Peter's station. The uneventful bus ride seemed just as long as it had the first time. However, I eased into the ride with grace, knowing that I could indeed get to the station and back to my bus stop any time I wished without turning into a puddle of panicky mush.

On my second attempt, I followed the trolley tracks several blocks further, but stopped at an electronics store in order to purchase a pay-in-advance cell phone. Even though Peter had given me his cell phone number that first day, I had yet to find a way to call him if I needed him in an emergency. As I walked down the sidewalk, ever mindful of the trolley tracks to my right, I hesitated only briefly before I went inside, hoping the experience would be easier than buying groceries.

Angels must have been guiding me, for I walked right to the cell phone counter, passing all manner of computer equipment and electronics paraphernalia, none of which I would have known how to work even if they had been in English. Thankfully, Peter had described what I needed that first day in Bruges. Quickly, I picked out a little blue cell phone, hoping it was the kind that could be activated on a pay-per-minute basis. Without much drama, I waited in line behind three people at the counter, keeping the usual distance per Belgium custom. At least I had already learned something.

Remembering my experience at the meat counter several days before, I said *"Dank je wel"* to the youthful clerk before he even had the chance to say something to me. In fact I said it several times, just to make sure he understood I was attempting to be polite. My head bobbed and nodded like a cork floating in a choppy sea. However, he ignored me, fiddling instead with one of the newest handheld games shoved in his direction by one of his coworkers. The two seemed more like high school students to me than store clerks.

After paying, I said, *"Dank je wel,"* again before adding, "How?" As I shoved the phone back across the counter to him, I repeated, "How?" once more. I had no idea how to insert the battery, how to activate it, or how to make the thing work. In fact, I have trouble enough with those things in America where the directions are in English. He answered me speaking Flemish for five minutes without checking my face for a hint of comprehension.

However, after he activated my phone, he turned his back to me and said to his coworker in flawless English with a very disgusted tone in his voice, "These tourists are so troublesome to me. Anyone can make a phone work. Whew!"

"Bless you," I crooned back to him as I reached out to pat the back of his shoulder as if he were a friendly dog, avoiding all Belgian customs for politeness. Then, more to release my frustration than anything else, I added, "Bless your efforts. Bless your attitude." Enough was enough as far as I was concerned. One of the coaches at my children's school years ago would say the same thing (or similar) to the basketball referees when a bad call was made. When said sincerely, it is very effective. At least in this case, it made me feel better. I would have loved to speak to him in English as I bought my phone. It would have been the first time in several days that I would have had a chance to have a conversation with anyone.

Instead, I chalked the entire experience up to his youth. One day he may be displaced in society, on his own spiritual mission, and quite confused. Or maybe not. Eventually I realized that often what people say to you is not about you, but is actually about them. I hadn't learned this at the time I purchased the phone, though; then, I still took absolutely everything anyone said to me as unconditional truth. Experience is a boon to inner wisdom. My own lessons were forthcoming, it seemed.

The third time I attempted to get to the city center, I achieved my goal. With lines highlighted on the map of Ghent, I found the older cobblestone streets with absolutely no problem at all. In fact, my previous two attempts had served me well as far as boosting my confidence. I walked along the same street, noting familiar unfamiliarity.

By the time I wandered into the older section of Ghent, I found St. Michael's Bridge, the most famous bridge in Belgium. As I walked across the stone archway, for some reason I felt very connected to something powerful quite beyond me. Upon reaching the top of the bridge, I looked over the iron railing directly at the Leie River, wondering at first why I had felt the need to be near it.

Elongated boats filled with tourists listening intently to the history of the area moved slowly on the river. For some reason, I had no intention of ever riding in one of those boats. Perhaps it felt to me like an open-air bus on water. Yet, it was more than that, I know. It seemed too touristy. Instead, I had to be near the water in order watch the flow find direction of its own accord, moving within the space provided as it coursed into the future. As I watched that day, the river drew me into time past, just as if I had memories of flat barges bringing wool and goods into the area. Of course that couldn't be, for I had never been in Ghent before. For certain, whatever I needed to know from my trip to the older city center would come to me via intuition instead of through the narrative of a guide on a boat made for tourists.

As I glanced back over my shoulder, the three towers of Ghent—Saint Nicholas Church, The Belfry, and Saint Bavo's Cathedral—loomed upward as if by sheer design their intention was to point upward toward the heavens. Beside me on the left were the Graslei and Koornlei, two streets alongside the Leie River. The most beautiful medieval houses of Belgium can be found near the bridge.

However, that particular day I was not interested in those medieval houses; something called to me just beyond the bridge to the right. My intuition was screaming to move on, beyond the tourists, beyond the towers, the bridge, and the river that I had worked so hard to find. At the time, I could do nothing else but follow my own inner nudging. I crossed back over the bridge walking toward Gravensteen, the ancient castle of many Counts dating from the early 1200s.

After paying an entrance fee, I toured Gravensteen. The castle was wonderful, especially since so much of it had lasted throughout all these many centuries. However, in one of the upstairs rooms was a museum containing metal devices used to torture people. If I had known, I would not have gone in, as there is enough torture in this world displayed every night on the news of war, killings, and theft without visiting rooms filled with ancient devices used for inflicting pain on each other.

The courtyard was much more open, bordered by the castle on one side and a very tall stone wall circling the other side, enclosing the area completely except for the entranceway from the street. I paused momentarily expecting some sort of energetic clearing to take place in the sunny area as the horror of the torture room still lingered with me. Instead, I began to feel a different type of energy permeating through me as I connected to the courtyard. I did not like it at all, but for a different reason.

In the museum torture room, the energy had felt like victimization, like being shackled and persecuted against one's will. In the courtyard,

I felt a plethora of different energies swarming around me. I intuited the vibes of someone being in control, just as a Count would have been. Then there were the vibes of people of all socio-economic levels attempting to please others. Also, the energy of death seemed indistinguishable from the earth itself.

Was I psychically picking up on events of the past? Or was my imagination taking me for a rather interesting ride? From what happened next, I truly think it was my intuition kicking in with a bit of environmental empathy, the ability to feel either the consciousness of the people living in an area, the history of the people of an area, or the energies of the land itself.

I walked on the ledge of the stone wall just as the soldiers of old might have. As I overlooked the courtyard of Gravensteen Castle, tourists mingled about. They were entering in groups, meandering into the castle rooms to get their money's worth. I was aware of how my feet felt on the stones below me, secure and solid. The sun played hide and seek in clouds overhead, which moved faster in Belgium than they did in Georgia. I also was aware of the history of the area, not specific in details, but through the intuitive sensations I began to feel.

Through my intuitive third eye, I saw a woman of about thirty-five years of age. With her hands tied behind her, she had been forced by a very strong guard dressed in chain mail to bend over what seemed to be a sturdy trunk of a tree formed into a cube. It almost looked like stone, but did not seem grey enough to me. Two men dressed in rather fine clothing stood nearby to watch, one to the woman's far right side and the other facing her head. Spectators of the community gathered around in groups, wearing the simply woolen clothing of the day's workforce. At a nod toward the woman's head from the man in charge, a rather strong-looking man lifted what looked to me like a rather special form of sword over his head and came down on the neck of the victim. Her severed

*head rolled off the wooden block to the feet of the man
in charge.*

That inner knowing, that subtle feeling which is quite beyond reality of the five senses, blew tsunami-like into my interior perceptions, gifting me with information I could not have known otherwise. I gasped so hard I had to hold on to the stone ledge to keep from falling off the wall. Too involved in the psychic moment, I have no idea if any of the other tourists noticed.

I'm convinced intuition in its finest form is the language of the soul, the basis of mystical experience. In the Bible, intuitive wisdom allowed the prophets to actually became prophets. It is what helped the saints be saintly. Through that still, quiet, holy voice within, Jesus knew to heal the two blind men on the way to Jerusalem by touch while he healed the blind man in Bethsaida with spit and mud. Often called "gut instinct," intuition exists to all humanity, but only if openness is first embraced. Very intuitive children, as well as adults whose intuition opens up later in life, often are not understood by society. Unfortunately, many people believe only what they have experienced or information they have obtained through the senses of seeing, smelling, hearing, touching, and tasting.

My own intuition had remained in the strong box of safety I created as a child years ago. Slowly, it awakened through the writing of questions and answers over several years. But until this particular day, I had not had this level of intuitive vision since I was a child.

As I walked out of Gravensteen, I felt like I had reclaimed part of myself I had lost many years before. For a while, I stood just outside the gate not particularly looking for what direction in which to walk, but knowing I would understand that inner calling better if I embraced the fact that it existed. A gentle breeze blew through my hair, cool and inviting on the hot August day. My eyes were closed in order to shut out the view around me, allowing an inner peace to enter my soul. Or perhaps it was coming from my soul. Or better still, for my soul. I had no idea.

Deliberately, I opened my arms wide to the heavens as if to make a funnel in order to receive some form of loving embrace from heaven itself. It covered me like a finely-knitted shawl draped around my shoulders, and the warming feeling of Spirit's love moved right into my heart.

In walking away from Gravensteen, I felt as if I was intentionally walking away from the heaviness of not being understood in my child-hood. This was what my inner knowing was telling me. That empty, absent feeling that had plagued me since my preteen and teenage years began to dissipate. Let the torturous emotional moments of not being understood stay in the past. Let them fade away like ripples on the River Leie as they slapped against the ancient stone and brick buildings. Some place deep within me seemed alive again, small to the point of almost being insignificant, yet bursting with life. Just as an acorn is filled with the potential of an oak that is yet to be, I also felt filled with impending expansion.

I walked along the cobblestone street without looking at my map. For the first time in Belgium, I wandered easily along the narrow streets, moving into what was called the Patershol, an area of Ghent that is filled with old brick buildings and cobblestone streets so narrow a car can hardly maneuver through them. Currently, there were many restaurants in this area, including one Peter had mentioned, Amadeus, an all-you-can-eat rib establishment. Mentally I noted it, wondering if I could ever get there for dinner one night. The red walls, antique books, and red checkered curtains appealed to me for some reason.

I meandered along, noticing how my feet balanced on the round tops of the cobblestones that filled the streets. Balancing seemed to be more important to me than ever, emotional as well as physical. Occasionally I reached out to touch one of the ancient stone walls as though if by touch I could be part of the setting, understanding the fortitude it took to withstand so many changes over the centuries. Although I had never liked close quarters before, this time the proximity of the buildings seemed to nourish me. Each building held secrets, many stories from centuries of people just trying to make a life seem like living; I related to that. My steps slowed meditatively, one by one, as if each step meant more than the previous one.

Light filtered through the clouds, searching for bits and pieces of the area in which to express illumination. Ever-present shadows dissipated into this sunlight on the corners of buildings as well as in brief interludes on the street. Once I even stopped, holding my hand into the sunlight then back into the shadows, then repeating. The experience of light and shadow was very real in not only the Patersol area but also inside my awakening spirit.

As I rounded yet another corner, I stopped suddenly before crossing the street. My feet simply would not move another step; it felt as if I had walked straight into a new thought. Glancing around me—first to the left, to the right, then straight ahead—I next looked back in the direction I had just walked. It was not the streets that startled me, nor the idea that I didn't know where I was and was not frightened, but a sudden idea that seemed to flood into my consciousness from somewhere beyond my current awareness.

"Oh my," I said out loud to absolutely no one. "I cannot believe how this area has changed since the Middle Ages."

It made no sense to me at all. I had never been to Ghent, at least not in this lifetime. Why, then, would I notice how things had changed? How would it happen that I was aware of an area from the Middle Ages, aware of the many changes it had endured without reading it somewhere or having someone tell me? I had no idea. What I did know was that I could feel the changes somehow inside my body, mind, or perception. Like shoots of daffodils in early spring, I felt surges and tingles pushing out of my own sullied familiar into a new light of day.

Pausing ever so briefly, I turned toward the direction of the shopping area, delighted to find a cluster of benches under the shade of a tree growing beside the River Leie. Pigeons were waddling about, hoping to find a leftover crumb or two. Frankly, I had no intention of feeding the pigeons. I needed to sit down before my legs gave out from under me. Instead of fatigue, I felt like information had begun to shift through me, as me, and beyond me—information about me as well as about the area in which I found myself. The fatigue came from not knowing exactly what this information meant. I was absolutely sure I had not experienced this level of inner awareness before, at least not that I remembered.

At first, I watched the tourists on boats floating down the river and back again, noting that not many of them were smiling but instead were listening intently to history lectures given in several different languages. I watched the wake formed from the boats lap up onto the brick walls of the buildings that had withstood the elements of nature at the water's edge. I watched the pigeons congregate, separate, and then congregate again as a middle-aged lady threw cracker crumbs to them. Ever so slowly, I closed my eyes, hoping to block out what I was seeing from what I was feeling intuitively. More than anything, I needed to give it a name. If I recognized this feeling, perhaps I could claim it better.

Eventually, it came, not as a reflection, not as an idea, but as a sense. It was the same sensation felt after a weary traveler returns to his or her place of residence. Like a child cuddling with a favorite blanket, it comforted me, embraced me, and actually engulfed me as wave after wave passed through my entire body before landing somewhere inside my heart. It felt like I was being held in a lover's arms, like the entire world was at peace. Even though the sounds of the city flooded my hearing, inside there was a peaceful silence that I did not recognize because I had not heard it in so many years.

There in the midst of a foreign city filled with buildings I had never seen before, tourists I did not know, and a language I could not understand, I felt like I was home. In some way, I had come home.

Home—but not just any home. Somewhere deep inside I was experiencing the type of coming home feeling that emanates from deep, spiritual love innate to each of us.

As I sat there on the bench wide-eyed with wonder, I pulled the small notebook out of my purse with the intention of writing clarity into the situation at hand. With pen in hand poised at the top of the page, I again closed my eyes in prayerful meditation, hoping the answer would come and bring me clarity. Was I coming home to Belgium? Or was I coming home to myself? I was not sure. In fact, I could not even get to the place where those two questions made any sense to me; therefore, I was not able to even write them on the top of the page. Indeed, I was a wanderer searching for that unknown, unrecognized loving something I'd had all the time but unfortunately didn't know I had.

When I opened my eyes, I fully expected the sights to have changed, primarily because I felt so different, even with the questions unwritten. Yet, all around me was the same as before, just different sets of tourists strolling by with maps in their hands and guidebooks tucked carefully away in shirt pockets. Smiling to myself, I wondered if they also would like to find themselves on a map somewhere. Also, I wondered if any of them even needed to.

My little notebook page remained blank, questions and answers not forthcoming. Even though I knew to trust God for the answers just as it states in Proverbs 3:5, I had to talk to someone about this. True to my female nature, I had to process out loud what I felt in order that I might understand it more thoroughly. Slowly, I pulled out my little cell phone and dialed Peter's number. Perhaps Peter would be able to listen attentively while I expressed my soul.

◆ ◆ ◆ ◆ ◆

"Vind je het leuk?" Peter asked, indicating the pile of ribs on my plate. "Do you like it?" At my suggestion, Peter met me several days later at Amadeus, the rib restaurant in the Patersol area of Ghent. Each of us had a slab of ribs covered with the best sauce I have ever eaten. Another bowl of sauce was on the edge of the table slightly to our left. A quick push would have knocked it all over the antique books lined up on the red shelves next to our corner table.

"Yes, they're absolutely divine," I answered truthfully. After cutting each rib apart from its buddies, the first one had become naked history, leaving its saucy remnants on my fingers, napkin, and plate. I hoped it would not end up on my shirt because of the inconvenience of having to wash it out in the sink of my rental unit.

"Wait until you taste the baked potato," Peter counseled. "You'll never want ordinary butter on one again." He dished out a second helping of the sauce meant for the potato, allowing the excess to melt all over his plate. "This is food for the gods," he grinned.

"And I thought the gods dined on golden elixir," I answered back playfully while I dived into another rib. "Now I know."

Peter was well into finishing his first slab of ribs, having enthusiastically gorged on them like a starving man. With careful deliberation, he swiped his lips with his tongue before sucking each finger clean. After a swig of beer followed by a belch, he held up a rib remnant, shaking it at me like it was a finger pointing out information I needed to know. "Paddy, life is like a slab of ribs. First, it's full of meat, some easy to chew and some a bit tougher, but all well worth the effort. It's our job to clean up the meat—enjoying the journey—before finally eliminating all issues keeping us from understanding wisdom found in the bare bones of the matter." His rib was moving up and down at me as if the words were coming from it instead of the mouth of a man enormously enjoying himself. Peter placed the rib into the refuse can on the table, grinning from ear to ear the entire time.

Frankly, I wasn't sure if he was talking about eating ribs or something more profound. From what I knew of Peter, his words always were filled with depth, even if they seemed illogical at the time. Often they came at me sideways, unexpectedly filled with some little morsel of truth I had not known previously. I paused from eating just long enough to look eye to eye at Peter, hoping there would be more to the story. Although wisdom is best integrated when truth is discovered for one's self, what I wanted right then and there was to be presented with answers to my question about what I had perceived days before—not ribs. Peter, though, was not buying into presenting me with any type of easy answers. His way of teaching mimicked navigating the path through a labyrinth; one had to do the walking singularly to reach center.

"Say what?" I answered back, forgetting temporarily that I still had half a slab of ribs to eat. Peter, however, had begun his second round of ribs and second potato. How he managed to talk and eat so fast was beyond me. His meaning was also beyond me.

"You said you wanted to talk in order to understand what you were feeling the other day when walking through the older, narrow section of town. Perhaps you simply felt your own version of the rib. Felt your own version of exactly what it is to be you. You may have felt your core."

"I'm a rib?" I asked incredulously. "Is that what you mean?" My voice trailed after the last question for I knew intuitively that was not at all what Peter was explaining to me. In order not to hear an answer immediately, I dived into separating more ribs, making each of them singularly important. With my fingers, I held up one that seemed to be filled with the most meat.

"If I eat the meat, then true essence is left?" I reflected to myself. Truly I did not want an answer. Not then. Frankly, it didn't matter what I wanted, for Peter evidently had no intention of answering me as long as I was thinking out loud. Slowly, I took a bite of meat, chewing it rather deliberately before swallowing the last bit of goodness. Licking my own fingers one at a time with a sucking motion that could be heard across the room, the truth began to dawn upon me. The dawning of a rib-truth-wisdom flashed itself into our candlelit moment.

"Peter," I said slowly as the words began to form from thoughts oozing out from my very soul. "What if my substance—my backbone so to speak—what if my inner realness has been so hidden over the years that I haven't recognized it? What if there is a firm, strong inner part of me I had not accepted before?" I took the bare rib in my right hand, turned it over and over just as if it were a crystal ball where I could gain the answers to my own questions.

"If my essential self is strong," I continued, "is the real strong part of me, then what in the world is the meat? What have I been chewing on all these years thinking it was all I was? All I had?" By this time, I had no intention of eating one more rib. Peter, on the other hand, waited for his third and last section of ribs. He stopped at two potatoes, however.

"Well," Peter formed his words carefully without the playfulness he'd had before, "What words of others have you taken on as your truth? What has been your sauce so far—your neediness—that caused you to eat hungrily as truth every word everyone has ever said to you, about you? Indeed, what caused you to hide from your strong self all these years? What is the fear?"

"Oh my God, Peter," I all but cried. "I have no idea. I have no idea. I have no idea." My words faded, each sentence softer than the one before, eventually falling silent into the space just outside of my heart. *Truly, I had no idea.*

By now, even Peter's appetite showed signs of abating into the deeper meaning of our conversation. As the waiter brought more ribs, Peter waved him away with a flick of his hands. With a playful intensity, he shook the paper towelette before cleaning the rib sauce from his hands, mouth, and beard. However, his demeanor became quite serious, flanked by a soothing tone of voice. "Paddy, you don't have to know all the answers to the questions right now. It's not necessary. Just ask the questions and then open up to the Universe for the answers. They will come."

Isn't that what I had already been doing by asking my questions in prayer and then writing the answer? Wasn't that exactly what my little notebook was all about? Questions and answers?

"Peter, I *have* been asking," I answered in earnest. Lowering my voice because of the seriousness of the matter, I leaned across the table to better look Peter directly in the eye as I repeated my statement. "I have been asking. Over and over I have been asking. But the greater questions do not seem to have ready answers." By the tone of my voice, anyone listening would understand the seriousness of my own words emanating directly from my heart.

"Sometimes, listening would be best achieved when done with the heart instead of the head. Perhaps you have only heard the answers you could understand. In order to hear the deeper answers—the deeper truth—it may be necessary to listen in a different way. Perhaps instead of answers to questions, what you need is solid truth. You need exclamation points." Peter's voice matched mine tone for tone in seriousness. "The only way to receive these exclamation points is by surrendering. You cannot find them by grasping." By now, ribs were a moment of history as our conversation began to ebb and flow into a more spiritual mode. Peter wiped his forehead with his napkin before using it to clean his glasses.

Already, I realized it was time to open up deeper to God in order to ascertain the security I craved so dearly. In fact, several days before, I had attempted to do exactly that.

"Peter," I explained, "the other day I went into St. Bavo's Cathedral to pray. Unfortunately, I arrived just after an organ concert. The sanctuary had been roped off. A young lady stood just inside the entrance taking some form of payment to attend the concert."

Peter was listening attentively. Yet a slender smile and an ever so slight nod of his head made me think that he already knew what I was going to say. Nonetheless, he didn't interrupt. I continued explaining my experience as a tourist.

"The Gothic interior took my breath away, especially the oak and white marble pulpit. I felt like I had been led to a special place with all the statuary, ancient Gothic interior, and the series of oils from the fifteenth century, *The Adoration of the Mystic Lamb* by the van Eyck Brothers. I just knew I would find my answers there inside all those religious icons. After I approached the ticket taker, I asked her where I could go to pray."

By this time Peter's nod had turned to a smirk. Evidently he did know what was coming.

"The young woman was indignant. 'Prayer has not been scheduled today,' she insisted in a rather authoritative voice. When I asked her if I could pay and just sit inside the sanctuary by myself somewhere, she took it as a threat for some reason because the concert was all but finished. After I asked her in a rather indignant voice why in the name of God prayer had to be scheduled by the church, she motioned for security, and I left."

"Although there are services at Sint-Baafskathedraal—Saint Bavo—every Sunday, for the most part, it is a tourist attraction." Peter's words came in bursts between heartfelt laughter. "There's a better place not so far from here. Another Catholic Church, ancient like this one, but without the exquisite artifacts that draw tourists. In fact, I meditate there often. I'll meet you tomorrow about noon, and we'll go. We'll take the buses from St. Peter's Station, so you'll be able to find it yourself next time."

The next day, the energy of Afsnee Kirk absolutely blew me away. The Church at Afsnee felt light, spiritual, and quite holy, a place for the heart to open with a quiet mind. Situated on the River Leie, it is officially called St. John Baptist Church. When I first entered it was like entering historical sacredness itself. The opulent icons I had seen at Saint Bavo were not present. Instead, the church seemed rather plain inside, as if to strip away any type of finery standing between a spiritual experience and me. Even though the Romanesque church originated in the twelfth century, the current building is not that old. It just feels that special, energetically wrapping itself around you, beckoning you to journey inward into the spiritual nature of yourself. It would not surprise me if the church had been built on an energetic vortex of the earth.

On that first visit to St. John Baptist Church in the village of Afsnee, Peter and I entered without talking. Since I am not Catholic and at that time had never been to a Catholic service, I was not aware of the traditions. Peter, though, had been trained as Catholic from infancy, so he knew what to do when entering. Like a shadow, I followed his example when he made the sign of the cross after dipping his finger into the holy water that served this purpose. Peter then sat on one side of the church, front row left. I sat on the third row, second seat, right side. It felt right for some reason not to be in the front row.

Unlike before, this time I had not ventured into Ghent with paper and pencil. Knowing I was going to pray in a church, I decided that I would best be served just to sit silently, stating my prayerful intention, and then totally surrendering to whatever answer would be forthcoming. The church was empty except for the two of us, silent and meditative. As I bowed my head, I formed the prayerful thoughts inside the depths of my heart.

I'm scattered, God. I feel like parts of me that I knew have been cast upon the secret places of the earth, dissolved, and disassembled as I knew them. Several days ago, I felt a feeling of home in an area I have never seen before, yet I am not home. In fact, I don't have a place I call home anymore, only a house where I live. But you know that, know that home is more than a location. Help me find that place called home within myself. Help me put together my pieces of self in a more righteous way that I listen to your voice of Spirit within my soul instead of the words of others that fragmented me so. God, help me get it together again. I have not heard your answers lately. Are you still there?

I don't know how long I sat waiting for an answer that did not readily come. I thought it was several moments, but later as Peter and I were leaving I realized we had been there for two hours. I'm convinced that the mystical union of self and Holiness is an experience quite beyond time.

What I do know is that suddenly I felt like I had to go toward the open Bible placed on a table to our left. The urge to do so came at me like a jolt of intuitive electricity. At the time, I had not even known a Bible was open on that table. It called to me not like curiosity, but like a directive I could not ignore. In fact, it was shouting at me, beckoning me forward as if an angel stood there with hands on hips demanding, "Okay, you asked. Now come over here right now and discover! Come. *Now!*"

Gently, I stood up, trying to be careful so as not to disturb Peter, who I thought was still meditating. I found out later that Peter had for the most part finished meditating long before then and patiently sat there waiting for me all that time.

I did not understand what I was seeing, for the Bible was not in English. To tell you the truth, I had no idea of the language in which it was written because I was so caught up in the moment.

"Peter," I said pointing at the open page, "Please read to me what this says right here." I was touching the book of Wisdom, chapter one, verse seven. The Protestant Bible does not have the book of Wisdom, so I truly had no idea what I needed to have read. What I did know with absolute certainty is that particular sentence had to be read to me; I had to know it. It was so important that I would have copied it down to have it translated, if indeed I had brought my paper and pen. It stood out from the rest of the verses energetically just as if it had been highlighted. Intuitively, the verse screamed at me of importance. That verse might as well had been jumping off of the page, flapping its little letters like a white dove strutting its tail and flapping wings in order to impress the hens during mating season.

"God's spirit fills the world," Peter loosely translated. His tone matched the holiness of the experience, above a whisper, yet with emphasis to indicate importance. He paused looking me directly in the eyes before he continued, "...that which holds things together knows every word articulated."

"...that which holds things together..."

I sat down so that I wouldn't fall out of utter amazement. The wisdom of the moment told me right there and then that even though I felt fragmented, that even though I felt like I had been scattered to the winds of change, that even though I had lost so much in the way of life as I previously knew it, God was holding my pieces in Holy Hands to keep me moving forward. Something out there, up there, in there, larger than I, greater than I, holier than I, listened to not only every word I wrote, but every word I said as well as thought. Through the voice of my soul, that still, small voice of God heard me, directed me. Better yet, everything would be just fine.

It was okay to feel scattered, for God loved me enough to hold my fragmented pieces until I could reassemble them. I was loved enough by That Which Is—the Great I AM—in order to be helped. No longer did I feel alone in the world. The voice would whisper from my soul or shout at me intuitively. If necessary, my path would be blocked in order to change my direction. Roads yet untraveled would open up. I would be able to get where I was going, eventually, wherever that was, in order to feel whole again. All I had to do was take baby steps forward while listening intuitively. Always, above all, l was to listen, to feel Spirit's guidance.

Peter leaned over to touch my shoulder. By this time I was sobbing uncontrollably. Perhaps that was the reason I let him. Though it was totally unnecessary to explain to him what I felt, I could not have done so anyhow. All I could do at that moment was to sob and allow Peter's hug of friendship, thankful beyond measure that I had someone who allowed me to express the depths of my heart in each tear without judgment. Immediately I started calling these experiences of overwhelming mysticism of Spiritual union my "little moments." Peter seemed to understand.

That connection—that spiritual connection that began that first day at a church where divine magnificence far exceeded visual splendor— stayed with me for several years before finally integrating as part of my consciousness. Just as that profound gut feeling had gestured within me to walk across the room to read the message in the open Bible, the directives continued. However, soon the inner directives became more complicated than just a walk across the room. With every intuitive nudge I followed, life as I was to experience it was beginning to turn into a series of profound "little moments." The God that holds things together had heard every word I ever prayed.

*"...the Lord your God may show us
the way we should go, and
the thing that we should do."*

JEREMIAH 42:3

◆

CHAPTER SIX

Profound Little Moments

"THAT'S WHERE I have to go!" I exclaimed suddenly, stretching my right arm in front of me, finger pointing down the Hill of Tara, across the wide Gabhra Valley, and up another hill in County Meath, Ireland. I looked toward the hill far in front of me before looking behind me at the late afternoon western sky. Already low, the sun hid behind several clouds alerting me of the short time we had left in the day.

"What?" Peter answered. At the time, he was intently studying Lia Fail, a single oblong stone called the Stone of Destiny on a grassy mound high up on the Hill of Tara, a pre-Celtic, Neolithic site. Rising from his squatted position, he first turned to look at me and then toward the direction I pointed. "I thought we were going to be here at the coronation place of pre-Christian kings for the Harmonic Concordance. I thought we decided this would be the most profound place to be." By his tone, I suspected he was more surprised than miffed I wanted to leave the area.

Two weeks previously, Peter had explained in an IM from Ghent to me at home in Georgia that there was to be a rather unusual alignment of planets in the universe on November 8, 2003. Many believed this Harmonic Concordance served some sort of alchemical opportunity for personal and planetary shifts in consciousness. Even though I had no idea about this type of planetary interaction, truth or not, the last minute trip to Ireland sounded like a grand idea to me. Frankly, I had nothing else going on in my life at that moment. Accepting Peter's suggestion, I just considered it another chance for an interesting adventure. After meeting at the Dublin airport, we immediately traveled to the historic Hill of Tara.

"You decided that, Peter. I just went along for the fun of it." I looked back at Peter, who now was standing in the center of one of two concentric circles that looked and felt quite filled with male energy. From my place in the center of a convex circle of earth that felt quite heavy with feminine energy, I added, "And it's grand, actually. The view is incredible. But that's where I have to be." Again I pointed out to the hill in the distance. "Not here." Although several other groups of tourists were laying blankets, setting up chairs, and making other comfortable arrangements to await the forthcoming full moon later that night, I could have cared less about staying in this area because of the intense pull from across the valley.

Peter's glance followed mine again this time. "You mean you want to go to the top of that hill?" We both were looking at the ruins of an ancient church standing like a firm sentinel of faith.

"Yes, there," I answered firmly. "It's not something I just want. In fact, I have to be there. Can you find it?" Every one of those intuitive white doves that lived in my stomach began to flutter. Each time something spiritually important needed my attention, those doves guided me forward into the holiness of God's directives just as if they were flying out of the church steeples in Ghent when the bells tolled every hour.

"Well then, let's go," Peter said, ready for an immediate adventure. He smiled as his glance moved from the ancient church ruins to me.

By this time, Peter had become quite used to my sudden changes of location, changes of heart, and changes of intention as I listened ardently to my intuition's directives. Because he understood this level of intuition, he was able to honor it. "Of course, I can find it. Let's go."

Hoping to outmaneuver the setting sun, we all but tumbled down the hill to the rental car, mimicking an older version of Jack and Jill. Our enthusiasm alone lifted us out of the grassy meadow, over the rocky wall border, and into a new adventure. My spirit soared in anticipation.

My heart tugs at me with fond memories of the naïve soul that I was, trusting Peter even though I had known him only a short time. My rational mind wondered how in the world I—a person who went into flight-or-fight mode so easily every time I felt the need to escape—would be able to travel anywhere I needed to go. All I knew was that something larger than I was, something spiritual in nature, with love, wisdom, and grace far beyond anything I ever dreamed possible, guided me. So far, it orchestrated the lighthouses at Topsail Beach, NC. It kept me safe that first month in Europe, providing me with much needed help time after time. It answered my written questions in the most profound spiritual manner. And now, for certain, it was leading me across the Gabhra Valley to the as-yet-unknown ruins of a church.

After Peter cranked the car, he paused just one moment before heading out of the parking lot. Although Peter had no map, he was able to navigate the narrow roads between the N2 and N3 primaries in County Meath successfully by using his intuition.

I said very little while he drove, for those psychic white doves were flying higher. The fact that I was here in Ireland with a guide following an internal spiritual directive seemed miraculous. I glanced at the intensity in Peter's face knowing he fully intended to get to the ancient church before sunset just because it seemed so important to me.

While Peter drove at breakneck speeds around the narrow, twisting roads, I thought of the ancient myth of Theseus and the Minotaur, and how the Minotaur had been confined to a labyrinth with its own curves and passageways. As my body slid to the right when Peter drove the car fast into a sharp left bend, I felt like Homer's version of Ariadne, who was said to have danced in the labyrinth. Happily, I danced within my own spiritual flow; the doves were still fluttering. I thought my heart would absolutely explode with connection. This place, even though it was not known to me, called so strongly it seemed as though Spirit would burst out of my body if I could not get there immediately. The vibrations started in my upper chest just at the base of my throat before quickly moving down into my stomach. I soon knew it was not anxiety this time; it was excitement.

As we crested the top of the Hill of Skryne, the road curved to the left, partially circling an ancient stone wall embankment on the road's left. Peter parked the car just beyond the old opening in the wall, out of the road, but not exactly in a place designated for parking. Across the street from the circular wall were a couple of houses and several buildings that looked like businesses, yet I did not see marked parking there either. Very soon Peter bounded up the narrow, steep set of steps in the wall's opening two at a time. I followed at a more careful pace, placing both hands on the walls on either side of me in order to push myself upward.

When I got to the top of the steps, I walked a couple of paces toward what looked like the front part of the ruin site. The sign nearby noted the medieval ruins as a church built by Hugh de Lacy of Skryne Castle in 1341. Mesmerized, I just stood there for a while noting how the walls were made of large stones carefully carved into oblong shapes. A steeple known locally as the Skreen Tower loomed in the back center of what was left of the church walls. Although the upper part of the one-hundred-foot tower no longer existed, it still stood straight and tall on the high hill as a beacon to all to witness its strength, to feel its defiance of the elements in order to remain a spiritual force in an oft wayward world. The glow of the sun hovering just behind the tower created a radiant halo in gold rays shining out on all sides. Even the grass under my feet felt holy.

Momentarily I closed my eyes in order to quiet my five senses, so my sixth sense could bask in the glory of the area. Tingles of excitement flowed through my cells like subtle stars twinkling on a moonless night.

I felt light—not lightheaded. Beautiful rainbows swirled though my third eye, into my soul, and back out again before turning in the most magnificent blue. I had become the sky. Or perhaps the infinite sky had become me. The blue felt like love to me, not the kind of love from a lover, but a love greater than anything I have ever known.

"Paddy," Peter shouted to me from his stand flanked by two stone walls at the front of the ancient church. "Look to your left."

Opening my eyes, I turned in place to look to my immediate left, seeing nothing except the top of the wall surrounding Skreen and lots of long grass that defied being mowed. "Look at what?" I asked.

"Across the street. Look to your left at the building across the street." Peter pointed in the direction he wanted me to look. "Look further," Peter instructed. "Widen your vision." With that, he chuckled like a wise man who knew a secret. He then entered the church.

I looked back and forth to my right and left before noticing the building just across the street built close to the road. The sign over the door read "Swan Pub."

I flashed back to the swans at the bench in Bruges that had led my vision from the words *Niet Kasteels* painted on a rock wall on the other side of the Minnewater, the Lake of Love. They swam gracefully toward the stone bridge just as if they were pointing to the Beguinage. And most of all, I remember turning toward them one last time as I crossed the bridge to my new adventures. Native American lore assigns transition, grace, love, soul, and balance to swan medicine. Just like I had thought while standing on the Hill of Tara, I was destined to be here at the ruins of Skreen. Again, a swan pointed the way. I took a deep, cleansing breath, surrendering to the experience forthcoming even though I had not one clue what was to happen.

"Yes!" I said with gusto, making a fist of my right hand and raising it into the air in a form of salute to the magnificent unseen grace and guidance I was getting.

"Thought so," Peter crooned back from his new stand in what looked like either an ancient passageway or window before turning to his right to continue his exploration.

As I walked across the long leaves of grass bending over in prayer-like position, I lifted each foot higher than normal, carefully placing it back down in front of me in meditative fashion. I felt like a young fawn in a lush pasture of Spirit as I walked toward the fifteenth-century tower flanked by two walls that beckoned like a mother's welcoming arms while saying, "Come here into my soul and be still. Then you will understand."

Honestly, I have no idea how long I stood facing the tower between the two walls. Peter was off on his own mission, enthralled by the fact that Columba, one of the Twelve Apostles of sixth century Ireland, was honored by a carved effigy on one of the remaining walls. I left Peter to his own discoveries about Columba and his work and life as a Gaelic Irish Missionary Monk who lived five hundred years after Christ.

Again with the feeling of walking on holy ground, I moved to the other side of the tower, settling down on the ground in order to watch the sun fall into the earth just beyond the hill across the valley. Thankfully, Peter left me to my own accord sitting there with legs crossed like an unknown Yogi with my back pressed against the ancient tower's stones. The tower base emanated strength, solidarity, and grace into my backbone. I felt just as spiritually connected as I had in Afsnee Kirk in Belgium.

This time, however, something was slightly different. The inner sensations I had learned to witness seemed to be more specific in their nature instead of just stronger. The feelings weren't just tingles, but seemed to be like effervescent bursts of spiritual energy floating into infinity. With opened palms, I placed the back of my hands on the tops of my knees, wanting to receive more. In fact, I wanted to be totally open to the grace of the moment.

Without much forethought, I became aware of a spirit presence near me. Without opening my eyes, I knew it was not Peter because the energy radiated with more light. Human energy is usually heavier. Just as I had done with the spiritual writing, I eased into a more relaxed state of consciousness in order to discern any message that might be forthcoming. With eyes open in this altered state, I intuited through my sixth sense what seemed to be a monk standing just to my left. Several others were nearby, but this one desired to communicate.

I am listening, I thought, and then added, *Thank you for coming.* For some unknown reason, I knew I needed to maintain gratitude, or I would not be able to communicate. Any other emotional vibration would mask his vibes.

Be still and know, the monk transmitted. *Be still and know God.* With that, the vision cleared.

Wanting to do exactly as he instructed, I settled my breathing into slow, deep inhalations and exhalations. Instead of trying to make something happen, I determined to let it happen, whatever it may be. I also trusted it would be exactly what I needed.

The feeling first washed over me like a lover's touch, warm and nurturing as it caressed my shoulders and embraced my heart. With eyes opened wide, I watched the sun's evolution of golden and crimson rays reaching beyond the clouds to touch the earth. Alternating, I closed my eyes to block out the visual magnificence in order to experience the alchemy throughout my body clear into my soul.

As I sat there in meditation, the sun's rays allowed Spirit's kiss of grace to peek from sporadic darkening clouds. The Irish winds slowly blew shivers of awareness into my body as I pressed harder against the ancient stones for strength. In that still space between thoughts, the inner sensation grew slowly at first like a lotus moves up from the muddy waters of psychological pain into the light of realization. It then blooms in full awareness of its own beauty. I lifted my palms upward from my knees as if I could grasp rays of Light, to seize the essence of what I began to experience in order to incorporate it into my heart before it dissipated beyond my understanding.

I could not hold the Light by grasping. Instead, I opened my heart, so Light filtered in between shadows in order to completely connect to the flow of life. I trusted myself to surrender to the full expression of the experience, knowing full well I would understand soon. The sun threatened to leave me, however, dipping slowly behind the Hill of Tara to my west. Still, I had the intuitive faith that this surging feeling wrapping me like Divine Love would bring some sort of realization in due time.

In the last wisps of light, I recognized the wall behind me not as the wall, but as part of something greater than I was. Slowly, I leaned forward to create space. Still I felt as though the wall and I were one, even though we were not the same at all. I felt the ground under me, feeling inseparable from it also. I stood, sat, and repeated the process in order to move my body in the space of my surroundings, still feeling just as I had with the wall—part of something greater and larger than myself. I touched the green grass, long and lush between my fingertips. I understood we were separate through my five senses, but with my heart I felt that we were the same somehow. As I moved my hand to touch my face, I knew I was not the grass, not green. Yet, I felt the lushness clear through my heart.

The experience continued with each thing around me, surprising me yet consoling me, comforting me with a love that defies description of any manner. Whatever was happening, I trusted the feeling completely.

Lifting my hands in front of my face, I looked deliberately beyond my open fingers and then to the sky yet again. The sky reached down and touched my open palms, running a vein of Spirit down my arms, blue goodness rolling right along with my spirit somewhere, somehow. I felt like I was the sun, rising and setting, just to do it again tomorrow.

Spiritual moments defy time. Time is a human construct, not a God creation. Therefore, I have no idea how long this feeling of spiritual connection stayed with me. What is important is that I felt it. I felt it in every cell of my body. I felt it with my mind. I felt it with my love. Spirit soared through me, as me. Emptiness became overwhelmingly full.

My heart connected to something greater than I was—something large, inviting, and very spiritually open. My eyes puddled with tears—holy water emanating from my own body. Would this have happened if I were not in this place in Skreen? Maybe so, if I had the intention to experience it with God's help. However, I did not expect this to happen. Instead I just followed that inner voice flooding my intuitive senses, open to whatever experience would come without specific expectations.

Yet, there I was in nature nestled among the stony ruins of an ancient church, listening to God through my open heart the best way I knew how—through my feelings. Without a doubt, I belonged not only to the earth, but to the Universe, to the cosmos. I belonged to the people I had hurt, to the people that had hurt me, and it was okay in some way far beyond my own awareness. I belonged to the family of God, belonged to myself—to my whole self.

"Peter, I belong to the earth. To the sky, to myself, to God," I tried to explain through my shuddering voice and profound tears. Peter had come around the building to see if I was still all right. Actually, I was just fine. Filled with Spirit, I felt like I belonged, and the feeling felt good, felt full instead of empty. The rest of my questions would have to wait, for Spirit saturated me with what I needed at the precise moment I needed it. As darkness fell all around us, my experience at Skreen looking toward the sun as it set over the Neolithic Hill of Tara filled me with wonder. At that precise moment, I was One with everything. I wanted this forever.

◆ ◆ ◆ ◆ ◆

After the trip to Ireland, my life moved rather smoothly for a while, allowing me to purchase a house in Atlanta and settle into a routine of frequent visits to Belgium. Because of international travel laws, I stayed in Belgium less than three months each time, making sure I was there no longer than 6 months per year. Even though I had moved to Atlanta, far away from my marital residence, it felt heavy to me, like I had to navigate in the midst of Stone Mountain itself. Each time I set foot on Belgian soil, I felt every cell in my body relax. I'm convinced there is more feminine spiritual energy in the Belgium area of the world than there is in Atlanta. On one day during one of my visits there, I invited Peter to come over to my Belgian efficiency.

"I thought you belonged to the earth, the sky, and to God?" Peter asked incredulously. "If that were the case, then surely you could find a labyrinth by yourself."

He leaned back into one of the four wooden chairs I owned, purchased in separate parts and put together in wobbly fashion with a screwdriver and a prayer. Peter's arms folded across his belly with fingers entwined as he tilted back in the chair so the front legs were extended in mid-air. He looked at me with a skeptical expression as if he could not believe what I was telling him. I knew better, however. Peter waited with pregnant pause for me to ask him for help again.

"It's the labyrinth idea, Peter. You know that. I have to find a labyrinth, to navigate to the center as a symbol of discovering the center of myself. I cannot find one by myself."

Peter smiled, yet to me it seemed more like a smirk covering some bit of knowledge I had not quite discerned yet. "You need to go to Crete then. That is the origin of the Minotaur myth. Remember the story I told you about the wife of King Minos of Crete who fell in love with a snow white bull sent to the king by the god Poseidon? Their offspring was a ferocious half-bull and half-man, the Minotaur, whom the Oracle at Delphi counseled to be kept in a labyrinth in order to protect others from its wrath. All this took place near the palace at Knossos in Crete. That's the origin of the labyrinth story. That's where you need to go."

"Okay then, I'll go. But you have to help me get there." Even though by now I had taken trains to parts of Belgium by myself, in no way possible did I propose to get to Crete alone. The mystical experience in Ireland had affected me profoundly; I fully intended to make it happen again. Unfortunately, instead of relying on my own intuition in order to discern the voice of Spirit leading me where to go or what to experience, this time I abdicated that personal responsibility, bowing to my own ego's demands and Peter's knowledge. Not only did he have at his disposal one of the highest IQs I have ever encountered, his level of persuasion could border on spiritual coercion if indeed he wanted to use it in that way. Instead of presenting the story of Crete and asking if

I were interested, his words were presented in the form of a directive that I should be following. I believed he had my best interests at heart.

Peter nodded. "I don't know what this trip will bring our way, but I do know it will be interesting. I'm sure of that. This four-day trip will be just what you need."

Initially, we were to leave on the train from the community in the southeast section of Ghent where I had rented an efficiency apartment for part of the summer. In the stillness of the morning we walked to the station before the little shops clustered together along the sides of the town in European fashion opened for the day. After waiting an hour for a train that never came, Peter learned the railroad personnel were on strike. There would be no trains in the Flemish area of Belgium that morning. Therefore, we had to go to the Brussels airport by car or bus.

"Peter, didn't the sign say that a bus will come by here to take the passengers with train tickets to the airport?" I asked. "Shouldn't we wait for it?"

"It's already been an hour, and I haven't seen a bus. Besides, I want to check the Internet airline schedules. I'm not sure I have the correct flight time."

"Good grief, Peter," I exclaimed. *"That is your job!* Our deal is that I paid for the tickets, and as our travel director, you got the best deal."

Peter prided himself on traveling inexpensively. On the other hand, I did the best I could in travel arrangements. I liked an iron-clad plan in traveling, including tickets in hand, assigned seats, trip cancellation insurance, and, of course, water as well as plenty of food just in case the world supply suddenly dwindles. Peter, though, tended to fly sporadically like an indigenous warrior on a walkabout in nature. Personally, I loathed his methods mainly because they seemed so free and unencumbered, ideals I strived for but could not obtain yet. Besides, I was not sure it was safe to travel alone as a female.

Sure enough, not five minutes after Peter walked the block and turned to the right, out of earshot and sight, the bus came to take us to the airport. I couldn't even set foot on the steps of that bus by myself; fear paralyzed me. Therefore, I waved the driver on, choosing to stay there to wait for Peter. Other passengers waiting along with me seemed relieved to get on the bus. I was miffed.

As the bus drove down the street away from sight, I stood there mad as hell, sandwiched between two large suitcases with my fists balled on my hips. After waiting about forty minutes for Peter to return, I started back to the apartment dragging both of our suitcases behind me down the bumpy Belgian sidewalks. By the time I got half a block down the street, Peter passed me in his green van.

"Peter," I screamed, waving my arms to catch his attention.

Peter, however, was not looking for me at the block midpoint. Instead he had gotten concerned after not seeing me standing at the bus stop straight ahead and, thinking I got on the bus without him, had turned the car around in order to go to the airport without me.

"Peter! Peter! Peter!" I screamed as loud as I could. Leaving the suitcases on the sidewalk, I ran into the street, chasing the van in order to beat on the back of it to get his attention.

A woman peeked out of her apartment early this Sunday morning, cracking the door wide enough only to determine that the woman running down the street screaming for someone to stop had nothing to do with her life at all. She slammed the door quickly, probably to protect herself from the excess noise coming from me, one crazy American who was running directly into a nightmare of her own making.

Peter slammed on the brakes, causing me to run headlong into the back of the van. Still he had not seen me. Instead, after hearing me beat the back of the van, he thought he had hit something. I ended up doing a body slam into his tailgate that almost knocked me to the ground. What I wanted to do was hit him. That's not my way, though. Instead, I loaded the suitcases and proceeded to sulk all the way to the airport. I pouted for well over an hour, saying nothing. Peter said nothing right back to me. The energy between us was thick, palpable, and quite testy. In complete silence, we arrived at the airport parking area shortly before our plane was due to leave.

"Don't go in there," I shouted suddenly as Peter made a U-turn into the parking lot. "You cannot get this van out of here. It won't fit," I screamed while pointing at the parking deck, noting that driving through that deck would be the only way to exit the lot. Without listening to me, Peter entered the parking lot anyway, pulling his van into the first spot available outside the deck. If he had entered the deck, he would have gotten stuck between the floor and the low ceiling. Our only way out was to back through the entrance. I had no idea how in the world we were going to exit after our trip. However, we had no time to bother with this detail. Our flight left in forty minutes.

After running down what seemed like every corridor at the airport, finally we got into the tangle of people squirming for the front of the line. Yet again, Peter had purchased tickets on flights with no seat assignment. We did get on the flight, but Peter sat in the front while I sat on the back of the plane because those were the only seats available. Perhaps that benefited us both for I had nothing to say to Peter or the people to my left or right. As the jet took off, I buried myself in a book, glad for the silence.

"Peter," I said in my most pretend-to-be-pleasant voice after we arrived at our destination. "How are we getting to the resort if you didn't rent a car?" Literally, I knew nothing at the time about last minute tours, travel agencies, or traveling in foreign countries. My knowledge of worldly travel consisted of trips to Belgium and back. I not only liked a plan, but I liked knowing the plan. Peter, on the other hand, seemed to gather energy like a tsunami when he traveled. No plans necessary.

"I booked a tour. How in the world did you think I got such a great deal on our rooms? We'll just wander outside until we find the right tour bus."

"Merciful God in heavens. *Wander?* It's almost nine at night, dark as hell, and we have to wander about looking for the right tour bus? *Bus?!* Does this tour bus even have a name?" My voice dripped with sarcasm, decorated with threads of anger woven into the blanket of disgust with not only Peter but specifically for allowing myself to go to this place without having maps in hand. Tourist books, food, and water would have helped also.

We turned to the left after exiting the airport and began walking toward a line of at least ten buses parked. After getting on two by mistake, Peter finally identified the correct bus. I couldn't speak with any rational tone of voice, because I was so miffed at the situation in which I found myself. Therefore, with teeth clenched together, I kept quiet. When the tour guide established that all were on board, the bus went from hotel to hotel, allowing happy passengers filled with hopeful expectations to disembark. The last hotel on the tour director's list was ours. After I finally determined which hotel room was mine (after dragging my suitcase up and down short sets of stairs where many sets of rooms hugged the hillside), I fell into a deep sleep, glad the day was finally over.

The first full day on Crete, Peter went to the beach in order to soak up sun. I stayed in my room reading an older copy of Rupert Sheldrake's fascinating *The Presence of the Past: Morphic Resonance and the Habits of Nature*. Happy as a lark, I met Peter for the buffet lunch and dinner. From his eagerness to try several helpings of each dish, I assume the restaurant lost money feeding him. The feeding frenzy took hours each meal.

Bored from staying in the room, the second day I went to the beach, doing it my way, of course. Lounge chairs and umbrellas were provided for an additional fee. Several Euros poorer, I secured my chair, my umbrella, and my little drink (lacking the fancy umbrella) from a waiter who insisted I owed him much more than I thought the drink was worth. With considerable effort, I settled down to read more.

"Notice the difference?" Peter asked, indicating the rest of the tourists around me on the shore. He had just wandered up from his perch in the sun to speak. "You look like you're sitting at the North Pole while everyone else is at the beach."

Honestly, I hadn't noticed the people around me because so far I had occupied my time getting settled. From inside my beach bag, I had donned myself with sunglasses, a wide-brimmed hat, and sunscreen I had brought from the United States because I always insist on smearing myself with the highest number protection available. I had on long pants and a long-sleeved shirt buttoned up to the top of my neck. On my feet were rubber-soled shoes with socks that had elastic in the tops so I could tuck my pant legs into them. I had no intention of getting any sun exposure at all.

After delving into the spiritual meaning of the melanoma I had several years ago, I realized it presented itself as nothing more than a strong desire for life as well as a profound nudge that I was to start living more authentically from my heart. Although I listened enough to delve right into the spiritual awakening that became necessary for me at the time, I still wasn't going to play around with the sun's rays. I protected myself to excess—great gobs of excess.

"Well, that's just the way I need to do things, I guess. Perhaps it's time for me to follow my own path, do my own thing." Truer words had never exited my mouth; however, I still had not applied the meaning to our trip. "Speaking of which, we've been here two days so far. Where is the labyrinth I wanted to see? Better yet, how are we going to get there without a car?"

"There is no labyrinth in this area," Peter confessed. "I thought we could just lounge in the sun. However, if you insist, we can go to the Palace Minoan in Knossos, which is nearby. From what I've learned, cars are available at the resort. We'll rent one tomorrow."

"*I* had the intention, Peter, to *walk a labyrinth*. I told you that!" With that bit of honesty flooding out of my mouth like I had spit out a dead roach, I dived back into my book, delighted to be finished with Peter and his conversation that day. Rupert Sheldrake's book about morphic resonance fields intrigued me mainly because I knew intuitively that when one of us on earth heals, discovers, or creates in a profound way, we set up what I call points of light that others can follow. I had always felt this happens energetically, primarily because of my strong ability to sense energetic fields. However, I hadn't read any literature confirming this until the Sheldrake book popped into my life.

During a dream one night before this trip, I intuitively heard the term "morphic resonance field." Because the term was unfamiliar, I wrote the words down on the pad I always kept by my bed for this purpose and for writing down dream information. After an online search, I learned more about the term, discovering Sheldrake and agreeing with what he wrote. It felt right to me. After I read his book, I became convinced that resonance fields assist inhabitants of the earth—and maybe beyond us—in our spiritual awakening, gleaning wisdom and changing the consciousness of the times into different vibrations.

So, if I understood Sheldrake's theory correctly, then everyone on that beach was affected with my very bad mood. I felt like Peter had coerced me into believing this trip would be spiritual in nature. So far, all I had experienced seemed to have nothing to do with mystical experiences.

The next day, Peter and I set off to find the Minoan Palace. Unfortunately, Peter made a wrong turn, and we drove around Knossos for well over an hour not having an inkling of an idea where we were or where we had to be. We wandered through old city sections, new city developments, and all in between. We were on wide roads, as well as roads so narrow that I hesitated to even roll down the windows for fear of laundry getting sucked into our car as it hung from lines on apartment buildings. I had seen the sign indicating the direction of the palace, yet I did not speak up.

That was my first mistake of the day.

After an exasperating drive that annoyed me to the point of near hysteria, I noticed we were back at the place where we had taken the wrong turn the first time.

"Peter, turn here," I said, indicating the way the sign pointed. Even now, with all of my frustration, my voice came out as just a whisper, as if I were truly afraid someone would hear me. Peter was determined to be in charge, not me. Therefore, he said nothing, ignoring me completely. Because I hated being ignored, I was miserable.

"Peter, you're going the same way again. You're going the way you went before, the way that got us lost. You are repeating the same mistake again. *Do not go this way.*" By the time the words got pushed out of my mouth, I was aghast, breathless with my own frustration. Unfortunately, Peter was still not acknowledging the fact that I had said anything.

"If you don't stop this car right now and turn around, I am going to get out and walk!" I yelled. By this time I was crying out of frustration. I had no map, no bottles of water or food, and no inkling where I was other than in a rental car in Crete with a man I wanted to dissect because he still was ignoring everything I had said.

Clearly, I had seen the road to turn onto in order to get us to the palace. In fact, by now I had seen it twice. However, Peter had evidently squared himself into a tiny corner of Ego-Land and made the determination that he would be able to find his way out of the city strictly through what I assumed was his gut instinct, intuition, or whatever it was that he used instead of his mind.

"If you don't turn right here, I'm going to take control of the steering wheel," I screamed at the top of my lungs, meaning every word of it. "I don't care how you do it! Get this stupid little car on that road we just passed to our left. Do! It! Now!" By this time I touched the steering wheel, not so hard as to make Peter lose his grip on the thing, but hard enough to pound it out of total frustration. I needed to get his attention fast.

Suddenly Peter turned the wheel away from me, probably more to get it back into his control than to literally turn left. Yet, he did turn left. Our right front wheel clipped the edge of the curbing slightly, but finally we traveled the road clearly marked as the direction to the palace. My emotions glared at me from inside my body, swelling up into all sorts of nonsensical thoughts. *He should have listened to me sooner. I knew how to go. Any idiot could see that sign to interpret the meaning even if he could not read Greek. I should be driving this damn little car.* On and on they went, pulling me down into that deep, dark well of anger. *If I cannot trust Peter, then whom can I trust?!* Obviously, trust had become a huge issue for me.

I thought trust was being able to rely on the character, ability, strength, or truth of someone or something. Not only did I not trust

Peter to get us where we were supposed to be that day, but I realized that for me the trust business—or more specifically lack of trust—had exaggerated itself into oblivion.

Oh, in many ways, I did trust Peter. I wouldn't have been in Crete with him if I didn't.

On the other hand I seemed to be on a learning curve about speaking up for myself, and trusting not only my instinct but also that I had the ability to stand up for myself when necessary. Not owning my own truth enough to even speak up for myself when necessary over the years had caused my self-respect, self-knowledge, and self-worth to dwindle into nothingness.

In one of Patricia Evans' books about controlling people, she describes a frog in a pot of water happily swimming around. Yet, the heat has been turned up under the pot. Unless Frog realizes this and leaves, she will be cooked to death. Just like Frog, I had been all but cooked to death because I didn't say what I needed to say or, for that matter, be who I was created to be. Because I substituted wants and desires of others for my own needs, I ended up not even trusting myself to go outside the house to get groceries, be in crowds, or visit strange places. But the greatest wisdom forthcoming had to do more with trusting myself to discern spiritual guidance from the pull of my own needy ego.

This trust issue forced the furious bull to surface from the depths of my soul. As Peter drove around Knossos, profound fury inside my psyche defied the dodging of the bullfighter, pawing and huffing his own fumes. I was angry. It wasn't fair that I had to abdicate my own ability to drive to someone else who obviously did not care about signs, directions, or pathways. It wasn't fair that my fear of reprisal kept me silent when I needed to shout, to rage. I hated having this much anger. It took up so much time, energy, and space within me, space I could have filled with love.

With all the force I could muster, I pounded the side of the car door just below the window with my right fist, a move that startled not only Peter, but me as well. "It's just not fair," I wailed. "None of it seems fair to me. Why can't we all just love each other?" I turned to Peter, asking the unanswerable questions bubbling up from the depths of my soul. Reaching across my chest with my right hand, I again pounded the top of the compartment between our seats.

Peter said nothing at first. Then, after I had stopped pounding, he asked in a gentle tone of voice, "What's not fair?"

"Everything! Nothing seems fair at all to me right now." I turned back from Peter in order to stare out the front window with a piercing glance like a laser beam that would have desiccated brick and mortar. "Just drive, dammit. Get me to that palace. NOW!" I had nothing else to say to Peter, to anyone, or even to God. Evidently I needed to be angry for a while, and I was doing my job quite well.

Miraculously, we arrived at the palace historical site within fifteen minutes. Although Peter and I walked through the palace in close proximity to one another, not once were we side by side. Neither of us had the need to participate in extended conversation with each other. No one could have even known we were friends.

Not one labyrinth was to be found there, not as far as I could see. Very few walls of the palace were standing. Even though the architectural ruins were abandoned upon its destruction in 1375 BC, intuitively I felt nothing with any specific meaning for me. The fact that the palace stemmed from an ancient seventh-century Neolithic culture did nothing for me either. Those walls that were standing were embellished with magnificent frescos, but to me they did not feel ancient. Even the paint looked new. Yet, the last room I entered completely captured my attention.

On the wall was a picture of what looked to me like a woman leaping over a bull. As far as I could tell, she and the bull had each been running at each other, very much like the matador and the bull of the visions I'd had when Peter and I drove aimlessly around Knossos. It looked like after grasping the horns of the bull, she had been propelled through the air by a combination of the bull's head thrust and her own intention and power. I stared at it for what seemed to be forever, not believing that something as odd as this could be presented exactly when I needed it.

"Look, Peter," I said, breaking our silence. "Look what she's done." I pointed to the picture on the wall, so engrossed that I had no idea Peter could not get the meaning.

"Flying over a bull?" he asked, alternating his look from the picture back to me. "That's important?"

"For me it is. She not only overcomes her anger, she actually soars over it, using its power to create an upward thrust." I kept staring at the picture, amazed at the synchronicity of what I was seeing. "She didn't let the angry bull gore her to death, but actually used it to fly through the air, soaring well over her anger. Could it be that anger cannot destroy me? That I could overcome it somehow?"

Peter stared at the picture for a short time, and then looked back at me. "Take all the time you need," he suggested. "Seems to me like you need to process for a while. I'll be right outside waiting for you." He then wandered off to his own discoveries, obviously delighted to create some space for my anger.

"Thank you, Peter," I answered back, appreciating his friendship. "Thank you for understanding." For several more moments, I opened up to the message of the picture. All that bullish anger, and this woman had just soared right over it. (It never even occurred to me that the person in the picture could have been a man.) "She flies over it, just like an eagle," I said to absolutely no one except God, amazed that the Divine would actually care if I were angry or not.

While walking over the palace grounds with Peter on the way to our car, several thoughts plagued me. Other than the picture, nothing of the palace remnants meant anything to me spiritually. I found no journey to the center of myself spiritually, no labyrinth that I could walk purposely to the center of while mimicking a meditating monk who only had on a robe and sandals separating him and his Lord. For sure, I did not experience the mystical in any fashion. Frankly, I had my intuitive, receiving doors shut tight and padlocked by my own disgust in being here in the first place. Intuition and anger rarely occupied the same place in my psyche. Crete was Peter's idea, not mine. All I had wanted was a labyrinth to walk. Yet synchronistically I had discovered a picture of a woman flying over an angry bull.

The path through the remains of the complex, multi-storied buildings did vaguely remind me of a labyrinth, but only because I wondered where it all led. To me, the meaning of the entire experience evidently was more about trust—about not putting myself into the hands of another or allowing my own dysfunctional, needy ego to determine my future, my path, or my destination. The bigger story of this little confusing adventure evidently held a greater meaning for me.

Several weeks after this Crete experience, I sat at my computer in my Belgium rental organizing photos of my trips so that I could transfer them from camera to computer. As I looked at the Minoan Palace photographs, I paused briefly, moving into that space between thoughts to see if any wisdom lingered from the trip. Perhaps if I sat still for a moment, the deeper meaning of the Crete experience would present itself to me through quiet meditation. Could there be a meaning I had not realized so far? Did the experience of seeking a labyrinth present itself to me with any sort of helpful wisdom for my future?

Pieces of a Bible verse floated into my thoughts from somewhere other than my conscious mind: "Lean not into thy own understanding." "He shall direct...." Because I did not recall the exact wording or the particular place in the Bible where the passage could be found, I went to the Internet for a search, finding the passage in Proverbs 3:5-6. : "Trust in the Lord with all your heart, and do not lean on your own understanding. In all your ways acknowledge him, and he will make straight your paths."

In going to Crete, I had for the most part gotten too wise for my own understanding. Not wise as in wisdom, but too wise as in ego. Even if I could not trust myself to physically get to the places I needed to be in order to facilitate as well as enhance my spiritual journey, after this trip I knew for certain it was not someone else's responsibility to get me where I needed to be spiritually; I had abdicated that responsibility for three decades while married. Peter was a friend—not a partner, not a husband—a friend who thought he was helping me by going to Crete.

Eventually, I was going to have to travel at God's intuitive direction, not create some false need to satisfy my exaggerated ego in defining myself as a spiritual warrior out there meditating in a labyrinth. Instead of following a spiritual labyrinth to the center of my soul, I had followed a tangled web of my own chaotic making just to satisfy my ego's need to force a mystical experience in order to be spiritually wise. My greater task evidently had more to do with anger at this particular point instead of mysticism. The entire experience had the word "stupid" written all over it.

My intent had been to force another spiritual experience into my life similar to the one I'd had in Ireland. Instead of another mystical experience, I got a dose of reality. Staring at the pictures of the ancient Minoan Palace on my computer, I began to smile. The little doves in my heart began to coo appreciatively as I finally learned what the Crete experience had brought to me. Mentally I shifted into neutral, allowing that still, inner voice of Spirit to be heard. When I was to travel, I would know it from now on. I would trust that voice of God to show, present, or create via dreams, intuitions, or synchronicities the places I should visit and the experiences I needed in order to heal. Several months later, I got the chance to experience this level of spiritual trust on a little island in the Mediterranean.

◆ ◆ ◆ ◆ ◆

"If I were this mad at Mama, one of us would never have survived!" I wailed into the telephone. I was in Malta talking long distance through a pay-per-minute telephone to my healer friend, Maria, at her office in Georgia. As the minutes ticked by, my desperation was costing me a fortune. But I didn't care about the cost; my intense need for help overshadowed financial security.

When I first had visions of Malta, I had no idea where it was, other than somewhere in Europe. I was almost right, although it is not in the continent of Europe but in the extreme western part of the Mediterranean Sea, just below Italy. Unaware of Malta's ancient strategic port history due to its location between Europe, Asia, Africa, and the Middle East, additionally I had no idea of the remains of Neolithic (or Paleolithic according to some) culture present in the nine-mile-long island. The Knights Hospitaller of Saint John of Jerusalem had fled to Malta from the Island of Rhodes in 1530. St. John's Cathedral was built for the same knights, and ruins of megalithic temples existed on Malta all without my knowing they existed. What I did know, and knew well, came from my dreams.

The young eagle stretched its wings, flapped them a bit, and walked onward. It turned its head back to the chicken coop, joyous to be moving forward. Already it had stopped imitating the chickens. One day the eagle came to a place that was unfamiliar. It felt the need to experience the new place, but had not a clue how to do that or where to go. In an attempt to help the eagle, the dreamer asked where the bird needed to go. "Malta," was the answer whispered from the eagle's soul. "Go to Malta."

After the dream happened three times, I contacted Peter to see if he would help me make arrangements to get to Malta. After the Crete experience, we had remained in contact, although not as often. Still, our conversations were just as spiritually deep as they had ever been. Malta might have been located at the end of the world, but this had nothing to do with the fact that I was going to go there anyway. The eagle located in the pit of my soul screamed, squawked, and prodded me via dreams until we finally made the arrangements. Peter decided to accompany me; he had never been to Malta.

When Peter and I walked in the area of Mnajdra, which looked to me like it used to be two buildings of some sort. An unidentified energy having to do with feminine culture was palpable—I truly felt that I stood in an ancient culture that had respected females. Nothing I have read before or after in all of my research supports what I felt that day.

Instead, I read that this temple area had to do with astronomy and calendar functions. The feeling, though, was strong.

Additionally, the same energy seemed to thrive at other sites, including Hagar Qim, which means "standing stones." When Peter and I visited the hypogeum of Hal Saflienti, I thought I would have to lie down because of what I intuitively felt.

Peter truly wanted to visit the hypogeum, an underground ruin in the small village of Casa Paula. From what he had read, the catacomb was discovered in 1902 by workers excavating an old well. On the day we wanted to visit, however, all we could do was make a reservation for some time in the future. In order to protect the site, historians had determined only ten people at a time could go down into the cave-like structure. Therefore, tourists had to purchase tickets far ahead of time.

"You'll need to come back in several days," the gentleman at the counter said. "Purchase your tickets now, and then come back. We are booked until then."

Peter noticed the alarmed look on my face. I was so close to the site, actually standing in a building nearly on top of the ancient ruin, yet I could not get a ticket to go down into the cave. My heart leaped inside my chest; my intuition was so strong that I needed to visit this particular place that I thought I would burst into tears if I couldn't go.

"Let me explain this to you," Peter said back to the man who wouldn't sell tickets for that week. "This is the reason we have to go inside."

Truly, I wish I knew what Peter said after that. However, he switched to his limited Italian, and then German, before finally settling on French in order to be completely understood. Peter's words were firm, with an undeniably strong tone of voice. He was not angry as far as I could tell, yet an intense dialogue ensued, with both men gesturing in animated motions using both arms in unison. At one point I thought perhaps the gestures meant something specific, but the words were flying back and forth in such rapid succession I gave up trying to figure them out. Instead, I decided to go to that peaceful place inside of myself, hoping my smile would seem nonthreatening to all around me.

Evidently, something worked, for another man came out from behind a desk, saying in perfect English, "Let me look at the daily roster again. Perhaps there has been a sudden cancellation we're not aware of."

With that, he got out his paperwork, grunted to himself a little, flipped pages, and then said, "Well, you're in luck. We have a cancellation tomorrow. Be here at ten sharp, and you can go in. We'll take your money now for tickets."

Peter and I each paid our fees, happy as larks to have tickets in hand.

"What did you say to him? How did you convince him to give us tickets? You didn't threaten him, did you?" I wanted to feel safe coming back to this site.

"Of course, I didn't threaten him! That's absurd," Peter all but crooned in complete control just as he had been in the previous discussion with the two men behind the counter. "I just explained how important it was to the American lady that she visit the most important site in Malta. I also told them how much I appreciated the government of Malta protecting all these bits of history. It's important to the world."

I looked at Peter, not knowing if he had seriously said those things or not. As I tucked my ticket into my purse, I got into the back of the tiny rental car, preferring to be chauffeured back to the rental house instead of riding next to Peter. For some reason, it felt right to be in the back seat, especially since I still harbored questions about what had been said. As I looked at Peter's reflection in the rearview mirror, I had to smile at his expression. Without a doubt, he was pleased to have gotten tickets.

The next day, as Peter and I waited for our time to enter the steps down into the chamber, eight other ticket holders waited along with us. An additional two women from a tour group were also waiting; however, they did not have tickets, but had only reservations made by the tour. They would have been numbers eleven and twelve. On and on the manager's discussion went until the time we had to visit was seriously compromised. Eventually, the manager let them go with us.

"Peter," I whispered. "Were they supposed to be here instead of us?" Guilt began to flap around inside my stomach like a fish dying on a hot seashore. As much as I wanted to see whatever it was beneath us, I truly did not wish to bump someone else out.

"Hush," Peter whispered back. "Keep good thoughts. It will all work out." With that, the ladies joined our group, and we descended into the multi-level catacombs named after the street on which this discovery was found.

Our tour director seemed knowledgeable enough. From a waiting room, we entered a walkway leading into the first underground room. This walkway reminded me of a boardwalk at the seashore, except it twisted and turned, descending level after level into halls, passages, and chambers. The entire underground structure covers approximately five hundred square meters on three levels. This upper chamber has carved cave-like recesses in the walls said to originally be burial chambers. The middle chamber consists of various smoothly-finished rooms. The lowest level is a room 10.6 meters under road surface.

The whole hypogeum was dimly lit so that the lights would not harm the ancient stone. However, it was adequate enough to cast shadows on the carved rock walls and flooring. The ceiling above us was decorated with red-ochre spirals and floral patterns that reminded Peter of other designs he had seen at ancient sites in Ireland. I became intrigued by a drawing of a bull in black pigment on stone near the Holy of Holies. I thought back to my experience in Crete with anger, and the discovery of a picture of a woman sailing over the back of a bull. I held onto the railing for a moment, trying to ease myself into a more receptive state in order to be totally present to the current experience. Anger evidently will eat you alive, I thought. It's also everywhere.

Along the way to the lower platform, our guide discussed the ancient maternalistic culture of the island. She indicated some ancient graffiti carved onto a rock wall over what she called the Trilithon that lead into one of the small caves. One picture was of a very fat woman holding an ax. I loved the image; I rationalized no one in the world could tell her what to do or put her down in any way. Our guide told us that a museum in Malta housed a rather large carving of the bottom half of another fat lady found on Malta. In this particular hypogeum, she noted, two statues of women were also found. At that point, I began to tune her out, not comprehending one word she said. All that effort we took to see it, yet I couldn't seem to listen to her at all.

Instead, I felt in my body what I intuited from the area around me. I could not bond to the idea that this hypogeum was always a burial ground, even though thousands of bodies were found when the hypogeum was excavated. To me, it vibrated more like an ancient place for worship or a place for authority of some sort. Perhaps feminine authority. Also, there was something unsettling, either caused from where I stood or from inside myself as I picked up energetic vibes from the area. Perhaps something instead bubbled up from my psyche to be healed. I had no idea.

That night as I tried to turn over in bed, my back seized in pain. Not only could I not turn over without excruciating pain, I could not move, stand, or walk. I called for Peter in the next room, but he couldn't help me. He tried to massage my back; however, it hurt too much to even turn over so he could get to it. Because the pain was so intense, only by the grace of God was I able to hobble across the room into the hall in order to use the toilet the next morning. I then climbed up the stairs by sitting on each stair one at a time, because I could not stand. The process took two hours. For most of the day I lay on the upstairs sofa with a makeshift bedpan by my side. Peter left for the day, leaving me with a sandwich, some crackers, an apple, and bottled water. All I could do for myself was panic.

I did a superb job.

It's odd how synchronicities come at just the right time. With nothing else to do while I lay in agony, I picked up a book about results-oriented visualizations that I needed to read for the metaphysical studies I was taking. According to the homework assignment, I was to visualize myself doing something that would require wellness, showing that, because I was accomplishing the visualized task, wellness had already been achieved. On the other hand, if I were to visualize myself *getting* well, then I would be creating the need to have illness from which to heal. So, on and off all day long, I visualized myself dancing up and down the stairs. Slowly, my back got well enough for me to more easily go to the bathroom downstairs. I kept up the visualizations. However, I still needed help beyond just visualization, so that night I called Maria.

◆ ◆ ◆ ◆ ◆

"No, Paddy," Maria explained in her calmest voice from over the Mediterranean Sea and Atlantic Ocean. "You are not angry at your mother. What I said is that you're channeling feminine anger."

"What do you mean channeling feminine anger?" I cried out in exasperation. "I am not trying to do that! My back has frozen in pain. That's the problem!" The phone was ticking, so with considerable effort and a prayer, I deposited more coins, hoping to stay connected to the only human lifeline I had at the time.

"Feminine anger. You are evidently so empathic that you've picked up feminine anger in your body. It's far greater than just your own anger. It came from beyond you, but landed inside of you."

"Oh God, Maria. How beyond? Where did this come from?"

Over the years of my healing, Maria and I had had many discussions about how I hold energies of other people (including family, friends, and even people passing on the street) inside my body. Although this is challenging at times, many consider it to be a psychic gift. At the moment, it felt like more of a severe pain in my back. The problem this time was that I could not distinguish my own energy from what I felt from others. Being able to know what it was I felt became the only way I knew to release it. However, at this point, chaotic anger presented itself as back pain. It had gotten stuck. I waited for Maria to use her own psychic healing powers to help me determine the source of this feminine anger.

"Oh, Paddy. You're channeling cosmic feminine anger through your body. I can't believe this. Hold on...I can help." With that, Maria lead me step by step through her healing process, first by feeling the anger while she did her spiritual energetic work, then by going to a neutral place while it cleared.

"When are you coming back to Atlanta?" Maria asked with rather an insistent tone to her voice. "Soon I hope. Change your plans if not. We have more to do on this issue." With that, Maria and I parted, just as I ran out of coins for the telephone. Yet again, the right help had come at the right time. It was just enough. By the next morning, I was moving well enough to go to St. John's Cathedral in the city of Valletta, Malta.

Although it was a push for me riding in a rental car that evidently did not have shocks as we navigated the bumpy roads of Malta, I compensated by pressing my left hand on the arm rest in the back left seat and my right hand on pillows I had piled on my right. Underneath me were the rest of the pillows from the rental unit. This way, as the car bumped along, I could literally press onto my arms and hands, allowing my body to swing freely without jostling. The trip took forever.

The cathedral seemed exquisite in all ways. Built as a conventional Catholic Church for the Knights of St. John, it houses priceless works of art that enthralled me. The marble floor was inlaid in specific fashion. It took me several moments glancing at the area beneath my feet before I realized I literally was walking on the tombs of the knights. What seemed to be thousands of deceased knights lay beneath the floor of the cathedral, or at least their monuments were beneath my feet. Even the dates, names, and designs on the floor grave markers were of carved marble and other stone. I've never seen such beautiful stonework in my life.

However, its beauty was rivaled by the display of silk and satin vestments with the most exquisite embroidered symbolism of the liturgical calendar I have ever noted. The only thing in the entire cathedral grander than this was the lavish Baroque architecture. I hobbled through the corridors into room after room, with one hand always supporting my achy back, noting the grandeur of the displays.

Yet, when I got to one of the rooms that held many rare paintings, I had to stop for a moment. The magnificence of the entire cathedral began to fade away with one specific realization—in the entire cathedral, as opulent as it was, I saw nothing honoring women.

Side by side, more than I could count, lay the most exquisite markers for the Knights of St. John, all men. Each of the splendidly-adorned vestments was made for a man, possibly by very talented but unknown women. I remember reading on one of the markers under either a tapestry or an oil painting that a man was admitted to sainthood because of his miraculous healing, which had been assisted by an unknown female whose efforts have faded into the male glory.

I folded my arms across my chest, wanting to keep anything male from entering my heart. Immediately, I hated all the opulence. Clenching my jaw hard enough to break nails, I knew with every taut muscle in my body I hated killing of any kind in the name of God. I also hated male domination. As glorious as this cathedral was, it had nothing to do with me, my life, or what I wanted spiritually. I wanted softness instead of the harsh realities of battle, ancient or current. I wanted simplicity instead of lavishly adorned robes worn by officials in charge of another's faith. I wanted nature to whisper words of comfort into my soul instead of having opulence glare at me from gold embellished statuary, structure, and artwork. From the back of my throat, I allowed a noise to erupt, slow and steady, emanating from some psychic depth I did not even know existed.

"Paddy," Peter asked, leaning toward me so others could not hear. "You growled. Just like an angry animal, you growled."

His shock could not have been greater than my own.

"Maybe I did, Peter," I answered back with no intention of owning my own voice. "Maybe I did."

With that, I left the cathedral to the tourists. Within a week from returning to Belgium from Malta, I flew back to Atlanta in order to see Maria.

It had been more than several years since I knew I would need to leave a loveless marriage that had no hope for resolution other than escape. Yet, there I was, on Maria's table, half lying and half sitting, with balled fists boxing air while I all but screamed as torrents of feminine rage detonated from my soul. Actually, I thought I would explode from it. More than two hours later, I had calmed down enough to interpret what Maria said to me.

"Malta was about helping you get to your level of anger. Paddy, when you are holding that much anger—even unaware—it is going to affect your body." Maria turned from me for a moment to clear some space between us before she continued. "If you don't acknowledge it, if you don't release it, then it stays stuffed down inside of you. You've experienced what that causes, haven't you?" Maria maintained a steady tone in the face of my rage.

"But why Malta, Maria?" I asked. "Why go all the way overseas to release this level of anger?"

"Paddy," she answered, turning toward me with a very sincere expression. "Perhaps you had to feel it externally, feel it intuitively, before you were able to recognize it as your own."

I knew she was right. Those doves began to coo appreciatively from their psychic perch in my soul. I did not know how, but I knew I had to move on with life without the anger. "I cannot stay in this place of anger forever."

I hated anger. All my life I have hated anger, mine as well as anger belonging to anyone else. As a child, anger from a parent meant someone was either going to be punished, yelled at, or both. In my marriage, I rarely spoke up, hoping that agreeing with ideals of others would keep anger at bay. Ignoring my anger, though, never made it disappear. Instead, it lay dormant, only to allow shreds of fury to occasionally escape through cracks in my psyche in the form of tears, self-disrespect, and low self-esteem. My anger waddled around inside my body, at times bursting forth as panic, pain, and despair. That afternoon, I felt like a human version of Pandora's box as I clawed, expressed, and raged myself back into a more peaceful place.

"That was not all your anger, not in Malta. But today, it was." Maria smiled at me, making sure I heard her well. "Like energies attract. You were able to attract that level of cosmic feminine anger because of the anger you held in your body from your own experiences. Malta was a great teacher. You were spiritually led to be there."

Maria was right. Malta was indeed a great teacher. Anger had flooded my senses in Malta to the point that I paralyzed my own movements: anger at killing for God; anger at feeling that this was a holy thing to do; anger at the entire divorce mess; anger at the choices I had made out of fear; anger at people for not understanding the trauma I had been through; anger at myself because I had not spoken up more. Above all, I held anger at myself for having the experiences that caused the anger in the first place. All those feelings and many more lay in an impossible tangle, waiting for me to trust myself enough to release them.

After I left Maria's office that day, I walked through the small wooded lot just beyond my own house. My favorite oak tree stood like a sentinel of truth, roots easing out from the trunk deep into the ground while leaves reached for the heavens. I kicked it as hard as I could, cramping my foot to the point that I walked deeper into this tiny piece of suburban jungle with a noticeable limp. With both hands I lifted the largest granite rock I could find, spitting vilely onto it before heaving it as far as I could. It landed only four feet in front of me as if to reassure me that my efforts had done it no harm. Then I grabbed the remaining remnants of an old garden hose curled up under a rotting pile of leaves. Swinging it around the top of my head, I proceeded to whip the dead leaves into piles of rubble.

"Why, God? Why?!" I screamed out loud hoping not only that the neighbors would hear, but also that my shrieks would swarm through the heavens above me as they flew out into the cosmos.

I wanted angels to sing to me songs of sorrow. I wanted the saints themselves to say they truly understood my turbulent experiences. I fully expected some ascended masters—okay, Jesus—to come down on the wings of a thousand doves to shower me with love and affection. Nothing answered me in return, not in any fashion.

"Do you understand what I have been through?" I raged. "Where in the hell have you been? Day by day, I feel like I have been emotionally drawn and quartered as everything I held dear—everything—fell from me. My house. My garden. My chance for love. My community. Everything."

Gasping for breath, I continued through deep sobs. "Why did that happen to me? Why couldn't I have seen it coming? Will my tears ever stop?"

With that last sentence, I felt to the ground, knees bent into the soft loamy earth beneath a brown covering of crunchy leaves. My hands covered my face as wet tears streaked down around the fingertips through the spaces between my fingers before falling into the dead leaves in total submission to peacefulness.

The oak did not flinch. The rock did not crumble. Anger did not eat me alive. Nor did I drown in my tears. Instead, oozing out of some deep recess hidden inside my own heart, I remembered something I had written during those long weeks of initial questions and answers I received intuitively in meditation. *Why all the tears, God?* I had written. *What do they mean? They hurt so much.* That day on my knees in the woods, I incorporated the answer into my soul.

> *As you journey through your life's space, fault yourself not for the tears that inevitably appear. Tears are not a sign of inadequacy or helplessness. To consider them so is to compare what you perceive in yourself as thorns with your perception of the world's way of blooming. Should a rose that starts its life with just stems and thorns reject itself when compared to the spider lily whose beginnings include a stem and a bloom? The rose will eventually bloom in its beauty with a delicacy and fragrance that will permeate the entire area. The thorns will be then of an insignificant nature. Does it not take the rose and the lily to make a garden? A direct manifestation of compassion, love, and caring, your tears are a release when you need it. They are love when you experience it, and they are grace when you need it most. Tears are a display*

of feelings deeply felt, but not actualized. These tiny little diamond treasures of emotion are genuinely sensed, compressed inside, but better served outside as a reminder of your loving nature, expressions of passionate understanding. When the tears come, acknowledge them with a smile, treasuring them as the gift that they are. See in them the myriad of colors that fill the universe, compressed into a single drop. Find within them the joy of being able to express that for which words are inadequate. Feel their wetness, and remember the joy of love that you share. Taste their saltiness as a connection to the power of the Universe that is yours. As they begin to swell, do not be ashamed, but think of the roses blooming in their original colors permeating the air with a pleasantness that will fill your heart with love. The tears are uniquely yours; treasure them. They are your distinctive gift.

Love washed over me like waves cleansing ancient sands of time. As I paused, I looked through the woods, into the forest, up into the individual trees with limbs reaching out surrounding me like the arms of Mother Mary's love. With palms held together like a child in prayer, I asked God to help me release the rest of my anger. No longer did I have the need to hold it inside my heart in order to have something to cling to, to have something—anything—to place in my heart in order to know I was real.

I was real—one of God's children. I was one of God's children here on earth doing the best I could with my life. I closed my eyes in prayer, fully expecting something holy to eventually fill the empty spaces left by the anger's wrath, the empty spaces left by the wrath's absence. I had no idea what it would be, but I longed for love to fill my very soul. I felt the rock upon which I sat; it felt solid, strong. I looked up to the sky, seeing its blueness peek around the tops of the trees while leaves moved gently into the winds of change. Just as in the experience in Ireland, again I felt at one with surrounding nature, though not as profoundly so. Still, it was strong enough to fill my soul with goodness and grace.

Just before I stood to go inside, a Red-shouldered Hawk indigenous to the area flew onto the lowest limb on the spindly oak just beyond the patio not thirty feet from me. Native Americans considered the eagle or the hawk, depending on tribal location, as messengers from God. From my own experience, I concur. His very presence felt like the breeze upon my cheeks. His eyes pierced grace right into my soul. "Surely goodness and mercy shall follow me..." I remembered from Psalm 23. "...I shall dwell in the house of the Lord forever."

That night the eagle in my dreams took flight.

*"The big question is whether
you are going to be able to say
a hearty yes to your adventure."*

JOSEPH CAMPBELL

———————◆———————

CHAPTER SEVEN

Fear Not

ON AND ON the weary eagle wandered before reaching the edge of a very sharp cliff. Ahead of her, the wide, blue heavens stretched out to meet the hills and vales of the earth. Far beyond her lay the other side of the stony fortress sandwiching the deep canyon between the two. The drop straight down over the sharp crevices seemed perilous, a sure death at best.

To go back into the coop, confined and pretending to be something she was not, was demise of the individual spirit and soul. She could go neither left nor right for the same reason. The journey had to be forward. The only thing she knew to do was jump, hoping by a frenzy of flapping wings she would either fly or fall to a quick death

The eagle spread her wings, took a breath, and jumped into the wide-open sky.

I awoke gasping for air in my bedroom in Atlanta. My arms were spread out from one side of the bed to the other, fingers moving through the air as if I were furiously waving to someone. Drawing them back into my stomach, I looked around the bedroom fully expecting to see the earth reaching out to crush me to death as I fell. Instead, the walls of my bedroom still held their desert sand color while the forever busy squirrels ran endlessly back and forth doing whatever it is that squirrels do on a roof at four in the morning. On the very top part of the high wall just in front of me, moonlight danced through the oak tree's leaves just outside narrow windows far above my head. This play of light and shadow seemed quite an accepted play of nature. However, I did not feel reassured about my own light and darkness.

I moved my arms and legs, assuring myself that I was human, not eagle. Then I lay very still in my bed, covers tossed aside because they had encumbered a dreaming bird's flight. My heart beat the rhythm of an athlete at the starting line. It eventually took a quick cup of chamomile tea to calm me down enough to fall back to sleep. The eagle's spirit, however, had not finished with me. The dream started exactly where it had stopped.

> *Over and over the eagle tumbled, crying out to God in terror to catch her safely in loving arms. The ground continued to rise up toward the panic-stricken eagle. A recognizable fear was exposed through the eagle's eyes.*
>
> *From that small still place of holy love greater than the eagle—and a lot wiser—echoed a voice of wisdom, "Spread your wings. You can fly."*
>
> *At first, the eagle hesitated, for she had never flown before. The ground got closer and closer, threatening to swallow the eagle whole. Over and over she tumbled in freefall.*
>
> *"FLY!" the voice commanded with absolute authority. "You can do it. Spread your wings and*

> *fly! Winds of Spirit are here to help. But the help only comes if you try to fly. Do it now!"*

◆ ◆ ◆ ◆ ◆

Just as the eagle had wandered and stood looking over the cliff, I wandered back and forth from the rental in Belgium to my home in Atlanta. I had no intention of ever getting the visa required to live permanently overseas. Europe simply did not call to me as a place of stable residency. Instead, Europe became a place to gather spiritual wisdom beyond my current state of being in order to heal psychologically. For me, the change of location presented a chance to see the world—as well as how I fit into this same world—through a change of personal perspective.

In order to be myself, in order to learn who that self was, and in order to be secure being myself, I had to do it in a safe location, but one that was previously unfamiliar. That way the daily reminder of the old voices, the old habits, and the old pain stayed at bay. *Fear won't kill you,* I reminded myself, *you just think it will.*

During one visit to Belgium not long after the eagle dream, I decided to set out into the world walking instead of by bus. The previous week showered the area with so much rain that I felt like I needed rubber boots just to get to the neighborhood store. This particular day, the sun kept peeking through the clouds, bathing the entire area with lovely bursts of sunshine. With umbrella, bottled water, and a map, I set out to walk to Leidermeerspark, a nature area near the community of Merelbeke. For me, the time had come to embrace the light located inside my own version of safety. My current challenge was that I had not one iota of an idea how to discover this little corner of safety within my psyche. Hopefully, just like riding the bus, tiny experiences into the world would provide me with a method of feeling like I had moved full circle into personal security.

Unfortunately, I found the park through the back entrance, winding through clustered areas of housing, underneath a railroad trestle, and finally on a dirt drive. Evidently, in getting there I had wandered onto the wrong side of the street, for as I rounded a corner, a bicyclist almost ran headlong into me. Startled, I realized by the tone of the young man's voice his own surprise expressed itself through angry words. In my most polite voice, I said, "Have a good day." I have no idea what his answer was to me. At the time, it did not matter because anxiety had already filled every available space in my body.

Leidermeerspark captured my heart. Instead of cement sidewalks and narrow streets like I had seen on trips into the city center of Ghent, I all but floated through the lavish walking trails covered with only footprints of nature lovers pressed into the natural earth. A tiny footbridge spanned a little stream while trees, grass, and benches beckoned all ages to experience nature at its finest. For a while I settled myself on one of the benches in order to watch the swans swim about in a small pond. They seemed so content, moving effortlessly through the water.

On the walk back to my apartment, I saw the most magnificent tree; it had a profusion of yellow blossoms that began life at the stem, then hung down in a graceful bow to Mother Earth. The flowers reminded me of grape clusters, yet the individual blossoms were long and slender, filled with florets shaped like angel trumpets. How I missed that golden goodness at first is beyond me. It reached far above me before branching out like rays of the sun gyrating in between long branches.

Leaving my paraphernalia on the sidewalk, I hurriedly crossed the grass in order to stand under this tree. The sign I tripped over may have said "Don't walk on the grass," but it was in Flemish, so I pretended it did not exist to my one-language-only mind. The closer I got to the tree, the faster I ran. By the time I reached it, I was all but breathless with wonder. My eyes beheld it, but my heart had the experience.

The steadfast nature of the tree's limbs caused them to remain solidly connected, yet the graceful, delicate temperament of the flowers allowed them to move as gently as fairy wings in the refreshing breeze. Many, many flower shapes were in each blossom, and the flowers engulfed the entire tree. My first reaction quite surprised me.

Too much yellow, I thought. But then I allowed myself the grace to not think, listening to my heart.

How can there be too much yellow? What was this about? Intuitively, I knew that was a judgment reaction that held no wisdom. Yellow, I mused, the color of the third chakra, the body's energetic center of self-empowerment. Mine had closed down so many years ago that even the color of yellow was overwhelming at first.

I gingerly allowed my soul's heart to awaken, a process that assuredly began to open the doors of inner perception. The tree dared to not only bloom, but to crowd itself with blooms. Yellow, the color of sunshine. Yellow, the color of the daffodils in the garden I loved when I was married. Yellow, the sign of inner security. Yellow, the golden halo of Christ Consciousness. The blooms were not rigid like a steel rod, but found strength through flexibility. They were not afraid to move with the windy currents of life.

And with that, I recognized my own painful situation. Suddenly, I could feel my own center through the etheric doors I had closed down as a protection years ago. It was now time to consciously move with my heart through my many fears in order to find my own freedom; no more closing emotional doors out of protection. I opened wide my spirit to receive the message of this beautiful tree.

I stood under the tree for a long time, enthralled by the play of light and shadow on my arms. Slowly, I reached out as if I could capture this light, capture the spirit of this yellow, blooming goodness. I touched the bark gently, as if the tree itself could communicate to me words of peace, words of security, and above all, words of love. No words were spoken, of course—just the feeling that I was part of something quiet but holy.

Briefly, the tree and I became one, a full circle of yellow wonderful. For the first time in many years, I felt safe. Truly safe.

While standing there those brief moments, I absorbed the energy of the blossoms, felt the yellowness of life, and felt the solid connection of the tree to earth. I incorporated the way it bent and swayed, undamaged, with the winds. I could feel the shimmering movements of the blossoms as they gently touched each other and resonated with joy as I tingled with anticipation of forthcoming healing. As I stood under the golden yellow tree, I felt the golden Light of Love surround me, enfold me, encompass me. I did not feel crowded, and did not feel like my boundaries had been violated, but felt instead like they were expanding. I was expanding into the freedom of yellow. Gently, I reached out to touch a flower with my fingers. I felt it, though, in my soul.

While on the plane home to Atlanta the next week, I pondered further the yellow tree's meaning for me. Yellow flowers have always felt to me like coming home. During many years of my childhood, I'd had an oblong garden in the backyard designed by my mother with the help of her gardener, but totally mine in all ways. Bricks had bordered the garden, angled sideways so that one rested upon the other, individuals in full loving support. Always, the daffodils pushed their way into the early spring, their beauty trumpeting shades of yellow glory into the doldrums of winter's edge. I loved those daffodils and made sure to plant them in my garden every spring as the years went on. However, that day on the trip back home, I realized I had not planted daffodils since the divorce. When I focused so very much on the shadows of life, the light was hardly noticed.

Not long after the jet touched American soil, the limo pulled into my subdivision. As we turned the last corner to my home, I noticed on the corner of my lot the maple tree I'd had planted over a year previously to replace one that had died. Yet, this time it was not the tree that captured my attention, but the circle of daffodils surrounding it. I had not planted the bulbs, nor had the gardeners who planted the tree. Perhaps they were there all along, but I don't think so. The coincidence was too strong.

"Stop!" I yelled to the driver, opening the door before he had a chance to comply. After running over to the young maple, I counted ten yellow daffodils in complete bloom circling the tree. Bending down, I touched each one, making sure what I was seeing actually was real.

Since it was late August, they were out of season, yet very real.

Yellow daffodils called me full circle that day, home to explore the idea that perhaps life without paralyzing fears was possible after all. Were that the truth in front of me, I would indeed have to face my own version of the eagle's cliff. In some way, perhaps it was time to fly into the world by myself in order to discover my own depths.

In prayer that night, I asked for just that. St. Gerard Majella said, "Who except God can give you peace? Has the world ever been able to satisfy the heart?" I wasn't sure, yet I did know through every cell in my body and every twinkling in my heart that God had an answer. And the way peace came to me was beyond anything I had ever imagined doing.

◆ ◆ ◆ ◆ ◆

The first vision happened on the way home after visiting an old friend in the mountains of north Georgia. Although I prefer this type of experience to come during meditation, or better yet during that delicious dream state of sleep in which my heart is opened wide, this vision came while I was driving my car. Annoyingly, my psychic vision and thoughts concerning driving safely collided into each other like two cars in a head-on collision.

Driving home after having a delightful lunch with my friend Ann, my thoughts sashayed back and forth between wanting to spend more time with her and my next traveling adventure.   Although I felt something wonderful in my future would call me into a new place either psychologically, physically, or both, I had no clue as to what it would be. Basically, I knew it would happen in some way because my prayers intended it to be so. I could feel it coming.

Just like the eagle, I was determined to fly into my own love, into my own life, into my own freedom to be myself, free of fears. At least I intended to find out how to live without the paralyzing fears that kept me terrified of buses, the unfamiliar, and of being trapped. Somewhere within my psyche or body or spirit, I realized there had to be something that was not afraid of the world and most people in it. In the Gospel of Thomas is written, "If you bring forth what is within you, what you bring forth will save you. If you do not bring forth what is within you, what you do not bring forth will destroy you." I had no intention of being destroyed. I was going to live—truly, authentically live. I knew the answer would come somehow.

The vision started out in front of my car while I was barreling down the four lane highway trying to keep under the speed limit. Even though I have never gotten a speeding ticket, on occasion I may have needed one. Anyhow, out in front of my car, so far I could not at first readily detect it, was a vision of what looked like a head.

Because I lived intuitively and understood the importance of discernment, I knew at once this was just a vision. Visions are symbols brought to you for a specific spiritual purpose. I think of them as a reality of another dimension, a reality of spirit, or a message coming differently from ordinary life in order to get my attention. Because I knew these things, I embraced the experience from the beginning.

As I continued to speed down the road, the vision got closer and closer, eventually looking as if it were going to land on the hood of the car. I had never seen this particular woman before; therefore, I had no idea who she was. Her neck was long, with head extended forward. I could see no hair on her head or hanging down the sides and back of her neck because it looked to me like her head was shaved. The hat she wore was quite distinctive, not something we would have seen in American history. It was cylindrical; the top was flat, slightly higher on the back side as if to compensate for the angle of her head. As I said, I had no idea who she was or what she meant. What I did know beyond a shadow of a doubt was that she needed my attention.

So did my driving.

After I moved to the right side of the road, I slowed down, making space for myself that would not threaten other drivers. After all, safety was my first intention at this point. Yet to be honest, the woman captured my attention big time. By the time I had moved to the slower lane, the vision of this woman's head had taken residence inside my car. As far as I was concerned, she needed to state her business and then leave. I've never believed in ghosts before, at least not in the way they are presented in the media, but I have had experiences with the spirits of souls who have gotten lost. At first I thought I was having this type of experience yet again. I was wrong. Well, almost wrong.

"What is it you want?" I asked the vision, who by this time seemed to be inside what is commonly called my third eye. In other words, the vision was not being seen with the eyes, but with that special sense the shamans of indigenous tribes use when discerning dysfunctional spirits, sensing predators, or generally when in healing mode. In common language, this woman's head squared itself right in front of my face, nose to nose.

"Heal my Nile," the woman's head whispered quietly to me. It was said only once, heard through clairaudience or psychic hearing.

"I heard you," I said. "Now, I am driving. Please leave."

With that, the vision of the woman's head vanished. When I got home, I immediately went to the Internet to discover what in the world this vision was. *Or who.* Actually, finding her turned out not to be as difficult as I thought.

Nefertiti lived circa 1370 to 1330 BC in ancient Egypt, the royal wife of Akhenaten, often spelled Akhenaton. She and her husband tried to change organized religion in the area, preferring to worship one god, Aten, and this was a monotheistic or henotheistic form of worship not practiced before in the area. Because Akhenaten wanted to establish his new theology in a new place, he and Nefertiti moved to Amarna, the city he had built for his god. Eventually it would not be accepted, and the city destroyed. In the nineteenth century the ruins were discovered by Flinders Petrie; until then, Akhenaten's reign had faded from history.

What struck me as most important about what I had read was that Nefertiti had lived as a very powerful woman. Literally, her influence still is remembered all these many centuries later.

What in the world, though, did this have to do with me? At the time I was not into Egyptian anything. I had never studied it, I had never read about it, and, for sure, I had never visited Egypt. For all I knew, Egypt had pyramids and lots of hot sand. Heal my Nile were the only words I intuited. Surely, the Nile did not require my healing touch. Even that thought made me laugh. How could I heal the Nile when I could not even heal myself? The entire thought seemed absurd. Even if I were to have some beneficial help to offer to the ancient river of life running south to north in Egypt, how in the world would I get there? A quick Internet search let me know quickly that excursions to this area of the world would cost thousands of dollars, something I had no intention of affording. *Heal my Nile* indeed. I endeavored to put the entire experience right out of my consciousness.

Not long after my vision, a magazine at the checkout counter of the grocery store had a picture of Nefertiti on the front cover. In a church meeting for women, she was mentioned by the leader. I saw an advertisement on television that had a replication of her famous bust now found in Berlin's Neues Museum. All of a sudden the woman seemed to be everywhere.

Now, she had my attention.

Three things stood in my way from putting what started as a minor-turning-major experience to rest. First, I had no idea what the words meant. Second, I could not afford a trip to the Nile. Third, well, how in the name of all that is holy could I get there by myself, if indeed I chose to go? One by one the answers came, even though I truly did not want them to come. All I wanted consisted of a life of personal freedom without so many fears. I already knew that would never happen if I didn't continue to listen to holy guidance.

Actually, as it turns out, I hadn't interpreted the three words correctly. The words continued intermittently during meditation and dreamtime; they also came when doing mundane things such as washing dishes or folding clothes. Coming as whispers so soft I felt them instead of hearing them, I realized eventually that a pause existed after the word *heal*. Therefore, the thought I had intuited had actually expressed itself as *Heal. My Nile.* The difference astounded me, allowing me to get out of the ego thought that my psychic talents could heal a famous river into a more pleasant thought. I could heal. The Nile could be a place to do it. I fully intended to go to Egypt, somehow.

God help me.

But how could I afford it? A quick Internet search of travel agencies with tours to the temples of the Middle Nile assured me that it would be easier to afford a small used car than it would be to pay for a trip overseas. Then it occurred to me that the trip might be cheaper from my apartment in Europe. During the next visit to Ghent, I discovered how I would go.

"Peter, you would not believe the experience," I blurted out enthusiastically. "The Egyptian woman with the brimless hat just flew into my face!" I reached inside the steaming pot of mussels with my fingers, abandoning all proper manners. The shells just could not be navigated with a knife, fork, or spoon. Juice dripped from the inner goodness down the front of my sweater as we sat in the late April sunshine at a sidewalk café in Belgium.

"Nefertiti, Paddy. Use her name. It sounds wiser that way," Peter counseled. His smile expressed an inner knowing. Somehow Peter seemed to know a forthcoming story much better than I did.

I hated it when he got educationally elite. Peter knew this. Perhaps that was the reason he liked to express himself that way.

"I've got to go to the Middle Nile. I have no idea how. I just know I have to go." I dropped the black mussel shell into the tin refuse container placed between Peter and me. Picking up another shell from the pot in front of me, I managed to slide the inner goodness into my mouth with a fork this time. Instead of dripping down my sweater, the juice slid down the underside of my palms before ultimately landing upon the white sleeves of my shirt. Even in late April, Belgium chills the bones. Layered clothing kept me warm.

"Did you pray about it?" Peter asked, knowing full well I had. "Ask for something you can afford. If you are supposed to be there, then there will be a way that shows up for you to make that happen."

Peter looked too smug, as far as I could ascertain. I felt very guarded, but did not realize why. I did know that Peter loved going to Egypt.

He added, "Well, I could go with you. We would have a ball."

"Peter, Nefertiti did not come to you. She came to me. It was my vision, not yours. I have to do this by myself. For the life of me I don't know how to make that happen."

"Well, don't worry then. It will happen. Just trust."

Not seven days later, I received an email in English from a travel agency located in Amsterdam, Netherlands, an easy train ride away. They had a last-minute tour scheduled to the Middle Nile on a five-star deluxe cruise ship that included all food, all transportation, and seven days cruising the Nile. It even included airfare from Amsterdam to Luxor, Egypt and an English-speaking guide. Best yet, it cost only $800.00 American money. Five days later I found myself in the air on a trip to Egypt with a lot of people from the Netherlands.

To have talked myself into the fact that I could survive a trip to Egypt alone had to be a sudden burst of insanity expressing itself as bravery beyond normal recognition. Realizing the temperature in that particular area of Egypt would scorch the air passages into my lungs, I hastily threw the only sun-protective shirt I possessed into my suitcase. I owned one hat, a safari lookalike with a wide brim that made me look like an enormous hat with a small body underneath it. It worked well in the suitcase, however, because it could be wadded up into an unrecognizable ball. Thinking it would help my anxiety, I had purchased a travel book of Egypt at the travel bookstore in the city of Ghent. Thumbing aimlessly through the pages of the book while the plane lifted off the ground, I knew for certain I had lost my mind. Every cell in my body reverberated with native drummers pounding out a syncopated beat of a warrior's cry. Without a doubt, I knew I would somehow be eaten alive. Either I was the bravest soul on the planet or the most stupid. I have never felt so alone in my life. Or scared.

I don't know what the rest of humanity does when they are frightened beyond their own senses. As I have read, some fight with every muscle in their body. Some run faster than they have ever run before. Others, like me, stand absolutely still, paralyzed from moving altogether for some reason only God our Creator knows. Actually that question will be the first one of many I am going to ask when I get to the other side of life.

Meanwhile, we of the freeze version of absolute terror express ourselves by crying. I have to admit that on that particular flight, I cried my panicky heart into exhaustion. Long, sorrowful sobs dripped tears from my cheeks down into the dinner of God-only-knows-what we passengers were served in tiny plastic portioned plates on the late morning to afternoon flight. I could not have eaten if my life had depended upon it, even if I had recognized the food.

About an hour or two into the flight, the stewardess came to the miserable man sitting next to me—the woman who was sobbing herself into a frenzied stupor—and began to speak vigorously to him in either Egyptian, German, French, Dutch or whatever it was. For all I knew it could have been in Swahili. I had no idea what they were saying, but both people quickly glanced at me during the exchange, while trying not to be noticed. After about five minutes or so of this intense tête-à-tête, the man started excitedly nodding. I have no idea what he said over and over, but it had to be his native version of "Yes, yes, yes!" He looked at me as if I would morph into a flesh-eating piranha before he hurriedly got up from his seat. Hastily he all but ran down the aisle to the back of our plane with arms raised up into the air exclaiming what I thought sounded something like a heartfelt thanks to God for his good fortune.

Evidently my panic had caused a bit of commotion on the plane. At least that one sane thought exploded out of the tangle of other thoughts battling for attention inside my head. *I'm going to die on this plane. If they feed me that tired old brown food again, I will get poisoned. I have no idea why I am here or what to do about it. It is safe to drink the bottled water? Oh God. Oh God. Oh God. Help me.* The stewardess handed me a wad of toilet paper for what I assumed was intended to be a substitute for tissue. I took it with teary grace as I looked to the left through the window away from the others into the cloudy sky. Truly, I wondered if I would ever be fortunate enough to see Light again.

"Hello. You must be Paddy. My name is Peter," my heroic friend again said with a smile as he settled into the abandoned chair of my former seatmate. "Do you need some help?"

The first time I heard those words I had been on a bench in Bruges. Never in my life had I been so glad to see anyone. Yes, I needed help. I needed the God of common sense to bring me droves of angels to fly me off into something that felt safe. Instead I fell into Peter's arms.

"Oh Peter. Thank God! You came. I didn't know you were coming. I am so glad you did come." I blubbered, all of my words falling out into the air from their cesspool of chaos. "Why did you come? Oh God, I am so scared."

"You wanted to do this by yourself, you said. Well, you still can visit Egypt by yourself. The tour will be fine for that. I will be here from a distance if you need me. You were so intent on going to Egypt. I just felt like it would be better if you had a shoulder to lean upon if necessary."

In hindsight, I wish I had known Peter planned to come with me from the beginning. But that doesn't matter. What matters became the lesson lined in golden letters, etched upon my soul: I was going where I needed to go. I needed help getting there. It came.

◆ ◆ ◆ ◆ ◆

Mother of all that is holy, please bring me some cool air, I thought. Every breath I took cooked the insides of my nostrils, windpipe, and probably my lungs. Frankly, I managed the intense furnace called Egypt the only way I could, by purchasing two bottles of almost-cold water from the tour driver each time we entered the bus at the temple sites, placing one at the back of my neck while gulping down the other one as fast as I could. Although I still did not care much for bus travel, the air conditioning inside made it feel like a protective fortress from the furnace outside.

"You are good for business," the driver said in broken English, grinning as he handed me two very expensive bottles of water. "You come back soon. Good for business. Allah is good today."

"That's good," I answered back with a smile, not having a clue as to what else I needed to say. After the first day's trip from the enormous cruise boat, each of my Dutch traveling companions adapted my one-for-the-neck and one-to-drink survival method. Although I had not intended to be a trendsetter, evidently I pushed the one-bottle-at-a-time status quo. For that matter, I would have poured it all over myself if I thought I could have gotten by with making a drippy mess inside the bus.

Not long after I booked the tour, our tour company emailed a small travel brochure that explained that the temperature in Egypt reached extraordinary proportions in May. However, I didn't realize the literature literally meant this hot. What I experienced in Egypt made even growing up in southern Georgia (where summer temperatures often soar above one hundred) seem like a walk through a frigid meat cooler. One hundred and twenty degrees of excessively dry, hot air, or so explained one of our tour guides.

Frying-pan hot!

As children, we often joked that the sidewalks were hot enough to fry an egg. In Egypt, the air could have cooked an egg before it even hit the ground. If by chance this egg did drop to the ground, it would have burned immediately into crispy cinders. Actually, I thought that could have happened to any of us on the tour at any time. In fact, it almost did. Many of my traveling companions from the Netherlands dressed in shirts with thin straps, shorts, and sandals. By the third day, every one of them mimicked hot dogs roasting on an outdoor barbeque—sweaty, puffed skin, covered with red blisters.

On the other hand, I never burned. I made up for it, though, by becoming quite odiferous. Since I only had the one long-sleeved sun protective shirt, every day we went into the sun, I wore the same outfit. Because the heat evaporated any type of sweat like water drops on a sizzling griddle, the long sleeves helped wick in the moisture. Perhaps the traditional sleeping-shirt type of clothing native to the trinket vendors—those aggressive Egyptian natives who assault tourists coming and going from the temples in order to sell all manner of souvenirs—helped them stay cooler. I had no idea.

Even the temperature of the water coming out of the cold water faucet of my bathroom shower scorched my skin when I touched it. In order to bathe, it became necessary to either fill the tub or sink from the cold water faucet, then wait until it cooled off enough to cleanse. The cooling process took well over an hour. Therefore, I did my daily bathing after the early morning excursions when the temperature on dockside of our cruise ship exceeded what felt like the one hundred and twenty degree mark. After three days, my shirt looked and smelled like I had been living in the gutters forever.

"I washed my clothes and Fred's clothes today," Mary, my Australian dinner companion, explained to me. "Cleanliness makes everything so much fresher. You could try it, too," she suggested, looking down her nose at my white shirt.

"Yes, what a lovely idea," I answered honestly. "Perhaps I'll do just that." Yet, for some reason I never found time enough to cool two tubs of water, one for washing and one for rinsing. It required every effort to be ready at five each morning for that day's tours. At least I had other shirts to wear after the morning tours, when our floating hotel again sailed down the ancient Nile.

During the trips to the Temple of Deir El-Bahri, The Temple of Luxor, and the Unfinished Obelisk located in a granite quarry near Aswan, Peter stayed his distance, allowing me to not only experience the bus ride alone, but to have the experience of walking the temple areas by myself although I was still part of the group. In this manner, I navigated the area singularly with the full knowledge that I had support if I needed it. We also did the same thing while touring the Temple of Kom Ombo, dedicated to the crocodile god, and the Temple of Edfu, located sixty kilometers north of Aswan. For the most part, our system worked well. On a couple of occasions I really did need Peter's help.

In the Temple of Karnak, I fumbled with my Egyptian currency, hoping to get inside the toilets in time. Since I saw no sign indicating how much it would cost me to enter, I handed the woman at the booth what I thought was paper currency for twenty cents. The Egyptian woman reached out to take my money with a smile that mimicked the Grand Canyon.

"Here, use this," Peter hastily said reaching out to grab my paper money before the Egyptian woman could. With his other hand he handed her another paper bill, smaller than the one I had but still with the symbol indicating it was a twenty. "All coins are of paper here, Paddy," Peter explained further. "You have to look at the size of the bills to know the difference."

"Thank you, Peter," I answered hurrying into the ladies' toilet room. Needing the facilities in an emergency, twenty dollars seemed like a bargain.

Never in my wildest dreams would I have expected a man—A MAN!—to be inside the woman's toilet facility handing out toilet paper to each of the females who entered. This man standing just inside the ladies' room in Karnak possessed the only roll of toilet paper in the entire room. As each female entered, he rolled paper around his hand before shoving it at us. Evidently, we were expected to use the paper after our business concluded before putting it into a jar nearby.

I took the paper and entered the stall, hoping the door shut tightly to protect my privacy. Carefully, I removed the outer layer of the paper and the inner layer that the man had touched, glad to have a couple of sheets of toilet paper left that would be sanitary. After concluding my business I went outside the stall, paper in hand, and stuffed it into the jar of used paper, water, and heaven-only-knows-what, doing my best not to touch any part of that jar. On the way out, I looked back, wondering if anyone other than me was appalled about this type of control given to men over the most private of female matters. Never would that happen in the United States. As I rejoined the others in my tour, I wondered if men in Egypt truly had that much control over females in other ways. The thought almost made me sick.

The second time I truly required Peter's help was during a visit to the Valley of the Kings, a burial ground for about sixty-two pharaohs located on the west bank at Luxor. Before our group entered the burial area, we gathered under an open-air shelter while our guide explained to us in English that under no circumstances were we to take pictures inside the tombs, because the authorities wanted to protect the tombs from the flashes of cameras. Even though the tombs no longer contained bodies, items needed on the trips to the afterlife, or opulent golden articles thought to increase wealth on the other side of life, they did have magnificent hieroglyphs on the walls describing what I assumed were the great deeds of the deceased. (Actually, they could have been pictures depicting the recipe for crocodile stew and I would not have known the difference.)

These walls would have made great photographs. The hieroglyphic drawings started near the entrance of the tombs and covered the top to the bottom of the cave walls, leaving no space in between. I got the sense that stories were told in the writing, for I saw several characters repeated in different poses. As I squinted in the low light, I wondered if the stories of the pharaohs had anything to do with spirituality. I did recognize an ankh, the symbol for eternal life that is often seen next to a character's lips. I also recognized the amenta, a symbol representing the underworld or land of the dead, typical of the West Nile burial area. Even though I wanted pictures to analyze later in order to discern Egyptian spirituality and use for photographic decorations, I fully intended to obey the rules of no photography. I moved as close to the nearest wall of the first tomb as I could without touching it in order to see in the low light. However, what I didn't understand about the guards' intentions during the visitation process almost got me into trouble because of my gullibility.

"I can take your picture as you stand by the walls," the Egyptian man insisted as he stood at the opening of one of the tombs, pointing further inside the tomb to a wall filled with hieroglyphs. "You get over there, I take your picture." He touched my camera case strap as if he would pull it off of my shoulder while simultaneously pointing to the interior wall.

"No, no," I tried to explain pulling my camera case from his grip. "I don't wish to have a photo taken." What I did not wish had more to do with not being manhandled by this man more than with possible illegal photographs. Quite confused because this man's actions opposed what our tour guide had told us, my gut instinct alerted me that I had stepped into a trap unaware.

"You have souvenir, then. I take photos." He again reached for the camera as if I had said nothing.

I looked past him, out the tomb opening, up the rocky cliff to where the soldiers with machine guns stood. Even though I had been reassured by our guide that first day that the men at each major intersection supported by all manner of weapons protected the tourists from harm, I truly wasn't very assured of my safety or anyone else's for that matter. Yet, I had gotten used to seeing the small armory at each major intersection. However, the men on the cliff above me looked ominous, as if they were patrolling for some reason. The weapons rested in both hands, ready to be used at a moment's notice. Only later did I learn that once, several years before my visit, a tourist did get shot by an armed man, not a soldier. Evidently the soldiers had been positioned to protect the tourists. But my problem at hand came in the form of this very aggressive man who truly wanted to take my picture with my own camera for some idiotic reason.

"I would rather look at the hieroglyphics on the walls," I said honestly. However, that also invited yet another level of aggressiveness.

"Then I teach you," the antagonistic keeper of the tomb explained as he stood firmly inside the doorway to prevent my exit. "You pay me well."

Like a knighted hero helping a damsel in distress, Peter appeared at the door of the tomb in just that instant. "I've been looking for you. You have to come with me now. Our group is ready to go."

I don't handle aggressive men well and, in my estimation, Egypt seemed to be filled with them. Unrelenting trinket merchants hovered outside each temple site insisting on selling tourists all manner of postcards, statues, or whatever necessary in order to earn a living. If by some act of naivety you did pause to examine statues, clothing, or whatever displays the pesky merchants had to offer, you were doomed to say "no" in perpetuity until your very words dried up in the Egyptian sun. Other aggressive merchants would block the door of the sales booths, preventing you from leaving. The best thing I could do to prevent this sales tactic when entering and exiting the temple sites involved walking as fast as I could while staring down at the ground under me. Never make eye contact and keep moving. I reminded myself many times of a linebacker pushing his way through the opposing team at a University of Georgia football game.

"Peter, what in the world was that about?" I all but cried. "I thought he was going to grab my camera. Why couldn't I just see the inside of the tomb by myself? I hate this!" My frustration climaxed into tears.

"In a way, he fully intended to get your camera, Paddy. See the armed guards watching us on top of the cliff? Well, pictures are not supposed to be taken, as you know. The aggressive man at the entrance of the tomb knew that. He also knew that if he conned you into letting him take your picture, the soldiers would confiscate your camera and give it to him. You see, it would be worth a lot of money to him at the market."

"That doesn't seem honest to me, Peter. Why would they try to con someone like that? Why can't they just be honest?" By now the tears flowed freely, but the heat evaporated them before they even made decent eye puddles of needed moisture.

"Are you really interested in seeing more of the Valley of the Kings? If not, the bus air conditioning is on. I suggest we go back to the bus."

"May the pharaohs rest in peace without us," I agreed. Besides, the driver had two bottles of water ready for me. I settled myself into the seat, water bottle at my neck, while a fine trickle of moisture steamed the hot coals in the pit of my stomach. I breathed in, out, then slowly repeated the process over and over. Closing my eyes, I found a small remnant of peacefulness buried deep within the catacombs of my psyche to claim.

When the bus doors closed just before pulling out onto the Egyptian road ahead, instead of feeling trapped, I felt protected and safe for the first time in Egypt. Valley of the Kings did not do one thing for me even though many on our tour were enthralled by the entire experience. Two Dutch women passed tissues to one of their friends who was having a nosebleed due to the dry air, yet their Dutch chatter felt to me more like jubilation than complaints. My Australian friends passed back sunscreen to several very red women who had dressed in shirts with straps instead of long sleeves. Their sunburns must have been hurting, for blisters were beginning to swell. However, the entire bus seemed filled with tourists' joy instead of agony. Because I could not share their delight, I finished the last of my water before adjusting the bottle at the back of my neck in order to look out the window as the bus moved onward.

The earth at the temple ground supported no life that I could ascertain. Instead of being fertile like the banks of the Nile we cruised down each day, it looked dry, barren, and lifeless. It felt dead to me—graveyard dead. In fact, every graveyard I had visited in Georgia over a five year period several decades ago when listing them for a historical society felt more alive than this particular area. The Valley of the Kings contrasted sharply with anything I have ever known. Truly, as I settled down into the bus ride, it felt to me like we had just left an area that had been robbed of everything precious through archeological and Egyptological exploration since the end of the eighteenth century. Even the land surrounding the tombs supported this feeling. Perhaps it had.

By the fifth day of the Middle Nile cruise, I had grown tired of stone temples, ancient hieroglyphs, and trinket vendors pushing their wares into my face each time I went into or out of a temple area. That particular day our plans were to visit the Temple of Philae, a rocky island that used to be in the middle of the Nile just outside of Aswan. The ancient Egyptians had built a temple on this island to the goddess Isis; however, it nearly became submerged by water after the first Aswan dam was built. Many nations banded together to help the Egyptians move the temple after the new dam created a water supply source for the people of Egypt. The new island was called Egilica (Agilica) and was shaped very much like the older island. The Temple of Isis was first protected by a waterproof wall before the massive stones were numbered and disassembled. They were reassembled like an enormous jigsaw puzzle. It was an engineering feat that rivaled the ancients. The entire project took just over nine years, opening to the public in 1980. I could not wait to get there.

Isaiah 40:31 reminded me, "...they who wait for the Lord shall renew their strength; they shall mount up with wings like eagles; they shall run and not be weary; they shall walk and not faint." So far, the only eagle I knew still flew inside my dreams, although she circled for the most part. She came to me while I was in Atlanta, when I visited Europe, and the first night of the Egypt trip, always circling around and around, going nowhere. Although I often awoke wanting to scream important questions at her about my future state of being (all beginning with the words "why," "when," or "how"), she only kept circling each night. Evidently what I needed from this trip would be divulged in due time. All I had to do was rely on my faith, keep walking forward, and occasionally run. I also had to not faint.

◆ ◆ ◆ ◆ ◆

"The Lord is my Shepherd" I quoted to myself as the bus doors opened. As I stepped down onto the parking lot where the small covered boats would take us to the Temple of Isis, I fully expected to be assaulted by all manner of aggressive trinket merchants. This time Peter chose not to take the tour, so I experienced it quite alone in a crowd of Dutch people who had no intention of speaking English, although they had the ability. However, no vendors appeared at the bus door but instead kept their distance. Some very official-looking armed guards who may have been soldiers patrolled the area, keeping what looked like shirt salesmen from peddling their wares. Therefore, instead of dodging those who would have sold me almost anything— and a lot of it—I could take my time walking to the open-air boat in order to ride to our destination across what looked like a huge lake. Although I could not directly see where we were going, I stretched tall into the heat, loving the area around me. It did not seem dry and arid as the other sites had been, but instead the air felt almost moist. Well, not humid as we in the Southern United States experience it, but moist in Egyptian terms, which simply means less dry. What I assumed was excitement began to vibrate inside my upper chest. This particular tour already felt like a profound shift in some way, yet I had no idea what that meant to me. The difference made the tiny hairs on my arms stand up from hills of goose bumps like the cliffside soldiers standing tall over the Valley of the Kings.

What I knew about Isis wasn't much. Supposedly, she was worshipped as a goddess throughout Egypt as well as in the Greco-Roman world. Sometimes called Hathor, she was depicted as the ideal mother and wife, and she befriended slaves, artisans, and the downtrodden. The wealthy, the females of the area, and the aristocrats and rulers held her in high esteem. Throughout the Greco-Roman world she was worshipped until Christianity changed the flow of religious beliefs. Her powers were considered to be mystical, her healing ability involved nature, and myths of Isis eventually created cults in the predynastic times prior to 3100 BC. All of that had absolutely nothing to do with me whatsoever. Until the particular day of the tour, that is.

Our group of about twenty-five pulled slowly from the dock out onto the calm water. At first I looked back, watching the dock fade into the distance. When it became uncomfortable to keep straining backwards, I glanced forward, leaning my head out from under the canopy into the open air. Nothing felt familiar to me at all, even though greenery flourished on the banks of the lake. The water rippled slowly away from the sides of the boat; I followed one small wave with my eyes until it faded into nothingness. I remember a distinct smell that day, probably something related to the boat's engine. It churned inside my stomach like bad air seeking its own destruction. I leaned slightly over the edge of our open boat hoping to breathe fresher air, yet even the openness felt constricting.

Perhaps the lack of a companion to rely upon started the panic. Perhaps the little tour boat puttering out into the open water triggered my reaction because of the unfamiliar. Maybe it doesn't matter what started it.

That feeling of being entrapped by the unknown swarmed upward from my stomach into my chest, choking my breath into shallow gasps of air. I did not want this to happen when I felt so alone in such a strange place. As the boat careened to the right out into the open lake, I frantically looked back to the shore, hoping to see something familiar, something safe. However our bus could not be seen; I had no idea if it had been moved or if it had simply left us stranded upon the waters of doom. Nothing logical flew through my mind, for the stories I told myself came from my own panic. Somehow I had to stop them. I had to get in control again.

"He leads me beside still waters." Over and over I repeated it to myself, alternating my breath into longer, slower bursts in rhythm with the words I spoke. "He leads me. Still waters." With both hands I had a death grip on the pole nearby that held up the boat's canvas roof. I could feel the trembling start from the tips of my fingers pressing tightly around the pole, throughout my palms, and up my arms. I squeezed the pole tighter hoping to stop the tremble. It didn't work though, for I vibrated more than our little boat engine did. My hands turned shades of pale as blood rushed up to my head and back down again. My vision began to blur, closing in from the sides and giving me the effect of seeing the world through a foggy tunnel. I surrendered to the panic with complete submission.

He makes me to lie down in green pastures, I thought to myself, seeking peace through staring at the green bushes and grasses growing next to the water on the temple island just ahead of us. *He leads me beside the still waters.* Over and over I repeated the only two verses I could remember from Psalms 23.

I realized our boat reached the dock when the passengers began to disembark. Still I sat, not sure I would even be able to stand. "The Lord is my Shepherd," I said out loud. "I can do this. With God's help, I can do this."

"Are you all right?" Mary from Australia asked. She and Richard had paused briefly on the steps of the dock to make sure I exited the boat safely.

"I will be. One day I will be. Until then, I am going to keep moving forward," I declared to myself as much as anyone.

"Then walk with us a little while. The Temple of Isis is not far ahead."

Mary began to walk the pathway toward the temple as I got out of the boat. She slowed her pace in order for me to keep up with her. As we walked a slight incline from the dock to the temple, the grass, bushes and the few trees dotting the area felt welcoming to me, far different from the desert intensity I had experienced in the rest of Egypt. Richard followed dutifully behind us.

"I just need to walk around some," I lied. "It feels good to walk."

Step by step, I entered the area dedicated to the remains of the Temple of Isis. Along the left side of the passageway, I noticed large carvings depicting various forms of Egyptian life. Although my breathing had not yet returned to a peaceful normalcy, my vision had been restored and the tingling down my arms had ceased to be problematic. Busying myself with picture taking, I focused upon the shots needed to document the journey I had embarked upon. Entering from the south, I snapped a picture of the imposing wall directly in front of me, composed of two towers with an opening in the wall between. Carved into the wall were Egyptian gods. I recognized the falcon-headed Horus who, with one other god, seemed to be giving something to a female I assumed was Isis. On my right and left were a row of columns, each filled with different carvings. The columns reminded me of life's most profound events, passages from one human condition to another.

Closing my eyes, I breathed in what I hoped would be calmness, breathing out what I wanted to be terror. In and out. Repeat. Thankfully no one stood nearby, for Mary and Richard had wandered off to get a better view of the massiveness of the temple ruins. Again, I felt very alone.

After opening my eyes, I moved forward into what I later learned was the Mammisi, the Birth House dedicated to Isis in honor of her son Horus, the falcon god. Actually, at the time I had no idea what I had wandered into. It could have been an interior chamber for all I knew. Everything I saw seemed massive. The walls were stone, large enough to have giant pictures carved into them. In the center of the room was a stone block. I had no idea of its purpose other than perhaps an altar. I had no idea why it was named for anything having to do with birth. It looked to be a sacred inner sanctum to me. Spiritual rebirth, perhaps? One of humanity's greatest miracles to me had to do with how in the world these stones had ever been moved to the newly-created island. Some looked to be as large as a small house. Cooperation between countries must have been miraculous.

"I will fear no evil," I repeated out loud from the psalm, "for you are with me." Another panic attack had begun. Nothing remotely fearful existed inside this ancient wonder. Absolutely nothing. Yet, my vision again threatened to shut down. My knees buckled right under me, causing me to lean against one of the massive stone walls I had been told not to touch. At the time I felt it better to lean than to fall on the stone floor. Landing may have been problematic. My expensive camera crashed onto my right foot, then rolled onto the floor when I placed my hands on either side of my temples and over my eyes hoping that by purposefully cutting off my vision it would safely fall back into place. The sobs came out in shudders, tears falling along with me into what felt like a deep well of nothingness.

I could not continue the rest of Psalms 23. Not in prayer form, not in thought, not in memory. Physically, I knew where I was. Spiritually, I knew I was protected and loved deeply. Emotionally, I knew the panic was yet again forcing its dastardly self into my own reality, unwanted and unneeded. I did not have Peter to lean upon. I could not see Mary and Richard. Even the tour director was out of sight. What could I do? How was I to proceed? I had absolutely no idea.

Gathering every bit of courage, willpower, and inner strength left to me, I picked up my camera, thankful that at least it still seemed to be in one piece even if I wasn't. Then I moved into another corridor, room, or area, still not having a clue as to what I witnessed. Standing in one place for heaven only knows how long, again I closed my eyes hoping to find sanctuary. It did not come. My breathing began to get shallow again even though I endeavored to control it through the counting method. How would I help myself this time? How does one find help when no help is available? How does one help herself if she does not have the self-realization that it is indeed even possible to do so?

When I opened my eyes, the first thing I noticed seemed to draw me into the carved relief directly in front of me. Frankly, I have no idea who that figure represented. What did capture my undivided attention was the three-pronged staff in his hands. In Egyptian mythology this staff, the was, depicted power and dominion. From somewhere other than my own awakened consciousness more of Psalms 23 flooded into my soul. *"Even though I walk though the valley of the shadow of death, I will fear no evil, for you are with me; your rod and your staff, they comfort me. You prepare a table before me in the presence of my enemies; You anoint my head with oil; my cup overflows."*

Complete calm flooded through me, from the tips of my fingers throughout my body, landing clearly into my soul. *"Your rod and your staff, they comfort me."* The power I needed to overcome my many fears did not have to come from me. Instead, it could come through me just as the answers did in my spiritual messaging sessions. Like the carvings of Isis throughout the temple, I also could have the wings of an eagle formulated from God's power for me, through me. I felt more connected to God standing right there just inside the Temple of Isis, but different than I ever had before. Instead of being mystically connected I felt connected in a different way I had never experienced until now, a practical way filled with personal power that came through me, for me. It felt strange, unusual, and even weird. Yet, I knew with all my heart it felt good, it felt like it was meant to be, and it felt like the purpose of this particular journey finally had been actualized. This time, God showed me firsthand what it felt like to be truly, solidly, forever connected to myself through the power of divine love. The next day, I got the chance to understand this level of God's protective power firsthand.

◆ ◆ ◆ ◆ ◆

Because our floating hotel had docked due to the closing of the dam that particular day in May, several of our tour group wandered in the area nearby, hoping to entertain ourselves for what ended up being a long twenty-four hours. Peter and I discovered an area filled with the little shops of the trinket merchants. Soon we wandered to the end of the row of shops because I wanted to purchase an Egyptian tablecloth. As opposed to the other experiences I had with the aggressiveness of other trinket merchants, this time I had no fear, probably because I had Peter with me. For sure, we had entered their domain.

As soon as I entered the shop, I noted the cloth tent walls were covered with all manner of tablecloths hanging from makeshift rods and shelving. Before my eyes could adjust to the dim lights, a man dressed in traditional Egyptian dress left his friends to come to me. Almost immediately, I started backing out of the shop, a response that stemmed more from protective recoil than thought.

"You have come to my business to shop," he addressed Peter. "We will conduct a transaction then." I was completely ignored.

"No, I haven't," Peter answered with a smile as his glance turned my way. "The lady has come to purchase a tablecloth."

The Egyptian never looked at me. Instead, he kept staring at Peter as he answered, "Then we shall negotiate on her behalf."

I couldn't believe what I was hearing. I gingerly stepped forward and started to speak, but the words got garbled in my throat.

Peter answered for me, explaining, "The American woman will choose and negotiate for herself. Please find someone who can handle this transaction." With that, the traditionally-dressed Egyptian backed off with a bow and a younger Egyptian man dressed in shirt and pants common to the United States came forward.

For a little more than two hours I was shown what must have been every tablecloth in Egypt. Small square designs, with no print. Large rectangular ones out of different types of cotton. Cloths with hieroglyphics, both large and small. Eventually, I chose one, and then bargained the price. After the price was set, we then had to bargain again. After bargaining for what I thought was the last time, the salesman turned to me saying, "I have five women to support. How am I going to do that well if I earn only this much money for the cloth?"

"Uh," I slurred, hoping something other than my thoughts wondering if his women were his sisters, wives, or children would come out of my mouth. "How did that happen?" I then said, noting Peter's concerned expression. "I mean," I said, correcting myself, "This must be a blessing for you. You are very good then at what you do to take care of so many important women."

Merciful God in Heaven, keep my voice respectful.

"Allah is good to me," he answered, again putting the tablecloth in my hands so we could continue our negotiations.

Not knowing how to answer him, I just agreed, "Yes, that is very special." Our negotiations resumed yet again.

Peter said very little, but stayed nearby. With the final culmination of our deal, Peter and the salesman had tea. I preferred to just watch, fearing the source of the water. Peter and the man shook hands, western style. Peter then walked out of the shop, his long legs walking fast through the rest of the insistent merchants who were aggressively trying to get him inside their shops. He ended up momentarily tangled in a wad of shirts, statues, and postcards, all shoved at him by other merchants in the area. Unfortunately, I had to wait a moment for the cloth I had purchased to be carefully wrapped and placed in a bag. By the time I had my purchase in hand, Peter was way down the corridor, having made a hasty escape.

I started to turn to leave, but before I could, our salesman had nodded to the five or six traditionally-dressed merchants who had gathered in the back of this particular shop during our negotiations. Before I realized it, I was surrounded by what I had assumed to be some of the most aggressive men on the planet. Facing me was the salesman from whom I had purchased the cloth. I could not leave. But I could have panicked quite well.

Remembering the experience in the Temple of Isis, I mentally repeated the line from the 23rd Psalm. "...*for you are with me; your rod and your staff, they comfort me. You prepare a table before me in the presence of my enemies.*" I breathed deeply into the verse, noting the presence of Power moving through me. I remained calm, knowing

I would be all right regardless of what happened.

"Because you are an American," the spokesman of this group began to ask, "we have a question for you."

I intuited the best way to get out of this situation was to answer their question, and then gracefully leave, if possible. "Yes?" I answered back, hoping I truly knew the answer.

Because I had spoken to this man for over two hours during the tablecloth purchase, I looked directly at him for what evidently was an important question for the group. I had no idea what to expect. My job at the moment had more to do with staying calm and allowing that Divine flow to come forth to protect me.

"As an American," he started slowly, his words carefully chosen, "What do you think of war and aggression?"

Merciful God, help me, please!

Actually, I had no answer to that. What does anyone with any type of spiritual common sense think of war and aggression? Yet, I looked from face to face at the men standing all around me. I felt not threat, but honest inquiry. Still, I had to come up with an answer somehow.

Just as I had with the spiritual question and answer sessions, I closed my eyes and breathed deeply into that spiritual state. Not having a pen or paper, I knew I would have to use my voice for the first time to allow the answer to come not from me, but through me because I personally had no answers. The Egyptian men were waiting patiently, piercing eyes intensely focused directly on me. I breathed in again, allowing myself to be filled with the grace of the altered state where the answers would surely flow.

Slowly I began to speak words that were whispered into that still, quiet place of soul's connection. "When you speak and I listen to you with my heart, and then I speak while you listen to me with your heart, there is deep understanding between us. When there is this special level of understanding between us, we then can have great respect for each other. When we have this great level of respect, then we can have immense honor between our different cultures. That is how to obtain peace."

When the words came, I felt truly as if they came from something outside of me, through me. Their vibration felt quite high like how you would feel with a choir of angels singing your favorite hymn. With open eyes, I looked deeply into the faces of each of these men; I felt love coming from me to them and from them to me. They started looking at one another silently, then back at me. Their spokesman finally said to me, "You are full of faith. You are worth five hundred camels." I walked slowly back to the ship unbothered by any trinket merchants, amazed at my own calm during the entire event.

That evening, while standing on the upper deck of the cruise ship watching the dense foliage of figs, bananas, and coconut palms on the east and west banks float by as we cruised down the Nile, the vivid stars overhead dipped down one at a time, filling my heart with Light. The moon crested overhead, throwing rays of understanding deep into the ancient Nile River, filling the world all around me with silver twinkles dancing upon the waters of life. For the first time, I knew that the terror I experienced so often showed up not because of its immense power over me, but because of my lack of knowledge of my own empowerment. I'd been trying to do everything myself instead of leaning on the power of Spirit to move through me, as me. I looked down into my palms, cupping them at heart level in order to catch some of the intense mystical light of evening, perhaps to grasp it forever. The moment, however, burned itself into my soul. God's Spirit indeed filled my soul from that moment on. As ripples of the Nile moved onward into its own direction beneath the boat, I knew passionately that I also would move into my own direction. The hollow places of fear I held within me were filling up with self-knowledge, self-realization, and self-actualization. Whatever life held for me, I knew for sure it would be good. I could feel it in my soul.

"Surely goodness and mercy shall follow me all the days of my life, and I shall dwell in the house of he Lord forever."

PART III

Living the Questions

> *"...I bore you on eagles' wings
> and brought you to myself."*

EXODUS 19:4

*"Don't stop searching until you find,
and when you find you will be
troubled, and when you are
troubled you will reign over all."*

THE GOSPEL OF THOMAS

◆───────────────

CHAPTER EIGHT

Auschwitz

"HAVE YOU LOST your ever-loving mind?"

Intensity flooded out of Peter's sentence like grease oozing out of a big thick steak sizzling on hot barbeque coals. Abruptly he stopped walking the paved footpath next to the Leie River before turning to stare at me with a screwed-up facial expression as if he had just heard an insane person speak total nonsense.

"No, I have not!" I threw my sentence back toward him in the same tone, knowing full well the words would scatter on the rough ground between us like seeds that never got nourished into full bloom because they fell among stones. However, they originated from a powerful place within me—strong, secure, and very determined. "I said that I am going to Auschwitz."

"When in the love of sanity did you decide that?" Peter modulated his pitch, but frustration still flooded from his tone. "With your acute sensitivity to the earth, people, and energies around you, Auschwitz will blow you senseless. More importantly, why in the world do you want to go there?"

"Peter, I want to go because I feel like I have to go. Just like every other spiritually important trip I have taken in Europe, I fully intend to do what I feel like I have to do. I know this process often defies logic, but it can be no other way. I'm going to Auschwitz!" With that declaration I spun around, escalating my pace back toward the small ferry beside the church at Afsnee.

For the past hour or so, Peter and I had been praying there again, Peter sitting on the front left row and me sitting on second seat, third row right, our usual places. Always I felt more spiritually connected at that church than almost anywhere else in Belgium. Today had been no different.

"Well, I wouldn't do that. If I were you, I wouldn't do that at all," Peter announced in a firm voice dripping with skepticism. His arms crossed his chest into a position of absolute authority. "I really, really would not do that."

Spinning around, I snapped, "I assume you're not going with me this time. Well, then, I'll let you know what it looks like. Better than that, I'll take some pictures and tell you what it feels like to stand in that place of human horror."

I could be as defiant as the next person—including Peter. Stopping just long enough to make sure I had been heard clearly, I resumed walking away. Peter, however, remained graveyard still. He looked like the statues of warriors I had seen in Florence, Italy, that held the severed heads of their enemies. In this case, the severed head would have been my own common sense.

By the time I got to the dock of the ferry to cross the narrow river, Peter still had not joined me. Shortly after we met, I had learned that when Peter processed something important, his forward movement ceased to exist. For him more than for anyone else I have ever known, the deeper meaning of unusual experiences or those sudden changes in life always seemed to be a signal for Peter to delve into finding more information. While he traveled intuitively, his spiritual acuity for the deeper truth always kept him firmly positioned if he did not readily discern the answers.

In other words, my sudden declaration had shocked the hell out of Peter. To be totally honest, it surprised me, too.

Partly because the ferry was not currently positioned on my side of the river and partly because I truly needed someone to help me get to Auschwitz, Poland, I turned around to face Peter and then planted my feet firmly shoulder-width apart with arms folded, mimicking Peter's stance as best I could. I said nothing, just stared at him for what seemed to be a very pregnant moment. Just try to sever my impulsive head with your rationality, I thought. If I felt spiritually led to experience something, nothing—absolutely nothing on this earth short of death—could stop me from doing it. I stared at Peter without flinching one muscle. Finally, Peter began to walk forward.

"At least tell me what gave you this idiotic idea," Peter implored just before reaching me. He held his hands out to his side, palms upward as if he truly wanted some type of logical answer. Yet, I had none. Peter's understanding about what my sensitive nature would experience at Auschwitz seemed perfectly logical to me. It also had absolutely nothing to do with the fact that I was still going. Because I had been psychically knocked senseless many times due to my intense connection to the energies of place and consciousness—and survived, thank you very much—I knew I would also overcome whatever I felt at Auschwitz, even though in all probability it would take great effort on my part.

Instead of agreeing with him, I simply explained, "I didn't get repeated clues, visions, or synchronicities this time. No strong voice of God bellowing out from the heavens with a set of personal directives for my healing journey. Of course, as you said, this has not been a rational decision. Frankly, doing this had never crossed my mind even though I have had recurring dreams about Auschwitz concerning twins and not being able to breathe. In fact, I don't know a lot about Auschwitz except that it was a human hell hole of death." My tone softened, so the truth of my words would be better understood through a more imploring undertone. Actually, the whole idea felt to me like whispered foretelling.

"And...?" Peter asked patiently waiting for me to clarify my sudden decision.

"And, actually, I feel a prayer will be answered. Or perhaps it already has been answered?" Momentarily, I turned from Peter to stare at a small skiff easing down the river beside the walkway. It seemed so peaceful, quietly moving with the river's flow with no visible motor. I have always found mystical matters so far beyond language extremely difficult to put into common words. Language seems excessively limiting to me when trying to talk about the Numinous.

I turned back toward Peter with a serious expression hoping he would understand. "During my prayer time inside the church today, I realized that I still saw the world through the eyes of a victim. Not being able to speak up for myself all these years caused me to live as others needed me to live and to know what others wanted for me more than I knew what I wanted for myself. I took that to God today, asking for a way to put all of that history into perspective. I need to heal from this. I need to move on in my life. To carry all of this martyr intensity inside my heart keeps me in a loveless state of emotional turmoil. I wake up at night in a dead sweat afraid that someone I have displeased will break into my house to hurt me, and I don't even know who this person could be. The least little thing triggers my divorce post-traumatic stress, causing me to act irrationally to others around me who do not understand that my body seems stuck in some sort of flight or fight mode." My voice quavered with the pain of remembering. It trembled more with the pain of realizing I still had not gotten to that calm inner feeling of peace. Still, even after the shaman's journey of healing I had evidently been undertaking, I had no idea who I was other than a woman who wanted to feel loved again. Tears dripped shades of mascara down my cheeks just as if something soiled inside wanted desperately to dissolve in order to find meaning, purpose, and self-respect again.

"I want to feel whole, Peter. I want to see the world through my own eyes instead of the eyes of what society expects of me or what my parents expected of me." With that declaration, tears mimicked the Leie, flowing from that inner riverbed of pain.

Peter leaned slightly toward me, listening intently to whatever it was that I was trying to explain. Gently, his hands touched each side of my shoulders, stroking my upper arms slightly as a way of showing his concern and support. He said nothing, allowing me to fill the space between us with murmurs of truth as I perceived it. He respected me enough to know the seriousness of my conversation, realizing that indeed some spiritual truth had happened to me in the little church just an hour before. This certainly did not come in the usual manner for me (through visions, synchronicity, or dreams) but instead just appeared as a knowing. A reality flooded my soul with an idea I had never experienced.

"Peter, time became nonexistent for me during this meditation. Somehow, I felt like I had become wind, or Spirit, perhaps, floating purposely through the cosmos. I felt totally present, as if I were seeing beyond reality through unfamiliar eyes of wisdom far greater than I am or will ever be. The most beautiful colors floated all around me—magnificent, tremendous swirling nebulas of red, green, gold, and blue energy. Everything felt purposeful in that holy place as if it were all filled with potential. There were no whispers of Spirit this time, no subtle thoughts that I intuited, and no visions of the future. When I came back to center—okay, stopped meditating—I knew I was going to Auschwitz. I don't know how this realization happened, but I just knew. It's just that simple. Perhaps it's just that complicated. It's just that... well...just that way."

Less than one month later, Peter and I were sitting side by side on a plane traveling to a location thirty kilometers south of Katowice and fifty kilometers west of Krakow, an area in Poland known now as Auschwitz.

Our customs experience involved a complete examination of everything near and dear to each of us. I don't think anything more could have been discovered if we each had been naked inside a MRI machine having our very bare bones witnessed by at least twelve men who did not give one whit about the entire incident.

On the car ride to our destination, Peter briefly glanced once again at his printed directions obtained through an Internet mapping system before deciding he would find Oswiecim, Poland, intuitively. Just as I had in Crete, I wanted to knock some sense into him several times, because we passed by the sign indicating where to turn to get to the Auschwitz area not once but twice, going well out of our way before we actually arrived. It's just not necessary to drive around your elbow in order to get to your thumb. I couldn't decide if Peter truly could not read a map, intended to have a nice little ride, or just preferred to go off on his own adventures while dragging me with him.

Instead of nagging, I tuned into the energy of the area around me. We passed by wooded areas and small farm gardens, yet I could not discern any type of what I call "fairy energy" there—that light, airy feeling of intense spiritual love found in spring gardens. The trees did not whisper their version of beauty to me like they usually did. I did not sense the deliciousness of the farm crops, did not feel the potential of the woodland undergrowth, nor did I get any sense of life expressing itself to the fullest. Instead, I would have sworn that the trees were stoic survivors who had forgotten how to live, laugh, or love. I hoped with all my heart it was not so.

What I did perceive felt more like pollution of some unrecognizable form. While Peter began to mutter to himself about the insanity of the direction we were headed, I glanced outside the window in order to make sense of what I felt. Yet, nothing made sense to me. Smoke from the many factories we passed in the distance hung close to the ground. It crept along slowly like fingers of death reaching out into the earth around it, grasping, attaching, and choking anything it could find with its polluted stench. The blue of the sky hid behind puffs of clouds squeezed together tightly as if there were no other way to survive. I locked my door hoping to keep the world at bay.

Eventually, we got to our little hotel; it took almost an hour longer than it should have. Although the hotel was modest by American standards, the entire establishment looked clean—yet I felt as though the hotel, the town, and even the air in the entire area held secrets one never wished to know. After a bad night's sleep, the next day we went to the concentration camp.

"Arbeit macht frei" stated the infamous German words formed from an arched ironwork sign suspended over the gates of Auschwitz. "Work will set you free." With the barbed wire that surrounded the concentration camp, the armed guards that had been everywhere, and the death and horror each of the prisoners saw each day, the sign must have been like nails into the prisoner's very soul. Just as if I would never exit if I walked under that sign, I hesitated on the exterior side of the gates, trying very hard to breathe deeply in order to steady myself. Peter stood beside me, deep in his own thoughts. In some way, it felt like I would be violating every prisoner's memory if I entered what was experienced as a human horror story now turned into a visitor's attraction. I hated it. I hated everything about it.

Standing there, I had a profound thought. If the proverbial devil himself walked into the back of the church looking and acting like one would expect, all would know the danger involved. If this same devil walked in disguised like a robed minister praising and shouting hallelujahs, then who would know the difference? As we both paused just after walking into the compound under that sign for the first time, Peter looked like he was seeing some horrid part of history. His facial expression toggled between having a bad taste in his mouth and absolute hatred of everything he saw. Even though he leaned forward slightly from the waist, his chin was tucked downward while he pulled his head back in a protective motion. I felt like I had entered the devil's warren, all nicely cleaned up and disguised. At any moment, I felt as though I could fall deeply into some pit of horrid human suffering, a lingering energy that would cause me to suffocate through the pain of my own heart's trembling.

Auschwitz was indeed very organized and quite presentable to the visitors. In the exhibit by the gate, we learned that more than 1.3 million people come each year to witness the place where 1.3 million people died either in the gas chambers, or from execution, medical experimentation, starvation, or forced labor. As we looked at pictures on the walls, read facts, and tried to watch the movie telling about the horrors of the past that had taken place upon those grounds, something in me began to shut down as if closing off my spirit would make what I witnessed have less of an impact.

I was wrong. I sat through the entire movie with my eyes closed. Nonetheless, frames of history passed through my consciousness, one repulsion after another. For sure, there is absolutely no way to make Auschwitz feel like less of an impact without being devoid of a soul.

As Peter and I walked the pathways between the solid, red brick buildings, I realized we could have been walking through a 1940s apartment complex. Perhaps the buildings were designed that way to disguise the devil, so to speak. Tall, thin trees lined the pathways like sullen soldiers; even if winds of change blew in gale-like fashion, I knew for sure not even a small branch would move.

Along one corridor we started going into different exhibits fashioned within individual buildings. One of the exhibits housed enamel-covered bowls, pots, and pans in various colors. At first, my thoughts centered along the lines of recognition, for both of my grandmothers owned and used these types of enamelware. The familiarity lasted perhaps only thirty seconds, for another paralyzing thought soon overtook me. Each of these pieces of enamelware had belonged to a family who carried them into the camp as possessions, hoping to use them in daily living.

My stomach turned into hard knots. Tears had not come yet even though I began to question the sanity of having listened to Spiritual guidance about coming to Auschwitz. Peter lingered with the crowd inside the exhibit; I waited for him outside.

The second exhibit we visited held displays of luggage, each piece piled up upon the others as if they were castaway trash. If I squinted, I would see names printed on the sides of the leather luggage for identification, written by the owners who erroneously thought their possessions would be returned to them after the train ride to Auschwitz. The luggage, as well as the enamelware, had been placed behind glass enclosures, inaccessible to anyone in the museum. We filed by in a line like dutiful tourists, looking, wondering, and hoping what we saw truly never happened. Yet, just like the enamelware, these luggage pieces each belonged to someone who truly, honestly, graciously wanted to be able to laugh, love, and really live. The reality of these two exhibits flew out of the glassed wall like etheric monsters reaching, clawing, and grasping at anyone to disbelieve their legitimacy.

The knot in my stomach grew larger than my abdomen—at least it felt so. This time, I left a bit faster than I had exited the previous building. Again, I waited for Peter outside. From the look on Peter's face, he also was falling into the deep, darkened well of witnessing the suffering that had taken place during World War II. Nothing could be said between us; we had no need to say anything, actually. We walked into many buildings together that morning, each brick edifice a stronghold of many horrific secrets. We saw piles of leather shoes people once wore. We saw prosthetic devices lying discarded behind glass windows like the abandoned arms and legs they were. My belly was churning.

In all honesty, I don't remember in which particular compound-building-turned-exhibit that we saw the shawls worn by Rabbis. I do remember distinctly that they were displayed in a glass case hung on a wall to my left. For timeless moments I stood there, not really staring at them but absorbing their stories as much as I could. Those silent whispers of knowing began emanating outward from...from where? I had no idea. I did not hear with my ears, of course, nor did I hear through some imaginary modes. I heard from my heart, heard intuitively some sort of rabbinical leadership that felt like undetected, unrecognized music sung in a foreign language. It made absolutely no sense to me whatsoever at the time.

I looked down at my feet, finding they were still there. I looked at my hands, checked my heartbeat, and even pinched my forearm, making sure I was present. I already knew I was, of course. What I experienced felt like something more along the lines of psychometry, a psychic ability to deduce facts from an item by touching it. Yet, I literally was not touching anything. Slowly, I became drawn to the shawl in the center of the display. My connection at this point felt palpable, as if the story of this particular shawl were reaching out to touch my soul in ways I had not experienced before. The shawl and I were securely connected just as if it and I were of one understanding. For a poignant moment I just stood there absorbing one event out of the history of this shawl. For certain, I knew that a man who wore it once had led singing for a group of people as they walked to their death down a corridor formed by barbed wire.

Shortly thereafter I left to explain my experience to Peter. I found him totally engrossed with symbols the Nazis had used to categorize different types of people. His intensity matched what mine had been several moments before. He stood over a wooden case with a glass top just under waist high, absorbing something he saw within just as I had done. Out of respect, I didn't interrupt him, waiting until he moved back slightly before I said anything.

"You feel something, don't you?" I inquired, not expecting details at all.

Peter looked up at me, then back into the case, then at me again. His blank expression looked as if he had left the premises. In all probability, he had. "Yes, I feel something," he said with no other explanation.

I glanced inside the case, wondering what it could have been that put Peter at such odds with his own presence. One of the symbols stood out to me—a symbol for resistance fighters. I never asked Peter about it again. If he had wanted me to know, he would have shared. Instead, we both walked out of that particular building into another one with a display that almost shut down my soul.

Just like before, Peter and I stood in line to get into the building. The line moved a bit more slowly than before, yet we did move at a steady pace. Just like we had in the other buildings, we wandered up a staircase and then through different rooms. I have absolutely no idea what those rooms contained, for the memory has faded. What I do remember with absolute clarity was positioned not five feet from the glassed window in the last room of that building.

What is this? I asked myself silently, thinking that perhaps the thin silken grey strands were something used to stuff furniture. The historical sign posted nearby did indeed indicate that these strands were used for different things. Because my eyes suddenly began to blur, I stopped reading the sign, so I cannot say how the Nazis purposed what lay behind the glass. As I stared at the masses of what lay before me, my body began to shut down. Pools of blood stopped moving. My breathing became shallow if not non-existent. My legs insisted I reassure them to be steady, so they would not crumble to the ground in despair. My spirit began to fragment.

Oh, God, please, no. Oh, Dear God of us all, please don't let this be what I think it is.

I could not see, for not only was my vision becoming narrow and fuzzy in order to protect me from what lay before me, but tears of horror flooded out from the depths of my soul, through my heart, landing in dirty puddles all over the world at the horror of what humanity has done out of fear of those who are different.

Human hair lay in piles on the other side of the glass wall. Not a little human hair, but piles and piles and piles of it. Enough human hair...well, I have no idea how much human hair I saw in front of me. But it belonged to someone. It belonged to anyone. It belonged to every one of us in this world.

"No...Noooo," I wailed, backing away from the glass right into the people standing behind me. I looked around, thinking how upset everyone else must also be. If they were, I couldn't tell. Could they not feel in their bones how this had happened? Feel the shame of humanity upon itself? Feel the emotional turmoil of the victims? I looked to my left, to my right, in back of me, and back again to the hair.

"No, no, no, oh God no. Where is your heart? Why is this displayed?" I gasped. Honestly, I wanted to take the entire exhibit out to some graveyard in order to bury it in holy remembrance of all those people who had suffered at the hands of others. Instead, I ran out of the museum in tears. Because I had no idea where the forward path would take me, I went out the way I had come, against the flow of people. Bumping, shoving, and generally making a nuisance out of myself, I kept hurrying to leave this insanity, frantically seeking relief.

Just before getting to the door that would lead me into the welcoming sunshine of present time, one of the personnel regulating how many people entered the building at a time said, "Madam, you cannot go out this way."

"Oh yes, I can, actually," I answered back to him with a grunted tone of a warrior about to take charge of a situation. What I knew for sure was that this man could not have kept me in that building even if he had the ability to overpower me. "If I stay here one moment longer I'll projectile vomit all over Auschwitz."

"Then please exit," he answered, stepping back from me just far enough to dodge any propelling thrust. As he opened the door, in his most hurried, commanding voice he shouted, "Go!"

Peter found me between the next row of buildings, squatted down in a frog stance, touching the ground with both hands. Perhaps by laying hands upon the very ground I stood upon, Spirit would move through me to heal the entire insane world somehow, me included. The horror of seeing that human hair felt to me like a violation of something just out of reach of conscious thought, as if perhaps someone had defecated onto a holy icon. Yet to witness it in an exhibit? To have been one of many filing by it in a single circus-like line as though we were viewing a Christmas display in the department store windows of New York City completely undid me. I just could not imagine anything so horrible.

Except the experiences of those whose heads were shaved at Auschwitz.

"Paddy, are you all right?" Peter asked, knowing full well I was not. I looked up into his eyes and then stood a moment to ground myself before speaking.

"Yes," I answered with hesitation in my voice. Actually, neither of us could have been described as having all systems right that particular moment.

"Let's move on then," Peter said. "There's a line to get into the next exhibit over there just ahead. Let's go check it out." Peter lumbered forward, leaving me either to follow or stay in the same place.

Never stand still. To survive here, you have to keep moving. The first of several thoughts began to move at me intuitively, without warning.

As we reached the exhibit near the end of the alley, I noticed a line of people that came out the front door then filed down the short set of steps before wrapping along the alleyway in front of the building. No other exhibit had attracted that much attention, at least that I could see. Just after we reached the sign posted outside of the building, Peter abruptly began to move away from it with the same type of determination I had undertaken getting out of the human hair exhibit. The sign indicated we were in front of the Standing Cells of Block 11.

"Oh God!" I shrieked, not so loud as to be heard by the mass of people wanting to get inside that particular building, but loud enough for God to hear my plea. What in the world would people be thinking in order to want to go inside that exhibit building?

This particular building had been used specifically for torture; the tiny cells were so small that prisoners had to stand continually without food or water until they died. The people in line wanted to see this. Evidently Peter could not. Neither could I. Following Peter's example in moving quickly from the torture exhibit, I clutched my purse into my heart, not to keep it from being stolen as much as to protect my heart from falling out of my chest.

Immediately, the psychic knowledge came to me that a minister of some sort, perhaps Catholic, had died in this particular manner. I knew this not from something I read, but from some bit of lingering knowledge out there just behind the veil of present time I had evidently tapped into without intention. Not only did I attempt to sprint away from the building of torture, I tried to sprint away from my own sixth sense, hoping to outrun everything I had just intuited.

Truly, I don't remember turning the corner or how I got to another alleyway. I do know my breath came in pants as if I had been exercising vigorously. My hands were clutched to my purse in a death grip, knuckles white. I found Peter standing just outside one of the brick buildings waiting for me. Like many other countries had done with other buildings in Auschwitz, Belgium had selected this particular building in order to utilize it for a museum. For what seemed like forever, we both just stood there not saying anything. Actually, nothing had to be said between us.

Finally, I said what could not be held any longer because the intensity of thought threatened to explode into shards of glass inside of me. "I don't know why that had to happen, Peter. I also don't know why all those people stood in line to see it. I truly don't understand."

"Paddy, we came to see Auschwitz, too. We are no different than the rest of the tourists, it seems." Peter looked at me with an expression that bespoke of puzzled inconvenience. Peter had to come back to center. Auschwitz still had the power to suck the very life out of anyone who still cared how humanity treats humanity, past or present.

"And I don't understand that either," I admitted. "I really don't know why I'm here. I need to know!"

Overhead the sky held cerulean color in its hands, shaking out wisps of blue promises streaming down to me that there still exists goodness somewhere, that hearts hold love, and that somewhere people care about each other. As I stood there looking up, I breathed into this cerulean goodness, closing my eyes, not to shield Auschwitz from my presence, but instead to feel heavenly blue permeate into my bones, so I could carry it with me. In and out I breathed as the words came back to me from Psalm 23:4: "Even though I walk through the valley of the shadow of death...." I could recite no more. Somehow, I began to feel calm, but not a real peace like daffodils in springtime, or an oak tree's shade, or even a meandering stream flowing through the currents of life. Instead I felt a silent lifelessness, like part of me had surrendered because it could not move forward.

My arms and legs felt heavy, as if they were fashioned of iron and lead instead of flesh and bones. My breathing wasn't labored, yet it did not feel light, airy, or even natural. The usual panic I felt when overwhelmed had not appeared; frankly, I don't think I could have even felt it if my own panic had presented itself that very instant. I felt very unresponsive to life, like a cold stone that would never be able to feel anything again.

Through the eyes of the statue that had become me, I glanced at Peter walking into the Belgium Exhibition. At that point, following him inside would have been quite impossible. Instead, I intended to delve into the heaviness I felt to discern how I had been affected by Auschwitz, especially the past two displays.

The blue sky above continued to send down rays of energy. To me, it felt like being bathed in waves of sapphire and indigo. Even though it permeated my body, swirling around like eddies in a woodland stream, what I can only describe as lifelessness inside of me still remained. Tuning into this inner insipidness just like I had with the robes of the Rabbis displayed in the museum I had visited earlier, I asked the question Maria taught me to ask when doing this type of inner inquiry: "Is this mine?" Just as I had discovered many times on the healing table in her office, I readily had an answer.

Unlike before, this time I knew it was not Auschwitz I had picked up empathically. Instead, the lifelessness that felt so heavy, felt so much like a statue afraid to move through life, and felt so disconnected from my authentic self resided inside of me because I had created it in order to survive my own experiences. The need to recognize this is what led me to experience Auschwitz. It was a most powerful teacher of inner wisdom.

Reaching down, I picked up a small pebble, holding it inside my cupped palms. Somewhere within my own psyche I had a rigid, fearful stone of some sort. Or perhaps I had more than one. Opening my hands so the cerulean blue could touch this stone throughout with light, I held it up to God in prayer.

Somehow, for some reason, God, I ceased to be me over the years. At this time, I don't know who you created me to be. I haven't actualized my gifted talents, not really. And even with those I recognize, I am afraid of what others may say if I use them. Help me turn this stone of lifelessness I hold within my self-consciousness into a stone of strength and love that I may walk through my life in my own skin, my own way, being my own created self as you intended me to be.

As I placed the stone into the side pocket of my pants, I quoted, "I can do all things through him who strengthens me." Philippians 4:13 nestled my mind like a cradle holding a newborn. Oh, the heaviness still felt very real to me, yet the light from the sky falling down into my soul warmed my heart with a new feeling that I could indeed eventually move forward in life without those inner stones weighing me down. Looking toward the door to the Belgium exhibit, I walked in, a symbol of moving forward into my own power.

The Belgium Exhibit at the State Museum Auschwitz consisted of three rooms, each filled with light accenting the brightness of the white walls, a remarkable welcoming contrast from everything else we had seen from the other countries' exhibits in Blocks 13, 15, 16, 17, 18, 20, and 21, which seemed dimly lit and foreboding to me. Perhaps because most of the exhibits had photos honoring those citizens who had died or happened to survive despite the inhumane conditions at Auschwitz, I felt like I was moving through energy so dark and nasty I wanted nothing to do but leave each building and walk in the mid-day sunshine. Therefore, the light walls in the Belgium exhibit seemed almost a relief.

Unfortunately, I could not read any of the displays because each hanging panel was printed in the two languages of Belgium: Dutch and French. Even though I asked Peter to translate some of it to me, he was not so inclined to translate all of it. He only told me briefly what a couple of the hanging panels explained.

Room one dealt with the occupation of Belgium given in historical time sequence. From what Peter said, the reactions of the population were also explained. Room three described all twenty-eight convoys of those interned that left from Mechelen, Belgium. However, in my opinion room two, which explained the gradual loss of Jewish freedom by seventeen Anti-Jewish decrees, was the most powerful one to know for future wisdom, personal and worldwide. From what I could ascertain, most of the decrees were copies of what looked like either fliers or published newspaper accounts.

With all my heart, I wish these could have been translated and made more readily accessible to each of the people visiting Auschwitz who spoke other languages, because personal abuse is so very much like these seventeen decrees. Loss of personal freedom is usually gradual. For instance, it's first presented as a way to be safe—or, in other words, this first step presents itself as an antidote to fear. This stage is similar to the allegory of the devil disguised in the church. The other steps build upon themselves, culminating into complete loss of activities, housing, community, and life. The Belgium Exhibition described all these seventeen steps by the Nazi movement very powerfully by showing the actual documentation. Humanity throughout the entire world could learn about the loss of personal freedom from this particular exhibit.

As Peter and I walked away from the Belgium Exhibit, I thought about my own story. Without comparing myself or my experiences to the horror those unfortunate souls at Auschwitz experienced, I used history as a teacher to discern some greater spiritual truth in order to grow closer to God for wisdom in my life. As I walked, I felt oddly detached from everything around me, which was actually a welcome feeling, especially after the reactions I'd had in several of the exhibits. I realized how not speaking up for myself over the years became a choice, albeit an unrecognized choice. For whatever reason, evidently at some point I had made the determination to please others to find love instead of learning how to feel love within my own heart. But love has to be known from the inside of one's self-awareness before it can thrive in relationship. Love should be the basis of not only all righteous human connection, but also the basis for self-actualization.

Deep in thought, Peter and I left the Belgium Exhibit, moving quietly along the row of remaining exhibits without wanting to enter another one. Each of us had seen enough in this area. Placing one foot in front of the other, I managed to keep walking down the alleyway between the compounds, hoping that if I kept looking at my feet I would not have the ability to see how many other buildings were around us. We passed several groups of tourists as deadly silent as we were. Auschwitz was one of the most quiet tourist attractions I have ever experienced, quite beyond words. Horror has no voice other than an inward piercing scream reverberating in one's soul. I had not realized that Peter had altered our course from the exit area to a pathway on the outside of the Auschwitz compounds. Before long, we were standing beside the only crematorium at Auschwitz.

Honestly, I don't remember the construction materials of the walls or the exterior of the building, but I do remember the roof being very low to the ground as if the earth had been piled upon the sides to keep gasses from seeping outward. The red brick chimney reached beyond the roofline; it looked tall and ominous to me, as if by sheer height alone it made a statement to all who could see it, nearby or from a distance.

"Are you going in?" Peter asked. By the time Peter finished his question, I was already entering the building.

Like a zombie on an unknown mission, no thoughts as to whether I should enter the building or just pass by ever came to fruition. Instead, I felt like a sleepwalker programmed into doing something far beyond consciousness. My thinking switched dimensions; thought and vision flew at me intuitively from somewhere—some dimension—other than my own experience, without conscious awareness. It brought with it sheer horror beyond any recognizable description.

Large, sturdy bricks formed the oven that remained inside. The interior chamber had been constructed of solid cement. The walls, floor, and interior roof looked completely unyielding; I didn't know how something could be built that impenetrable. Even the hypogeum carved out of solid rock far underground in Crete wasn't this dense. Anything trapped inside this chamber had no chance of survival.

As I entered the gas chamber, I wondered why in the name of all that's holy it still remained. From what I had read, almost all of the crematoriums had been destroyed quickly after the war. Yet, this one still existed. Later, I learned that it had been reconstructed for the tourists.

The cement felt solid under my feet, as if it literally could not be destroyed. I knew it not to be true, yet the feeling permeated my being that the cement structure felt like a sarcophagus. As I entered the second interior door, I intuited a whispered thought from ancient times before I was born.

This is not a shower.

On I walked in my zombie trance, as if some force beyond my own consciousness pulled me deeper into the chamber of death—alone, but not alone. It did not matter to me if Peter followed me inside or not. In fact, I don't remember one way or the other if he came into the inner chamber, the one where tablets were dropped creating the gas that killed those who were not ready to die.

Plop, fizz.

Sensations of others, of myself at another time, grasped at me intuitively inside the chamber, silent thoughts wanting to be discovered, wanting to be purged. I huddled near a column at the wall, not wanting to move while simultaneously wanting to run, to go home, and to escape.

Hold your breath. Do not breathe this.

I leaned against the wall, holding my breath just like the people I had intuited who really were not ready to die had done so many decades ago. Finally, I gasped for air, knowing it was over. Looking around me, the people of my vision—the people who were starving, who were without clothes or in rags, the people who were as afraid of dying as I was—were not there. Yet, I felt them, I heard them, and I witnessed them. I felt part of them, one with them. I had loved them in my childhood dreams.

And I cried with them.

None of this made any sense to me whatsoever. So into the intuitive moment, I had been unaware of the other five or so people inside the crematorium, who evidently were as naïve as I was for going inside in the first place. I knew I was not alone, but I felt alone, felt as if my entire body had disappeared, felt as if no one could ever approach me again. I tried to feel the solid cement underneath my feet in order to energetically anchor myself, but I had to look down to make sure it existed. Devastated, I felt unreal, quite absent, and absolutely abandoned.

As if in a trance, I left the building, pausing shortly before the open red brick oven. The cement that had previously felt so solid underneath my feet felt far below me, as if I were a spirit floating through the room. I looked at the emptiness in front of the oven, but witnessed through some sort of strong psychic sense beyond current reality a particular body being shoved inside the oven like a useless piece of trash tactlessly discarded. Somehow, I intuitively pierced a veil between time past and time present. I felt like I was in spirit form watching my own body being shoved mercilessly into the oven.

But how could this be?

Placing each foot in front of the other carefully in order to not fall into total despair, I walked out of that death chamber into the light of my own day. Looking up, I wanted to scream at the magnificent blue sky, begging it to overshadow what I had just felt. Who was that woman who tried not to breathe in order to save her life? How had I attached to her spirit as she hovered over her own dead body watching it being shoved deliberately and without compassion into a furnace?

Was her spirit me?

More than any other time in my life, I needed a hug from someone, just an agape-type hug in order to feel love, to feel compassion—for that matter just to be able to feel. I needed to be touched, to feel my own body's warmth and make sure I was still alive and real. I looked imploringly over to Peter wanting physical contact—to be held, to be soothed. Peter, however, was not inclined whatsoever. Perhaps he had fallen into his own well. The words of Jesus rang into my soul: "...I am with you always, to the end of the age." (Matthew 28:20) That would have to be enough.

Standing there in the open air just outside the crematorium, I breathed in deeply. I gazed up to the sky, then to the green treetops nearby. Looking at the several others who were exiting the crematorium, I wondered how they were affected. Just as silent as the other tourists in Auschwitz, they made no noise, not even to each other. Even the tourists in Auschwitz seemed to be divided and conquered in ways beyond common understanding. Communities still do not survive in

Auschwitz. Quietly, they walked away. Peter had moved to the pathway nearby, ready to leave. Evidently he had seen enough. I turned my glance from him back to the crematorium and then further down the alleyway where the museums had been made out of prisoner barracks. I joined Peter at the path in order to exit Auschwitz.

"If you think that was horrid, you should go to Birkenau," the man standing just next to us declared. Honestly, I have no idea where he came from. His words startled both of us because of the suddenness of his appearance. Frankly, I was not even aware if he had come from inside the chamber or if he had just stopped to speak when walking toward the gate.

"What is Birkenau?" I asked, having never heard the word before. "Why did you say that?"

"Auschwitz II is also called Birkenau. It's another concentration camp just nearby. You really should go there. You really should." With that he turned to walk away nonchalantly.

Peter and I looked at each other for a pregnant moment. Our visit to Auschwitz had only taken about four hours. Since it was early afternoon, we still had plenty of time for another experience. Of course we would go to Birkenau, if for no other reason other than the odd way in which the choice was presented to us by a perfect stranger. From a map of the area, we learned the distance to reach Birkenau required only a short drive.

Even though in my naïveté I had not heard of Birkenau, Peter did know of it from his study of World War II. As we navigated the couple of miles from one horror story to another much worse, Peter explained to me that Birkenau had existed for the sole purpose of bringing captives from different places in Europe in order to determine the fate of each prisoner. While Auschwitz had been designated as a work camp, Birkenau existed as an extermination camp.

I lost myself at Birkenau.

"And this, our life, exempt from public haunt, finds tongues in trees, books in the running brooks, sermons in stones, and good in everything."

WILLIAM SHAKESPEARE

◆

CHAPTER NINE

The Unbecoming

THE ENORMOUS RED brick entrance to Birkenau stretched out to each side of the compound like two massive arms of threatening Nazi wrath daring anyone who entered to ever hope again. Peter and I each walked singularly through the large opening in the middle of the towered archway like trespassers who did not wish to be discovered. While our voices remained silent for most of the visit, our hearts hung heavy like weighted anvils suspended within our souls.

This entrance is called the Gates of Death, and justifiably so. The energy of Birkenau felt like a massacre: dead, intense, and horrifying. Just on the other side of this entrance remained the infamous railroad track upon which the transit ended. As I stood just inside the gate to Birkenau, I noticed the railroad tracks stretched forward from the massive gate entrance before coming to a final stop, the end of the line for most people crammed into the trains during the Holocaust.

Long enough to satisfy forty to fifty railroad cars, the tracks originally culminated right in front of the two largest crematoriums. However, they had been destroyed at the end of the war, replaced by the International Monument that looked rather like a smaller version of an ancient Greek amphitheatre constructed of massive stones. Messages from many countries were carved into the stone along the outside.

As I looked to my right, my left, and straight ahead, I knew for certain that the left side of the enormous compound had housed women, the right side men. The information came to me intuitively, for at this point I had not read any of the information signs posted every so often along the sides of the railroad tracks. Not many, if any, of the units on the right side remained. The intuitive vision I had of those united on the right side looked like makeshift barns to me: cold, drafty, and unhealthy to the point that not even animals could have survived a winter inside one of them. Not many were still standing on the left side of the tracks either, having been destroyed during the liberation by the Russian Army. Slowly, I walked forward into the *virnichtungslager,* the extermination camp of so many people. At first I preferred to walk forward in the middle of the tracks toward the monument just ahead. The gravel stones moved under my feet, an unsteady feeling at best. I reached into my pocket with my right hand in order to grasp the little stone I had carried from Auschwitz. I clinched it tightly as I moved forward, as if by holding onto it I could steady myself through its firmness. By the time I got halfway to the end of the tracks, I stopped walking. Literally, I could walk no further because my intuition kicked in with feelings that threatened to overtake me.

> *I hear words I do not understand today—words of authority, angry judgmental words that fill me with horror. Even the horrid stench of that goods transport type of railroad car I had been pushed into with all those other people did not compare to the abject terror I feel as I stand here being shouted at, pointed at, and segregated into groups that would die soon and groups that would die later. I know that. I know*

that with my heart, my soul, and my...well, I just know that. The children, though! Someone come save the children. I try to hide the twins behind my back, hoping...hoping....

My vision stopped abruptly as I brought myself back to present time. I squeezed my little rock tighter. Again, just as I had at the crematorium, I looked about for Peter for support. Other people were milling around the Birkenau Camp, but not nearby. The towering barbed fences still remained, separating the tracks from the unit areas. However, Peter had moved in another direction; my help had to come from my own inner connection to Spirit in whatever form I could find it. In this location, self-support seemed almost impossible. Oh, I knew God transcends all problems, all experiences. If the kingdom indeed is at hand as Jesus taught, perhaps he was not standing where I stood? I moved forward several steps and then to the pathway to the right of the tracks, where I stopped again because the visions came in a different form from someone else's experience.

The words were foreign again, but not German. Yiddish, perhaps, but still indistinguishable. They came from a holy man of the Hebrew faith who wore some sort of shawl or cloak as the designation of a Rabbi. In a calm voice, he directed his flock to sing. Keep singing, he insisted. I could feel his love radiate outward from him, even in the face of the soldiers from the Third Reich. Keep singing. As they got off of their specific transport car, their shaky voices mingled, reaching some form of golden light harmony far beyond what I could imagine was humanly possible in this situation.

The singing voices continued whispering silently in my intuitive ear, not consciously, but silently as if I were to be reminded they remained. The words were indiscernible, yet the intention of spiritual connection through methods of another faith highlighted the simple voices that continued to ring through the ages. I had to move on, for to have any more of these psychic hits would have brought me to my knees in some sort of spiritual apoplexy. I moved to the right with the intention of walking down a long, straight, narrow road perpendicular to the tracks. The road had been encased by barbed wire fence along each side intended, I supposed, to keep some out and some in. Truly, I could not think of that, for the road itself grabbed at me like nothing had previously.

Literally, I felt like I ran slap into an impermeable energetic wall forcing me to stop after taking only ten steps down that road. This made absolutely no sense to me whatsoever. How different could this particular road have been? *What happened along here?* I wondered. Almost immediately, another vision assaulted me.

> *Keep singing, the holy Rabbi said. His flock walked onward down the road, singing as they clung together. At the end of the road, the men were separated from the women. I saw visions of women who tried in vain to remain modest by covering their nakedness with their arms and hands while sitting on benches; their heads were shaved. I intuited piles of their confiscated possessions being sorted by Nazi workers in another building. Selection processing had begun just as if they were....*

I could not go further either with this vision or in this particular direction. By this time I was leaning on the large sign next to the tall wire fence. I could no more make myself read that sign than I could walk down that road. "Merciful God," I said out loud. I could hardly breathe, the vision was so dastardly. Abruptly, I turned aside, almost knocking Peter down.

"I cannot go down there," Peter said simply. "I will not do it."

"Neither can I," I answered quietly. "But evidently he can." I pointed to a young man who walked with total authority down this particular road that lead to death inside the Birkenau compound. Deliberately, he all but marched forward as if nothing could stop him from doing it. It seemed to me that visitors at Birkenau each have individual intentions, all of which are to heal, to remember, or to process some inward horror lodged inside their memory, their experiences, or their soul's journey. Truly I believed Peter and I were no different.

While Peter moved into a grassy, wooded area to pray over the ashes of the crematorium victims he read were scattered nearby, I moved to the women's side of the concentration camp. Fortunately, no other visions came to me while wandering there, but I did go inside one housing unit that pulled at me. Even though it had not rained that day, the long brick structure felt wet to me, cold and damp. Hesitating briefly, I walked inside the door, noticing a fireplace. I could go no further inside that building. Only one thought came to me from outside of nowhere, or perhaps from inside of anywhere.

Oh, the children. God please protect the children.
Are the twins all right?

The voice felt to me like the same one I had felt in the crematorium at the other Auschwitz camp, the same one who had witnessed her body being shoved inside the furnace as she floated nearby in spirit. It also felt like the same voice of initial panic beside the railroad tracks as she and her companions exited the train transport car. Although I could not cognitively hear the voice of the woman, could not literally see her or even imagine what she looked like, I knew she was tall and thin. I felt her vibrationally, as if she and I were connected somehow through a spiritual veil united with a singular golden thread of love's recognition.

Frankly, I wasn't sure if knowing the details of her experience would have the power to disconnect that particular thread or if walking away from the entire experience with the intention of never thinking of her again would cause this golden thread to dissipate. None of that mattered at the moment. The afternoon sky above me slowly became cloudy, choking the rays of sapphire and indigo from my awareness. The winds blew icy shudders into my bones, causing me to pull my jacket closed in front. Again, I clutched my purse to my heart, fingers pressed tightly around it to steady myself, to hold onto something tangible in present time. I tapped my pocket, making sure that little rock still served as my foundation. My intuition saturated me completely that day just as if I had been tarred and feathered by memories I knew nothing about until now, memories perhaps inside some recessed file folder of my soul. I had to get out of my visions, get out of my sixth sense, and get back into my own thoughts.

Hurriedly, I walked to the back of Birkenau, hoping to steady myself on either the steps of the monument or one of the low walls, or at least touch a tree. The little stone in my pocket felt quite insufficient. I needed something beyond my own knowledge, beyond my own strength, and beyond my own awareness to bring stability. Birkenau existed solely as a location for death. I felt the horrible truth from not only the remaining structures, but from the very earth sobbing beneath my feet.

"Peter," I implored, hoping to get his attention. He moved toward me just far enough to hear what I said. "Would you like to sit here with me for a while?" I thought perhaps having someone near would help me settle into my own thoughts more.

"No," Peter answered, glancing down at me sitting on the stone steps of the monument. He then looked back to the trees and grass to his back. "I am going to stay over here. Ashes of so many people are said to be scattered here. I just feel like I need to be with them." With that, he walked back into his own processing.

If I could have cried, perhaps my tears would have been cleansing, yet no welcoming tears came to me on the stone steps that afternoon. I took out my pad and pen hoping to get some answers in written form. I felt like the gravel between the tracks just in front of me had moved under my ribcage between the pit of my stomach and my heart.

What are these rumblings I feel inside? What are they all about? I wrote my questions on my little tablet and then waited for my hand to move.

Remember the Journeyman's story.

The answer evidently had to come from my memory and not from my hand. I placed the pen and paper down to my right next to my purse. Noticing that the little rock had slid to the back of my pocket, I reached inside and held it for a moment. The story of the Journeyman had to do with stones—so many, in fact, that they were his undoing. The myth I had previously received in meditation held so much wisdom for me, I remembered it well.

> Once there was a journeyman who traveled his path of life. Like any other journeyman, his road was often filled with twists and turns of the beautiful love of God's creation, as well as the occasional debris of emotional challenges that must be overcome. Yet he continued his forward movement of life, for this was his purpose. He was, after all, a journeyman.
>
> One day, as he rounded a bend in life's direction, he suddenly found his way blocked by a very tall mountain. Since all forward movement in his life had stopped, he felt completely lost. In order to locate the correct path to complete his travels, he had to reach the top of this mountain. In climbing, his trials were many, but he was steadfast in his effort. Whenever there was an especially difficult move on the rocky, jagged climb, he took his well-worn tools and, with all of his might, chiseled away at the unconquerable stones in order to create a place for his hands to hold and his feet to push. He then carefully placed the stone debris in his backpack and pockets, simply because he was afraid to let the stones fall away. In his mind, the stones had been obstacles. The only way he could be sure they were removed from his path was to chip them away and carry them with him.
>
> After a while, he was so loaded down with the discarded rocks that not only was his body tiring and in pain from the extra weight of the stones, but he had reached a point where he could barely hold onto his present position on the mountainside. Inadvertently,

a very small rock fell from above, landing in his pack. The extra weight brought him to his knees. Because he could no longer move due to the excess weight, he began to wail that the last rock had completely undone him, never realizing it was just one of many that caused his problem.

I reached over to the tiny stone I had carried with me all day, thinking about what my own stones had been. How many troublesome issues had I clung to over the years? Like the Journeyman, what were the stones of my own undoing? I held the rock cupped between both hands, willing it to speak to me, to let me know what I no longer needed.

Slowly, hard stones began to crumble into separate pieces as fragmented parts shifted into more recognizable form. I looked down around me, but the stone steps I sat upon were still as solid as they could be. The stones that were crumbling resided inside of me somewhere deep within my own psyche; I could feel them grumbling like a volcano's wrath about to be purged.

Yet, instead of being jubilant about finally being able to differentiate my true self from the despair I clung to as self-definition, I was uncertain about the change this realization would bring into my life. I slid to my left, hoping to find the stone steps a bit softer, yet they felt harder, uncomfortable, and quite painful. I slid back to my right, angling my legs toward the tracks just in front of me, determined to let Birkenau reach into my soul. The stone issues rumbled as the volcano of truth got ready to purge. Like a woman holding tightly to a life raft in a turbulent sea when the waiting shore lay just ahead of her limited vision, I held onto the sides of the stone steps. Over the years, evidently I had protected these dysfunctional interior stones well.

As an introverted child, I longed to relate through my natural tendencies of in-depth conversations, a strong interior life, and solitude, which is totally different from loneliness. Most of the adults in my family, however, did not recognize introverted characteristics for the naturally quiet beauty they are but instead felt like they were a form of shyness disorder that had to be overcome. The extroverted ways I had been coerced into living seemed false, ludicrous, and totally unnecessary to me. Slowly, I recognized a false directive grumbling within the bowels of my psyche that orchestrated my every movement: "To succeed in life, you have to pretend to be extroverted." Nothing could be further from my truth.

The first stone rumbled upward from the volcano of truth, complete with its hot molten lava. I could not sit on the steps any more. I had to stand. I looked to my left at Peter wandering in the grassy area completely in his own world. I turned to face the tracks again, wondering how they just stopped. Did they ever go anywhere else? Would I ever know why I was here on this planet?

What I did know with every fiber of my being was how to be the gracious Southern lady at parties, in social engagements, and in the company of my family. Like so many other women who were raised in the late 1940s, 1950s, and early 1960s, I had been taught the consciousness of the times: appearance is far more important than how you feel inside. The art of courtship was a high-stakes presentation, and it was imperative for one to display herself correctly.

Also, my generation had been caught between the June Cleaver directive for women to be the perfect housewife while never ever getting flour on their best dress or heels and the Gloria Steinem directive that screamed at women to be out there in the world as doctors, lawyers, or any other professional; we were sandwiched in the middle, not knowing how to break out of our own initial molds. Our mothers and grandmothers diligently taught us how to act according to the standards of their times. In contrast, the feminine consciousness of the late 1960s demanded we become professionals because we had that right. Left with our initial set of directives from our feminine ancestors, I, like many others, got caught in the chaotic middle, not having a clue as to how to navigate through our own perspective of the changing times.

Memories of a favorite uncle taking videos of each of his nieces and nephews at my grandmother's house on Christmas Day flooded into the open Birkenau air. I hated those home movies with a passion because I felt like I was being compared not only to the beauty of each of my cousins, but to the entire Southern society like an oven-browned goose displayed upon a silver platter. The new clothes my maternal grandmother gave us for Christmas each year were intended to satisfy some unrecognized need of hers to have grandchildren that looked refined and socially accepted. Her ideals had started in her era of the 1920s when the emerging culture taught women to work on what was called the "art of fascination" in order to be visually charismatic. Thinking she was helping her granddaughters, she taught us everything she knew about the art of feminine presentation.

What I wanted more than anything in the world then—as well as at this time in my life—was loving reassurance that came in the form of either a comforting hug, words of compassion, or, perhaps even better, deep listening with another as we shared the depths of our hearts. Because I was too young to know the difference, I had believed the stories I was told about how no one would love me unless I looked especially pretty at a gathering, unless I acted like I were a premier actress on center stage, or unless I made the best grades. I believed it when I was told I was too sensitive for life on this planet, was told to get my feelings off of my sleeve, and was told to keep my own desires to myself.

Stone number two crumbled from the depths of my false persona. I reached back with my right hand and threw as hard as I could. My little Auschwitz rock landed just short of the train tracks.

Breathe deeply, I thought to myself. *Breathe into yourself indigo, sapphire, and love. It's out there, just on the other side of the clouds.* My emotions were still solidified into a stoic demeanor, even though I knew this second stony story of my life had been brought out into the open air in order to be healed. Instead of feeling relief, I still felt rather exhausted, as if I had carried a heavy tombstone on my back all these many years with etched words that read "Do everything in your power to become who you are not. Conforming to the expectations of others is the only way you will be loved." Exhausted, I sat back down on the stone steps of the memorial. With a strong breath, I settled into a more calm state, willing myself to listen attentively to that small, inner voice of wisdom just in case it spoke to me.

Alternating between eyes closed and wide open, I became spiritually aware of everyone visiting Birkenau that day. Each visitor seemed beautiful to me even though their clothes were not spectacular, their faces were often screwed into intensity from processing the moment, and their hearts were heavy with the Holocaust horror. Through my fuzzy vision, everyone seemed connected with invisible silken threads, like lines of spun sugar blowing into winds of change. What a sharp contrast between the ways I perceived them and the way I had perceived my own self. No prayer seemed to come to me for the moment; however, the entire experience felt like deep, heartfelt prayer from the depths of my own spiritual soul.

While sitting on the stone steps of the Birkenau monument, I realized I also had some of those threads of spiritual unity. I could feel them inside my own heart where they had been hidden all those years underneath these heavy stones which now crumbled away. Instead of insecurity betraying me with its sad heaviness, I felt as if feathers of a dove opened up inside my chest waiting to fly into my own future, waiting to fly into the loving arms of God. My sense of peace did not last long, however. The third stone rattled right out of the psychological sack very quickly: For most of my life I had lived as others needed me to live instead of as God created me to be.

Who in the world would allow his or her self to be placed inside a household, a marriage, or even a community to be used as a pawn to satisfy someone else's inner needs, especially when doing so robs her of her own spirit? Frankly, I just don't think that could possibly be the reason for life. Yet, it's safer as a child to sometimes stay silent, even though the need to speak authentically rattles up from the throat's depths. Instead, the needs are swallowed—stuffed down into the throat chakra—so they can be nurturing manure for a thyroid goiter to grow healthy and strong enough to eventually render a choking death from the wayward nourishment. Oh, I became a master at this process, so much so that the silence morphed into saying what I intuitively knew others wanted to hear because it made them so very happy, content, and well-defined. Instead of golden threads of Oneness with God completely acknowledging the beauty of my created self, my threads were the ropes of a marionette held captive by anyone I wanted to please.

Anger rose up from me like a geyser engulfing this particular stone, as the heated energy of shame melted into smothering, molten lava. Instead of being directed at others in my life, this particular stone's wrath was directed inward for letting this happen. Oh, I wanted to stay angry, to scream words of disgust until even the cosmos rippled disgust right along with me. However, they would not come out of my throat because they held no truth. I had been, done, and become what I thought was expected of me to the point that it killed everything I knew about myself except my connection to God.

This self-anger singed anything it touched, burned holes in my happiness, and caused a rigidity to stay in place within my own life to shield myself from my own wrath. Sometimes I believe it is easier to forgive others than it is to forgive yourself; yet I knew that giving up the illusion that my life could have been any other way would be the only way to put out the inner fire of self-anger. Often, just recognizing the problem becomes the way to healing. I fully intended to put this third stone to rest regardless of how long it took.

"Are you about finished?" Peter asked. Without me realizing it, he had come up behind me ready to leave.

"No, I'm not ready," I sneered, thrusting the anger I felt at myself toward the only human in Birkenau that dared speak to me. "We've only been here two hours. When I walk out of this place, then you will know I'm ready to leave." I turned from Peter back to the railroad tracks, wondering if I ever would be ready to leave.

Thinking I would still be in a state of Oneness, I glanced up to the visitors approaching me parallel to the track in the midst of Birkenau, hoping again to see the threads of connection like I had before. I only saw people like me visiting a concentration camp. Instead of peace, I felt raw, as if my spiritual essence had been smoldered by my own carelessness. Just about the time I thought things could not get worse, the fourth stone appeared from the depths of my psychosomatic being. This one hurt like hell.

I did not feel loved by anyone on this earth or beyond, myself included.

Instead of processing that Oneness and Love are the same thing—a holy union of God and person that is blessed by total acceptance—for many decades I processed God through the same understanding I had with my own life: One had to please others in order to feel worthwhile. *If I don't do what you want me to do, I will not be loved,* I had integrated as a false truth. God became a judgmental, persecuting being out there somewhere waiting for me to trip up daily, at which time He would zap me into a hell of my own making. The more I became myself toward the latter part of my marriage, the more I felt unloved because I felt guilty for being myself, a direct opposite of what should have happened. Religion had become just another set of rules and regulations to me. Please, and be loved. Displease, and you are loveless. Unfortunately, this desire to be loved morphed into an acute state of neediness that consumed my very essence.

With this realization, the fourth stone cracked wide open from the back interior of my heart where it had lay dormant for most of my life. The next thoughts came from that still small voice inside, just like the questions and answers I had been receiving in deep meditation that bathed me with their substantial spiritual truth. Hastily, I retrieved pen and paper from my purse to write down the divine whispered thoughts.

> *Neediness consumes every waking moment if you allow it. Reaching out from the unloved depths of personal psyche, it stretches itself like plastic wrap clinging to everything, every event, as well as every person in your life. Weathering change like an ancient windmill on a barren plane, neediness adjusts direction of its own perspective by self-advocating a desire to move to something or someone more fulfilling.*
>
> *Neediness clings to the gratification of parents, lovers, or relationships in order to determine what to*

wear, what you like, or what you wish to study, as well as your own opinions before you even knew you had a God-gifted right to have different opinions. Like a trained puppy on a neediness leash, you walked not into the directions of your own dreams, even if you had some, but into the direction of dreams assigned to you by the people you wished to please.

Neediness never wallows in the shallows of your life, abdicating responsibility of personal choice, but demands to be forerunner each time a new decision is to be made. Will he/she love me if I wear this? Think this? Do this?

The need to be loved—neediness—reconciles its own existence each time gratification comes its way through a compliment, recognition, or even a smile: If you do as I wish you to do, you are just what I need. Thank you for not speaking up. Or perhaps the opposite: I did not ask you to do that. What in the hell were you thinking?

Neediness robs your sense of self blind, causing you to wander aimlessly from one set of instructors to another, squeezing the very lifeblood from the depth of your soul. Your spirit lies dead, beaten to the ground like fall chrysanthemums on a stormy night. Here's the thing though: regardless of how much you give of yourself to others, regardless of how much you do for others at your own expense, or how many things you substitute for self-authenticity, it's never going to be enough. Neediness never, ever receives enough.

The certainty of this message for my life rang clear and true like the church bells of Belgium pealing across communities reminding those who have ears to hear to pause momentarily in spiritual authenticity. Just like it had happened previously, the sentences came from beyond me, through me, and for me. There, sitting quite alone on a corner of the monument in the midst of one of the surest places of abuse on this Earth, I had been gifted my own epiphany. I felt its authenticity throughout every cell in my body.

Slowly, a softening occurred, one that began unexpectedly through gentle paths connecting body, soul, and spirit. Until my shoulders began to relax, I had not realized how stiff and tense they had been from the weight of dysfunction. The blessed softness curled deliberately from the top of my head down my backbone where it culminated at my first chakra like a contented kitten sleeping before a warming fire. Shifting my legs from side to side to make sure they were still operational, I stood tall, stretching my entire frame as a bridge between the ground upon which I stood and the cosmic infinity where all possibilities exist.

With great intent, I lifted both of my arms parallel to the flat monument, then straight above my head with open hands reaching up as if I could fill my softness with holy substance. The sensations that surged through my body bounced out from my soul, gathering with them all expressions of personal spirit that felt so delicate, so genteel, and so very authentic. Even though this sensation presented itself as glorious, it was beyond any awareness I had at the moment. In other words, what was it? How would I recognize it again?

As I walked straight ahead on the abandoned railroad tracks, I pondered these two questions. So many people had been brought to this place, forced into a Holocaust defying description. Only a few had survived. In some way, through my own lack of self-awareness, I had created personal situations that, for the most part, rendered me heavy with emotional dysfunction. More than any place—other than Ghent, Belgium, where I visited during my years of spiritual journeying— Birkenau felt more familiar than it should have. Putting one foot before the other onto the gravel between the iron tracks, I intended to move forward somehow, to move forward into something that felt uniquely me, however it might be presented. This time the stones between the tracks felt solid, quite connected, and welcoming under my feet.

With deliberate caution, I looked to my right where so many women had suffered. I then looked to my left, down the roadway that felt to me as if it led to hell on Earth. This time, however, I kept walking toward the tower above the red brick expanse up ahead in order to move beyond the Gates of Death into a new life for myself as I left my own stones behind.

Just as I got within several yards of the end of the tracks, something soft and delicate caught my attention because it contrasted so very much with the energy of the concentration camp. Between the iron rails, someone had placed a single red rose nestled upright in the stones between the tracks.

At first, I reacted as if this rose were an apparition. After all, a red rose has become the symbol of love throughout the world; Birkenau was not about love. For a brief moment, I stood still just staring at the softness of red, the color of paper hearts given at Valentine's Day. Over the years I had learned to be still, to move into that silent Oneness of complete surrender in order to discover the higher meaning of those special objects, animals, books, or situations presented to me through Spirit to increase my own wisdom. This was no different.

Moving to the other side of the rose, I squatted down in order to get eye level so that I could take a picture. From that perspective, the rose essence seemed larger than it actually was. The tracks looked as if they culminated into a point far ahead. Barbed wire fences, compound buildings, and literally everything else that bespoke of Holocaust horror paled into blurry focus. The rose stood steady like a lighthouse sentinel beckoning one to journey within.

After placing my camera to my left, I reached out with both hands to cup the rose petals into my palms. That same genteel softness I felt while sitting on the stony steps of the monument radiated out from that rose up into my arms. Swirling, tingling, and joyous, the rose energy cascaded into gentle waves of a moist ocean lapping onto the dry shores of my heart.

At that moment, I knew. Truly, I knew because I could feel it completely for the first time. Finally, the cleansing tears began to flow.

Like an acorn buried deep within the fertile soil awaiting precise conditions of God's nourishment before it morphed into the mighty oak it was created to be, within my heart I also had a seed of authentic essence. Perhaps my own kernel of awakening had lain dormant for many years awaiting its chance to grow. Maybe it had been bristling with desire all my life, awaiting only personal recognition before glowing like a full moon's radiance into all areas of my being. Honestly, none of that mattered to me then. What did matter pulled me forward into a new day, centered me when my emotions created temporary chaos, and presented me with a choice daily of whether to view the world through the eyes of a victim or through the soul of my own love. The words written by Leonard Jacobson rang true to my heart: "The path of awakening is not about becoming who you are. Rather it is about unbecoming who you are not."

Cupping my hands together, I moved them from the rose onto my own heart, as if by doing so I could retain forever the love I had just felt. Just like the rose standing within its own loving nucleus in the midst of Holocaust history, within my heart love resided as my soul, as the essence of my spirit. It resided as God, as God's Love within. By creating space inside by releasing the stony issues of my past, I had created space for Love. I felt it everywhere.

Turning from the rose, I walked out of the Gates of Death that day much different from the way I had entered. All the love I had sought through subjugating myself to the will of others had never manifested the way I needed it to be. Instead, all the Love I had ever needed and would ever need had been created with me, as me, and for me. As I approached the rental car, I glanced once more back through the gates into Birkenau. The rose could still be seen nestled into the rocks, securely placed for anyone to experience. I put my hands over my heart, knowing Love, real Love that felt so powerful and so Divine that it only could have been described as Rumi did: "a drop in the sea of God."

Peter was waiting for me in our rental car. "Well, seems as if you're now ready to leave." His tone was matter-of-fact, quite centered and peaceful.

"Yes, Peter," I answered back, my voice all but crooning. "I am indeed ready to leave it all behind." I closed the car door just in time before Peter backed out of our parking space.

By the next afternoon, I was on a plane back to the United States.

Even though my intentions were to leave Auschwitz behind that day, trading self–abdication that fragmented my soul into a thousand pieces like shards of glass on the basement floor for the wholeness only Love can heal, Auschwitz called to me in my dreams for months to come. The anguish of the woman I had intuited who died in the gas chambers, who clung to the twins as if all lives depended upon it, who cried with me in silent intuitive whispers of her own story, had to somehow be assuaged. Would the newfound sense of God's Love I felt inside be strong enough to put her dream-presence pain at peace?

With all my loving heart, I hoped so.

"Darkness cannot drive out darkness;
only light can do that. Hate cannot
drive out hate; only love can do that."

REVEREND DR. MARTIN LUTHER KING, JR.

———————————◆———————————

CHAPTER TEN

The Choice

I WATCHED IN abject horror through the spirit of a woman whose soul shuddered in sorrowful dread.

She waited, knowing it would not be long before the twins crossed the veil to be with her. Mengele placed the instrument down on a tray near the two boys lying side by side. The woman watched as blood oozed from the neck of the twin farther from her. Once the twin's throat was severed, Mengele removed an organ as the body gasped then turned cold. The brother watched in speechless terror, unable to move, unable to untie the binding straps so he could run. The woman opened her spirit wide like two loving arms to receive this young soul in order to escort him to a better place.

I heard the crack of three hearts breaking.

"OH GOD HELP ME!" I screamed. The words formed inside my heart and squeezed through my throat, but instead of discovering their own sound, they rumbled aimlessly into the silence of the night, unheard. Once again, the dream came to me unexpectedly, just as it had for several months before Auschwitz to several weeks afterwards. Each time I hoped it would be the last time I ever had to experience this again, yet it persisted like sticky flypaper that could not be purged from my own sleeping psyche. Each time I dreamed this particular dream, I wanted to scream out obscenities to God for letting such evil happen in the world. My silence was deafening, oozing out into the bedroom where it hit the walls and then reverberated back to me before I caught my breath. My hands were clammy, my heart raced, and the tears ran down my cheeks like swollen torrents flowing down an unconquerable mountain.

Yet again, I vowed through intense prayer that it simply had to stop. This time, instead of tearfully pleading to God to make the dream stop, I screamed it right out loud in the privacy of my bedroom.

"Okay, God, you have my attention!" I shrieked with my fist balled into the air as if I could intimidate the Divine into giving me some help. "As you know, I have tried two counselors to get to the bottom of this dream, to no avail. I have looked for a meaningful message within it with no results. I even went to Auschwitz! It's between you and me now. Show me, tell me, or guide me—your preference—but this dream has got to stop. Now! I. MEAN. IT!" In a show of determined anger, I threw the bed pillow across the room where it hit the top of the dresser, knocking to the floor pictures of my happy, adventuresome self riding a camel in the Middle Nile.

Instead of acting loving or surrendering, this time I flat out demanded to get some sort of answer to the dream. Evidently it was not going to stop until I got to the bottom of the meaning. Oh, I had already tried dream analysis, but no particular message could be ascertained. This dream came to me intermittently during my sleep from somewhere other than the normal dream state. Frankly, it felt like a memory. But that was quite impossible, for I was born after the Holocaust, not before.

Or was it impossible?

Approximately two months before the trip to Auschwitz, not long after this particular version of the dream had started, out of desperation early one morning I padded down the two sets of steps in my split level house in Roswell, Georgia, to get to my computer. (I left the coffee, herbal tea, and anything else that would serve as a normal morning's delight in the kitchen. Not only was I much too awake to require a caffeine stimulant, but what I needed was probably more along the lines of a soothing cup of chamomile tea. Even that seemed like overkill; I was much too angry to even swallow.)

After what seemed like a very short Google search for the words "past life" and "past life clearing," I had found someone named Luke from Tennessee who taught online shamanic methods. He also offered healing and intuitive counseling sessions by telephone. Even though I found others purporting to do the same thing, this man seemed quite genuine to me. When I read his website that early morning, a sense of peacefulness overcame me. No other site had caused that reaction. After swallowing my fears, I sent him an email asking for help, but now here it was almost five months later and I had not heard from him—and the dreams had continued.

Unbelievably, the morning after screaming my little tirade of a prayer to God to find help for the dream, the shaman I had previously contacted replied to my email to see if I still wanted to do a healing session. Oh, yes, you bet I did! Hopefully my prayer would be answered soon, so I could finally put this particular dream to rest. We scheduled an appointment for later that week.

"Tell me about the dreams you've been experiencing," Luke said over the phone. His voice sounded soft, as if every word he spoke came to him in whispers of faith. Although I'm not sure what I expected, his tone of voice was reassuring, as if it emanated from a state of Oneness. Instead of charging at the problem at hand like a warrior armed with sharpened sword and heavy shield, his tone was gentle and non-assuming—Christ-like in many ways.

"First, may I ask you something?" I inquired. Before I could proceed to whatever our clearing would entail, I had to know why after these several months he had contacted me that day instead of months before. "Why did you feel the need to contact me now instead of months ago when I first asked you for help?"

"My wife and I get a great number of emails asking us for healing help. Obviously we cannot handle them all, so we make a pile of those we think we can help. Today Spirit spoke to both of us to contact you. Timing is perfect."

"Well, I am overwhelmed. Indeed, the timing is divine, at least for me. For years I've been open to past life regression. I've even cleared some of the past life energy I have been holding from other experiences this way. However, until now I have never encountered anything this overwhelming or this detailed."

"Yes," Luke said in his soft, powerful shamanic way. Nothing else was said about the matter. He simply waited for me to begin to explain my problems.

I wondered how much I would tell Luke about the visions I'd had while at Auschwitz and Birkenau, yet before I could make that determination, I ended up blurting out the entire psychic episode detail by detail. He listened attentively.

At first, I started by explaining the dream of the doctor experimenting on the twin boys with the woman in spirit hovering nearby. When I initially dreamed this particular dream, I had no idea the doctor in the dream was Mengele; I discovered his name in a photograph that matched the man in my dreams through a Google search. Then— because I literally could not stop the words from bubbling up from my soul—I began to explain my visit to Auschwitz and Birkenau, even though the dream in question first started prior to the Poland trip. When I mentioned entering the gates to Birkenau, I could tell the energy between us changed, yet I had no idea why.

"Luke," I asked, interrupting myself. "Should I go on? Are you still there?"

"Yes, I am here. I am going to call you back though. I need to call you back."

I had no idea why Luke had to call me back, yet I intuited for certain that it was not because of something happening inside his house, but something happening inside of Luke. Shortly, he did call back. Our conversation resumed as if no lapse had occurred.

After I finished, Luke paused. In stillness, I trusted all was as it should be for those silent moments. When he began talking in what seemed to me to be a very secure tone bathed in Spirit, I felt within me the truth of his words. Evidently, the woman whose vision I had intuited as she got off of the train hugging the twins to her side was part of a past life energy I was holding. The other vision I'd had while in the gas chamber—where the same woman tried to hold her breath hoping she would outlast the gas and not die—was also this same specific past life. The spirit of the woman who watched her body being shoved carelessly into the furnace was the same life or afterlife. It was also she who had hovered in spirit over the twins lying next to each other while the death doctor did his experimentations. By the time Luke finished explaining these things, they all seemed connected to each other, parts of a story of a woman's last days of life in Auschwitz. Her final experiences lacked the mercy of personal choice.

Thankfully, before the session with Luke began I had replaced the receiver on the phone with a set of headphones in order to leave my hands free. When Luke finished doing what he needed to do in order to heal my body, soul, and spirit of the energy of this Auschwitz woman with the twins, I was on the floor, headset intact. For the life of me I have no idea how I got there; the current space of time and place had been overshadowed by the healing events of another time and place. I have no memory of what Luke did; I just know it was righteous.

After I came back to my current reality, I asked Luke if the singing had anything to do with my own past life.

"Singing?" Luke asked incredulously. "Tell me about the singing."

Until then, I hadn't mentioned the singing that I'd heard from the Rabbi who'd led his flock down that horrid corridor I could not enter. I also hadn't mentioned what I intuitively felt when I saw the

Rabbinical robes on display. Luke listened with rapt attention before explaining something he had intuited, known, or dreamed most of his life.

As he explained to me, Luke felt like he had been a holy man of some sort brought to Birkenau against his will. He intuited that he had led the people in his train car in a specific holy song in order to help them endure the horror they were experiencing. He remembered walking down a corridor, and down a long road, singing.

The coincidence between our conversation and what I had perceived and felt at Birkenau and Auschwitz concerning this holy man was too strange to have been anything other than absolute truth. I know I could not have conceived this type of synchronicity. Perhaps Luke did on some spiritual level when he and his wife decided that I was to be contacted that particular morning. Perhaps in some way on an intuitive spiritual level I had also when I chose Luke to contact months before out of all those who purported to be healers on the Internet. Over the years I have learned not to question these types of synchronicities but to be grateful, joyful, and completely in tune through prayer, making sure I stay steady in God's protective love. This type of faith, love, and trust never fails.

Never.

After our session, I decided to email Luke the picture of the Gates of Death that I had taken. I also included a picture of the other gate in Auschwitz with the iron over it displaying the German words meaning "Work will set you free," and one more of the railroad tracks into Birkenau where I'd had the visions of the woman with the twins and the Rabbi. Later the next day, I got an email from one of Luke's internet-savvy business acquaintances who explained that Luke's entire computer system and printer had blown out as the pictures were being printed. I had to resend them to her, so she could print them for him. Later, Luke sent me an email thank-you note saying that he'd had a fear of gates all his life and could hardly go through one without being very cautious. Until that day, he had no idea why the fear plagued him so. When he saw the Gates of Death, he understood. He ended up doing a healing session for himself and his wife.

For a while after this experience, I zeroed in on past lives, past life regressions, and the phenomena of people holding energy as if they'd had specific experiences during another time and place. Dr. Brian Weiss brought these phenomena to light in his first book, Many Lives, Many Masters, in which he explained his experiences with a female patient who recalled her own past life under hypnosis. As a traditional psychiatrist, Dr. Weiss was skeptical at first—and then astonished when this memory helped one of his patients heal from anxiety attacks and recurring nightmares. As strange as the experience felt to me, I also began to accept the validity of remembering past life trauma.

Even though after my healing I never dreamed this specific dream again, to this day I still feel deeply about the experiences of Auschwitz. It's more than just the strong memories of a specific experience, more than just what I intuited when I visited, and more than just a profound empathy for those who suffered and died. Birkenau exists as part of my soul. The frightened woman with the twins of my dreams and visions lies deep within me as part of my soul's experience. I know it to be true somehow. Yet, to go day by day thinking of myself as this woman will never bring me any sense of peace. I cannot look back while traveling forward. Her experience was just too horrific. Instead, I think of her in the third person as I endeavor to incorporate her bravery, her love for her twins, and the courageous manner and deep faith with which she carried on her loving intention of protection even after death. Thanks to Luke the Shaman, as well as my own prayerful intentions, this woman's energetic memory no longer is with me.

Even so, one question lingered for me, twirling through every nuance of consciousness, every thought, and all self-awareness I possessed: if her experience was indeed mine incorporated into soul's wisdom of my spiritual being, where then is that bravery now? In other words, what does that strength of character feel like today as me? For most of my life, I have lived as if my life depended on being as others expected me to be because I was afraid to be different, afraid to be unique, afraid to be authentic. Could this also be a carryover from the Holocaust brought into consciousness now in order to be healed?

That indeed was the issue to be delved into, not just a past life memory that sneaked upon me during my deepest dreams. But I had to transform my own fear of being myself, especially in the presence of others who had stronger personalities. Somehow, I had to use all the persistence I could muster in order to transform that lingering feeling of victimization into one of personal empowerment strong enough to withstand any backlash I might experience when being the authentic soul God created me to be.

The problem was more of recognition. What did personal power feel like? Even though my faith and love for God strengthened my every waking moment, I needed to know what it felt like to trust myself when others doubted me. What did it feel like to stay secure in my own self-truth when others insisted I be another way? As I pondered these questions in depth the week after my past life healing, all thoughts morphed into one basic directive. I vowed to get myself to the most energetically powerful place on earth to discover for myself what absolute power feels like to me. Perhaps then I would be able to recognize it as part of my own being.

I was going to fly to the Great Pyramid in Cairo, Egypt.

◆ ◆ ◆ ◆ ◆

Hobbling back from the toilet, I steadied myself with both hands as I leaned on several of the seats in our plane so I could sit down. The thought of going to Cairo early that October scared me senseless, so much so that I entertained a supreme case of nervous digestion. My torso churned itself into an orchestra with each instrument playing a different tune; kettledrums in my heart overshadowed the screeching violins of my stomach. On one of my many trips to the toilet, our plane hit an air pocket while I turned sideways to reach for the toilet paper. Evidently the sudden drop caused my back to jam into an unnatural form better suited for slithering snakes than post-menopausal women. When I stood to straighten my clothing, intense waves of pain mingled with extreme fear like two jockeys vying for position right before the finish line.

What I wanted out of this trip was to finally understand personal power. Instead, what I felt seemed more like a hobbling cow on the way to the slaughterhouse. Just before I reached my seat, I inadvertently grabbed the shoulder of the Egyptian man sitting just in front of me instead of the back of his seat. Startled, he hastily pulled his shoulder out from under my hand, a move that caused me to stumble, rear end sideways, into Peter's lap.

"Good gracious, Paddy, get a grip on things," Peter cautioned. "We're almost in Egypt. You cannot just indiscriminately grab the shoulders of men to steady yourself!" With that admonishment, Peter slid out from under me to the outside window, a move that allowed me to slither my pain into a seat too tiny for comfort.

"I should have left you at home, Peter," I said to myself more than anyone else, knowing very well I had no way at all of navigating Cairo as a single woman. Oh, over the years, Ghent, Belgium, had become comfortable to me. For the most part, I knew the areas of the city, knew my bus routes (even though I never did learn to love riding in one of those metal coffins on wheels), and knew how to entertain myself in the museums and historic sites. Egypt was different, though. Men were in charge in Egypt, as I had learned in my trip to the Middle Nile. Very aggressive men seemed to be the norm of those I encountered. I did not then—nor at any time in my history—learn to love aggressive men (or antagonistic women, for that matter). Egypt seemed to contain aggressive men exponentially as compared to anywhere else I had been in the United States and Europe, though, and if I were to visit the pyramids successfully I had to figure out a way to navigate through the aggressive trinket merchants, cab drivers, and any other men I might encounter who would insist upon, for their services, more money than bank vaults contain. Therefore, I enticed Peter to come with me as my traveling companion, especially since Peter had already seen the pyramids several times.

From what little travel literature I had read about Egypt, transportation from the airport to the respective hotels would be better provided by limousine drivers instead of cab drivers. Therefore, at my insistence, Peter booked us a limo. We fully expected our driver to meet us just after the customs nightmare.

Because the customs officials went through their duties with the determination of a Bengal tiger on the prowl, it would not have surprised me if one of the thousands of people crowded into this one room could have been eaten alive at a moment's whim. Shoulder to shoulder, we stood. Once as many as three people pressed against me. As an introvert, I longed for space, for order, and most of all, for forests with mountain streams. Instead, what I encountered was beyond anything I had ever experienced. I've read that Cairo International Airport supports approximately 14,000,000 passengers per year as the second-largest airport in Africa. Frankly, it would not have surprised me to learn most of them were standing in line with me.

The sound in the room was deafening even with my low level of hearing. No one seemed to simply speak in a normal tone of voice. Instead, anytime anyone wished to express him or herself, the sound magnified exponentially in decibels that, had they been baseballs, would be home runs over the bleachers, past the parking lot, and well into the city before they softened enough to finally rest upon weary ground. Unlike any country I'd visited previously, this time the officials took our passports and our entry papers, and kept them for what seemed to be time enough to call home, order lunch, and dress for an evening out. Of course, I stood where he shouted at me in English to stand, but only after I had asked him to repeat himself twice. Only after he pointed did I understand; the sound in the room was not conducive to hearing anything specific. The entire episode rattled my bones to the core of my existence.

Then, of course, I had to navigate the toilet procedure in the Cairo Airport. In one way the process reminded me of the public toilet usage in Belgium—one has to pay. In Belgium, I always carried Euro coins for this intended purpose. However, neither Peter nor I had Egyptian currency with us. We fully expected to be able to use Euros like we had in the Middle Nile region. Instead, the young woman blocking the doorway to the woman's facilities kept shaking her head "no" when I presented various denominations of Euros. By the time I began waving the higher bills at her, Peter suggested that he go to the currency exchange counter at the airport to get the proper currency. Meanwhile, I stood there with legs and fingers crossed, hoping he would be back in time.

Again, just like at the Middle Nile temple area, someone stood just inside the ladies' toilet handing out paper for our personal usage. I would have run like hell had I not had to go so much. The only differences here were that the toilet guard was female instead of male, and at least I had brought a little packet of tissue with me this time. After Peter brought her back some lower-denomination bills in Egyptian currency, I finally got some relief.

After thoroughly searching for the non-existent limo driver, I pointed Peter to a line of limousine stands inside the airport where one could rent a ride to any destination. While Peter went to bargain us a ride, I chose to sit down with the luggage. Actually, I had to sit down because my back had shifted from a curvy snake position into total discord, apparently with an intention of never moving again without pain. Eventually he returned with an intensity that matched the decibels of the building tone for tone, except, of course, Peter almost whispered. When negotiating in Egypt, one cannot get emotionally involved. Instead, a calm demeanor, a strong intention, and a firm attitude suit the procedure best. Evidently Peter also was on a learning curve with this one. Thinking the price had been set, we endured a rather interesting ride in an older, non-limo car operated by an independent contractor who could well have been someone just off the street.

I have no idea if there are expressways in Cairo. Perhaps there are many, but we certainly did not travel on one. Already in overwhelm from the plane ride, the airport, and the back injury, I rode through Cairo with my eyes closed, opening them in brief bursts only when the limo-imitation stopped longer than expected. What I saw through the windows of the car consisted of great gobs of humanity, houses and buildings sandwiched between enough stoplights to mimic a fireworks display on a hot, sultry summer day. Eventually we got to our hotel unharmed. However, that's when the real fireworks happened.

In the Flemish area of Belgium, tipping normally doesn't occur because salaries are set by the government. At least that was how Peter explained it. Therefore, when we got to the hotel, Peter did not tip the limo driver because he did not realize it was expected. Our driver all but exploded with hands waving in the air, words half English and half what I assumed was Egyptian. Perhaps it's just as well we didn't understand him. Thinking he could settle the matter easily, Peter motioned for me to drag our luggage into the hotel to check in, and he would follow.

I hobbled into the lobby to begin the check-in process. Shortly afterward, Peter entered, followed by the limo driver who was still shouting and waving his arms in the air as if he wanted to swat flies. Peter could not get away from him. No one at the hotel tried to help us. Surely this had happened before. Maybe all were used to it; definitely we were not.

Peter asked me in a whisper how much tipping would entail. Although I am not a world traveler or did not consider myself to be one at that time, I told him that in Atlanta the better restaurants expected a twenty percent tip. Peter figured the amount quickly, counted out the Egyptian money, and handed it to the driver thinking this would settle the matter.

It did not.

"What do you expect me to do with this little bit of change?" he said in exaggerated English with a tone that would slice your throat. Waving the money in the air for all to see, he continued. "I have many women to support. I depend on my income. This is an insult. You are insulting the entire Egyptian culture with your presence."

"My God," I muttered under my breath. Literally, at this moment I feared the man would assault us with the entire hotel staff watching.

By his stance, I knew Peter had not been able to maintain his usually calm demeanor. His arms were crossed, his face flushed like a ruby red beet in the sun, and his breathing came in short puffy bursts like a steam engine gearing up for a long haul up a very steep mountain. Frankly, I thought Peter would have bolted by now. Instead, he gestured to me to do the bolting by taking the suitcases to the rooms because I had already checked in for both of us.

Later, we learned that tipping in Egypt could become a bargaining process. This time Peter had no intention of letting this driver browbeat him into giving more money. In place of bargaining, Peter began speaking to the driver in a firm tone that gradually began to escalate in intensity as he all but threw words at our driver like fastballs in the latter innings of the World Series. As I glanced back to the hotel desk where the two men stood arguing with one another, I realized that Peter's engine had revved to the point that his words danced through four languages. He started in English, because that was the common language between the two men. Soon, I noticed Flemish words spewing out of Peter's mouth, then German, and, of all things, Latin. I was proud of Peter's capacity to remain centered even though I could tell he had become very angry. His head reached out further than his chest as if by being closer the words would more deliberately sideswipe the face of the driver. The only thing I knew to do was pray.

"Help Peter!" was the only prayer I managed to mutter. "For that matter, help us both." Simple words, but they were said in absolute earnest. Centering in the comforting thought that I knew Peter would get some help in some way became my only job. Actually, considering the circumstances, I did that very well.

Not long after my prayer, what I assumed were two security men dressed in business suits entered the bullfighting arena Peter and the driver had assembled. Instead of going to the room, I peeked out from behind the corner, alternating between wanting things to be cool and not wishing to miss any of the show. Shortly thereafter, the two suited men escorted the driver out of the hotel. Frankly, if we had given the man our entire sum of cash, the deed to our houses, and the birth certificate of a first-born child, I still think he would have been very unsatisfied.

Approximately thirty minutes after we settled down in our rooms, Peter called me. A basket of fruit from the hotel management had been delivered to his room. Because I had not gotten any fruit, we both believed it was the manager's way of apologizing for the inconvenience. Positive thoughts helped us calm down. For the rest of our day, that became our only objective. After all, tomorrow we were going to be out there sandwiched between the world of tourists and the ancient world of Egypt.

◆ ◆ ◆ ◆ ◆

"You would like to take a camel ride," declared the man perched atop what seemed to me to be one of the tallest animals in the world. That camel looked to be well over eight feet tall. I could have maneuvered my entire 5'1" frame under its belly and never have touched any part of it.

I had hobbled to the back side of the Great Pyramid hoping to be able to find some solitude and space to myself in order to figure out the profound energetic thrust intuitively shoved at me. My back had not gotten better overnight, mainly because the mattress felt as if it were made of concrete. Unfortunately, I slept on my right side all night without moving, a position that required me to literally roll out of bed the next morning instead of sitting upright. At best, I angled slightly forward like the hour hand of a clock that moved just past noon. As long as I could hobble at my own pace in the hot desert sand, I could make slow progress. However, this annoying camel driver kept putting his ride in front of me in order to block my path.

"No, I would not like a camel ride," I answered for the umpteenth time. "No camel. No ride. NO CAMEL RIDE!" I turned to my left, slowly, in order to move away from him.

The camel-riding Egyptian moved in front of me again quite effortlessly. If it is camel nature to plod securely in sand, then camels and I have nothing in common whatsoever.

"You can have a picture taken of yourself on this beautiful camel," my annoying camel owner announced as he gestured with the hand nearest me. "You can have a fun ride. I am available now for your riding pleasure."

You're in Egypt, I thought to myself. *Be kind. Represent the United States well.* In my firmest voice I said, "I do not wish to ride your camel. NO!" Again I turned from him, thinking that would be the end of our non-negotiations. Instead, he plodded away from me only to turn back toward me so that I was eye to thigh to that camel, its drooling mouth right above my head. I gasped just before the driver moved him to my side again.

"I can lead him. You will not have to manage that. This is your one chance to ride a camel in Egypt. Take this opportunity. Now we can negotiate price."

In my entire life I have never seen anyone with such persistence as I did those trinket vendors in Egypt. Yet, this man seemed to outdo them all, especially since he kept blocking my way with a humongous camel.

"I have already ridden a camel in Egypt. In the Middle Nile region," I said, thinking that would end the conversation. Instead, just the opposite happened. The camel driver decided that I liked camels so much I needed to experience his version of one. He became more determined than ever to get my money and give me a ride.

I thought of running, but with my back the way it was, I could hardly walk. Even if I decided to ride that particular camel, I had no idea how I would get on top of the thing, even if it squatted down like I had seen in the movies. My right leg seemed to want to drag a bit from the hip downward. If I threw it over a camel's back, probably it would keep flying through the air quite free and unattached to whatever it was that had squished, severed, or squandered itself out of righteous order in my lower spine. Besides, even if I could run, I imagine camel dearest could have outrun me with absolutely no effort at all. Bottom line, the man wanted my money.

"I'll tell you what. I'll give you five dollars American money to leave me alone for the rest of the day."

"But if you ride, I will get more of your money," the Egyptian man said with a broad smile stretching both mouth and twinkling eyes toward his ears.

"That will not happen. Not today. Not tomorrow. Not while I am in Egypt. I am now offering you five dollars in American money to leave me alone for the rest of the day." By this time, I waved my five-dollar bill in the air like a Georgia peach blossom in a spring storm.

My camel driver paused a moment before he leaned sideways off of his camel as he reached for the money. "You have a deal then."

Just before he was within reach of the money, I pulled it back just out of his grasp. "Now, in America where I am from, when we strike a deal, when we exchange money for a bargain, that is the final matter. We do no more negotiations. Can you honor that?"

The smile naturally came back to his face this time. Evidently, Egyptians love this type of bargain exchange. Frankly, I hate it with a passion. But, as the saying goes, "When in Rome...." I waited for his answer.

"All day then. I will honor your request to leave you alone all day."

"Then the money is yours. May the rest of the day be as you would like it to be." As I handed him the money, I took my turn smiling. At least I had purchased a moment of peace from this one specific man who genuinely seemed rather pleasant in retrospect. My camel driver friend, however, was not American, but Egyptian. Evidently they do things their way in Egypt.

"I prefer Euros," he announced. "I wish to have Euros instead. They are worth more here." He held the American five-dollar bill in his hands like it had morphed into worthlessness right before our eyes.

"How can I give you Euro currency?" I exclaimed in my best-behaved voice. Actually by this time I wanted to shake the man, but that attitude would have done me no good whatsoever even if I could have pulled him off of that too-tall camel. I opened my wallet as a gesture of honesty, making sure he could not see anything inside. "See, I am American. I have American money only."

Clearly he finally understood I had no Euros to give to him. He paused, nodded his head, and then said, "Okay then. I have your American money. However, it is not enough. I cannot leave you alone all day for this little amount." The smile had returned. Obviously this man delighted in our exchange; he was having a ball.

Now it was my turn to have fun. Really, why not enjoy this particular journey. So, I began to laugh. Real laughter, not the fake kind that one uses to make light of a situation, but the real kind that comes from a delicious story just told.

"Then give it back to me. Our deal is broken now. The honor of our agreement is broken. I have no more money I can give to you at this time. Please give my money back to me." I reached out my hand to receive my five-dollar bill knowing full well it would not be given to me. By this time, the entire episode was hilarious to me. Here I was at the Great Pyramid, trapped in the middle of a sandy desert by a man on top of a camel who wanted me to ride an animal too tall for me to even fathom getting onto with my painful back.

"You and I can keep our honor," he said. "I have enjoyed our conversation. Now you may have my word that I will not ask you for a ride again." He tipped his head at me in friendly gesture.

Just before I hobbled away, we made eye contact, soul to soul. I liked this man after all, for I could see friendly depths in his dark eyes. Like the rest of humanity, he was just someone trying to earn a living. "The money I gave to you is a gift, you know. A gift intended for good will between us. Please accept it as such." With that, I walked away very proud of myself for standing my ground in a loving way without letting my annoyance get the best of me. As I glanced back one more time making sure I indeed had a clear pathway to walk away from this conversation, the camel owner tipped his head at me once more. Respect flowed between us like ocean currents. Throughout the entire day at the pyramids, every time this man and I made eye contact, he tipped his head in gracious acknowledgement keeping his part of the bargain. I always tipped my head in a similar manner. Somehow it seemed to me like more than just a money exchange had taken place between us during our bargain. Perhaps I would call it simply a profound recognition of souls that transcended country, culture, and intention.

◆ ◆ ◆ ◆ ◆

The enthusiasm of the people in line to enter the Great Pyramid of Giza overshadowed the concerns about the process involved. One had to purchase a separate ticket, a procedure that involved walking across the area in front of the pyramid in order to stand in yet another line. The process took hours of time, for the tickets were not sold all day long but at intervals during the day in order to control the number of visitors entering the pyramid. I sent Peter to buy mine for me when he bought his, mainly because I did not wish to walk more than absolutely necessary. Besides, the closer I got to the pyramid entrance, the stronger the energy I felt; I needed time to adjust.

At first, I thought it might have been panic rising yet again, even though my panic attacks after the past life clearing had lessened to a great extent. Still, my breathing became shallow, my eyes began to blur, and the old familiar tingling started from my fingertips moving slowly up my arms just as it had before. This time I had no intention of letting it get the best of me. In order to do that, first I had to bring into consciousness my own fear in order to dissect the monster it threatened to become. In other words, I had to figure out why in the world my body acted as though I had swallowed a personal vibrator stuck in the "on" position before I would even be able to enter the Great Pyramid.

By the time I maneuvered the stone steps to the tourist entrance—a small narrow passageway located below the original entrance—Peter still had not gotten back with my ticket. When this happened to the others in line, the guard would insist the tourists leave the line while pointing to the ticket booth. Fully expecting to experience the same thing, surprise overtook me when this same guard pointed to the stone ledge just to the left of the entrance telling me to stay there and wait a while. Perhaps because of his training he recognized my need to calm down before entering the dark passage to the interior of the Great Pyramid. Or maybe, instead, he thought that I would give up waiting and abandon the entire event. Whatever the reason, I considered it another instance of having spiritual help. Because I truly did not wish to anger the guard or navigate the stone steps more than once, I dutifully limped to the wall in order to squat down on one of the stones of the pyramid. Actually, nothing better could have happened at this particular moment, because it gave me time to pause and consider the energy that overwhelmed me so much. This guard had actually presented me with the gifts of time and location that I needed very much.

Never in my entire life had I felt energy this strong, a problem exacerbated by the fact that I did not recognize it at all. For a while, I felt as if I were submersed into the power of a thousand irritated warriors surrounding me, yet this energy did not feel warrior-like at all. It felt peaceful, like a lack of being threatened, as if it were a current of electricity that one might use to create light or heat.

Gently, I touched the stone upon which I sat, grateful for the experience to have this moment of personal space to use my sixth sense in order to process the entire experience. Slowly, I realized the power I felt seemed to emanate from the pyramid itself. Instead of panic, the intense power of the pyramid was what was causing my body to react the way it did, absorbing the vibrations to the point that they felt like my own. My job, then, was to accept that I could be near this power, accept that I could be inside this power, and accept that I could be totally submersed in this power without being destroyed, without feeling trapped, or without feeling like I had disappeared. The power felt just this strong to me.

People went in and came out. Each time, the guards would confiscate the cameras, but not the cell phones. I wondered if they realized that many cell phones had the new photographic technology. Of course, just like other places in Egypt, money exchanged hands in order to secure the cameras while the owners visited the interior of the pyramid. Only one woman argued with the officials, who remained calm, professional, yet forceful the entire time. Perhaps God and angels watched over me that day, for truly I needed to see people come into the pyramid and come out safely before I could even think about doing the same thing.

Eventually Peter returned with our tickets. Doing as we were told, we entered only when the guards gave us permission, securing our cameras with the woman at the entrance by exchanging our tip for a numbered ticket that matched the one placed on our equipment. Frankly, the process seemed well orchestrated even if the multitude of expensive cameras were shoved in random order to the back of a ledge behind the small table. A nagging insecurity lingered about ever seeing my camera again.

The inside of the tourist entranceway was not memorable to me, nor were the staircases leading in two directions, up and down. Instead of just bravery, what I truly needed was a map that clearly stated "You Are Here" in various places inside this pyramid. No such help could be found; our navigational ability needed to be self-directed.

As our trail of tourists passed the conjunction of the ascending passage and descending passage, an interior guard beckoned me to pay him, so I could experience the special privilege of entering the passageway downward. At first, I almost believed it possible that we could have gone into that direction even though a boundary clearly was placed across the top of that staircase to keep people out. Then, quickly, I remembered when visiting the Valley of the Kings being told definitely not to go anywhere other than the passageways open to tourists because of safety issues. Frankly, I don't understand that part of tourism in Egypt where one official tells you the rules and others tell you it is okay to break them if you pay him. I had no intention of breaking any law in Egypt, much less getting trapped forever in the bottom of some dark corridor in a stone structure older than time itself only to be discovered by grave robbers a thousand years later who wondered why I did not possess a camera. Hastily, I turned away from him in order to join the other tourists. As I walked away, this particular guard still demanded I pay him money for permission to break the law.

While I have only vague memories of stone walls, staircases, and dim lighting, what I do remember vividly floods into my very being like the lingering darkness of a childhood nightmare. The pyramid had light, but not much. Instead of being brightly lit, it seemed ominously filled with shadows that shifted silently of their own accord. Even though I wished to pause yet again as I had on the side of the entranceway ledge in order to incorporate, discern, and generally make friends with the overwhelming force that had begun to emanate all around me, I had to keep moving. Tourists were not only in front of me, but behind me; I had to keep up with the flow of traffic. Frankly, I did rather well maintaining my speed along with the others as we stepped upward inside this stone marvel of ancient antiquity, even though our passageways seemed to keep getting smaller and smaller. The middle incline, however, challenged not only my aching back, but also my soul.

Instead of steps, the ascending passageway inclined upward at a 26-degree slant, interspersed with narrow ridges to keep one from slithering back down like a greased pig on a playground sliding board. Because the stone ceiling hovered only four feet above the floor, anyone brave enough to venture upward and onward had to maneuver this challenge while bending over at an almost ninety-degree angle in a squatting position like a waddling duck. That position gave me no trouble at all, for it felt a lot more comfortable to my back to ease myself into this narrow tunnel in a squatted position than it would have in a full stance. I had no trouble reaching the hand railings added to the walls, because the width was only 3.5 feet. By the time I had crawled halfway to the top, the tunnel seemed to become exponentially smaller to me, like a 124-foot drinking straw carved inside solid stone. I completely ran out of air.

Obviously, I had slowed down considerably, for other tourists began to pass me, a process that required astute body contortions. The tourist wanting to pass would first announce his intention. I would then bank my back onto the right wall, balanced on my right leg while holding my left leg down and behind me as close to the wall as possible. Pressing my left arm to the ceiling helped maintain the uncomfortable position, although I had to simultaneously press my right arm to the floor to protect my back muscles from overexertion. This allowed the passing tourist to slither forward on his left side. Each time, we looked like two yoga novices who struggled to correctly get the poses. The entire procedure was quite intimate as our faces were less than twelve inches apart.

At first, I considered going back down in order to abandon the entire pyramid experience. However, the dollar bills I had spent to get this far flashed in front of my mind with a sad Grover Cleveland lamenting, "I have tried so hard to do right." Indeed, it would not have been right to have stopped. I had to get as close to the interior top of this pyramid as I possibly could. My soul pushed me forward while my emotional body pulled me back, like a tug-of-war between two sumo wrestlers.

I definitely needed more air. My breath came in long audible gasps as what little oxygen I could find squeezed into my lungs only to be thrust out too suddenly. Whatever panic I felt at crawling through this teeny tiny tunnel of a passageway obviously suited for only the most daring of slithering-adept humanity settled entirely in my chest cavity, where it threatened to squeeze my lungs to death. Again I paused my crawling, not because I wanted to, but because I thought I would pass out from lack of air. Rasping inward, thin threads of air visited briefly a few of the lung cells grasping and screaming for relief before dissipating into unusable oblivion; I then rasped again. How in the world were the rest of the tourists managing to breathe? It exhausted me to even think about it. In fact, one extremely tall young man traveled up the tunnel in a greatly stooped position with his arms dangled in front of him in ape-like fashion, holding a baby that could not have been more than two months old. Not only did he move at a rapid pace, but the man sang a lullaby the entire time. I could not have sung if my life depended upon it. After witnessing this father, it hit me that my lack of breath had more do to with the situation, rather than the actual conditions. The tunnel did not lack oxygen, evidently, because everyone else could breathe. The problem had to be my personal sensitivity to the narrow tunnel, lack of light, and movement from open air into whatever lay before me; I was beginning to feel like a stooping whale that had been swallowed whole by a long, thin eel. With this realization, I determined that I would keep moving forward, even if I passed out while trying. This was a distinct possibility.

When I finally got through the ascending passage into the Grand Gallery, the seven-foot width and over twenty-eight foot ceiling height still seemed very confining to me. The lighting was brighter than the previous tunnel, though, although still dim. Shadows from the other tourists exaggerated onto the walls and floors, elongated wisps of darkness competing for space. For this reason I still did not breathe easily, probably because the stone steps ascended for another 153 feet, a distance that required physical stamina.

By the time I dragged my exhausted self into the Kings' Chamber, Peter already stood by an open red granite container identified as a sarcophagus. Unlike the ones displayed at the Egyptian Museum in Cairo that had been excavated from the Valley of the Kings, this one had no ornamentation on the open stone sarcophagus, no hieroglyphics on the smooth granite walls, and literally nothing else that remotely resembled the burial chambers at the Valley of the Kings. For some reason, the entire pyramid did not feel like a resting place for a deceased body, and did not feel like a monument to the fourth dynasty Egyptian Pharaoh Khufu or anything of the kind. To me, the entire experience felt as if I had entered some sort of physical remnant of what used to be a place designed for a ritualistic purpose involving spiritual transcendence of heaven and earth to be noted by specific people.

As I entered the King's Chamber, I paused not only to see my immediate surroundings but to catch my breath. The first thing I noticed high in the wall just ahead of me was blue sky and air—blessed air—filtering through a rectangular air vent. At the time I wondered if it had been added, or if the body of the fourth dynasty Egyptian pharaoh Khufu needed air as much as I did. For a while I just stood there imagining a stream of blue grace bathing my lungs with good, clean air. Unlike the October air outside, the interior chamber seemed cool, almost refreshing.

While my body readjusted itself to the new surroundings, I noticed the people with me inside the King's Chamber. Most entered, looked, and left as if they had something important to do. One couple for some unknown reason moved slowly around the granite block walls of the pyramid with hands seeking goodness-only-knows-what through an energetically probing touch. For a while, I stared at them while my curiosity intensified, hoping I would get courage to move with them or at least ask them what in the world they were feeling with palms touching granite walls. I'm sensitive enough to discern the energy emanating from different stones and plants, as well as in nature, but I truly wanted to know if this couple could determine something other than the energy of ancient granite.

Instead, I noticed three others sitting on the floor with backs resting at the edge of the far wall; they were meditating. Frankly, for lack of anything else to do, I decided if they could sit down, I could, too. Peter had become so engrossed at the open sarcophagus that even if I had initiated conversation, he probably wouldn't have heard me. Sitting down would provide me with much needed back relief while giving me time to figure out why in the world I had felt that I had to come all this way to get inside this particular granite rectangle of a room inside the Great Pyramid to learn about personal power.

At first I naturally assumed the answers I sought would readily come, just as they had in my spiritual question and answer sessions I'd experienced throughout my European trips. With pen and paper in hand, I paused, ready to receive. Nothing happened. The stone floor beneath me upon which most tourists marveled just felt like an old flat rock to me—a very hard flat rock. I intuited nothing. I shifted sideways to my left a bit so my right leg and right hip would have less pressure. Then, closing my eyes in order to block out visual senses, again I tried to go into deep meditation in order to uncover what in the world I was supposed to learn in this pyramid experience.

Nothing happened. I heard no words; I heard no whispers of spirit beckoning me to write something profound. Instead of just sitting there like a heron waiting for a fish to swim by, I thought perhaps I would discern what I needed to know through another form of intuition: the

226

feeling state. But what I felt came from an aching back that sent waves of pain through my right hip, down my leg, and back again—nothing like the deep sensations of mysticism I expected.

So, I opened my eyes to see what everyone else was experiencing inside the King's Chamber. Just like several other tourists, Peter seemed to be inside his own world, having moved from the sarcophagus to the corner of the room in order to find the stone blocking what was thought to be airshafts. The meditators to my right still meditated deeply. The couple who were evidently experiencing some sort of pyramid laying-on-of-hands upon the granite wall had all but worked their way back to the exit. Of course, tourists came in, left, and were replaced by others doing the same thing.

Still I sat—or almost sat. I shifted entirely onto my left hip in mid-position between lying down and slightly reclining as if I were waiting for a handsome prince to seduce me with grapes one by one. Since this provided me with only a distinct sense of awkwardness instead of relief, I made the decision to sit upright again, leaning back on the wall for support with my legs angled straight out in front of me like a floppy Raggedy Ann doll exhausted after a hard day at play. By this time I had abandoned the intention of writing, for no specific words came through me from a Higher Source as had happened before. I could have stood to signal my intention of leaving to Peter, but I decided to wait a bit longer just in case I got an idea, message, or any kind of significant meaning. With this decision to stop trying so hard to receive some sort of insight, something inside of me relaxed enough to intuit.

It's always your choice.

At first, I thought someone near me had said these words, yet no one seemed to be remotely paying any attention to me, much less whispering thoughts into my consciousness.

Personal power. You always have a choice.

This time I knew for sure that these answers presented a chance for me to understand some tidbit of wisdom I needed to learn. However, I had not asked anything specific. Instead, I had just assumed I would have the opportunity to experience power, for hadn't my own intention in coming been to learn what personal power felt like? "Okay, I'm listening," I whispered out loud, hoping that more would be forthcoming.

This particular dialogue wasn't anything like I had intuited before. The energy behind these words truly felt beyond words altogether, although "mystical" and "powerful" come close. This energy was not evil in any way, for I had made sure this would not be my experience before the plane ever left Europe. The prayer of protection stayed with me moment by moment the entire time I visited Egypt. Even with this constant knowledge that I could rely on the presence of God to keep me safe, I carried with me at all times scriptures that reassured me if and when I needed them, like Psalms 16:1: "Keep me safe, O God, for in you I take refuge."

Because I had absolutely no idea what the energy felt like, I decided to ask. "What am I feeling?" I asked silently, for the dialog needed to be between God and me in whatever form God presented it to me. "What am I feeling?"

The answer came immediately, yet not through the silent whispers of inner stillness. Instead, it blasted me with power, power that could be described as from or of God—power from God in personal form. My back arched against the stone wall and my hands flew up into the air and then down again, while my soul inflated like a helium balloon.

What I felt came as the power of God available for personal use, a spiritual self-empowerment. For the first time in my entire life, I not only knew in my mind that I was part of God's creation, a child of God, but I felt the connection in my heart deep down through my soul into my very being.

When the realization came over me, I could not stop the giggles from coming. They emanated from the depths of my being, from some still point I had never before recognized as part of me but greater than me. Absolute, total joy flooded over my entire body, wrapped around my heart, and flew out of my mouth in happy little bursts of spirit. Not that it mattered to me whatsoever, but the meditators ceased to be focused, deciding instead to give me an awkward glance or two before continuing their silent processing; I had obviously interrupted them. With more joy than I have ever had, I felt me as me, as if an I AM of my own divinely-created presence found itself delightful, found itself delightfully recognized, found itself delightfully present in human form, and most of all found itself simply to be. So there was my I AM: a post-menopausal woman with a crooked back determined to hobble all the way up the pyramid in order to sit on the floor of the King's Chamber to discover her own empowerment through God's love and grace, and upon recognition, giggling about it. The laughter shot out of me in tiny explosive chuckles of ecstasy before bouncing off the solid granite walls like bubbles frothing out of an uncorked bottle of champagne.

For the first time in my entire life, I felt very real. I looked down my legs, awkwardly angled in a V-shape with thigh tissue that expressed itself expansively, and I loved every fluffy cell of them dearly. I noticed my hands, how the wrinkles and brown spots had begun to mimic not my mother's, but my grandmother's hands, and I loved not only mine, but hers also. I loved the people across the room who by now had decided to feel the stone wall in squatting positions. I loved the meditators, the tourists, and even the Egyptian officials who had the power to make my camera disappear. I even loved the annoying camel driver who intended to keep his word along with my American five-dollar bill. This wasn't love that I had in my head, nor was it love that I had in my heart. This type of love came from my spiritual soul center, my still point. It radiated outward and then drew back inside again, allowing me to know, to feel, and to actualize my own love. Most of all, I felt like God was not only inside that pyramid, but with me, as me, as the others in the room, and as even those who chose the dark side instead of the Light. At that moment, it all felt like God to me—far beyond rationalization.

It is your choice as to how you wish to incorporate this.

This time the still, small whispers of spirit rang true into my consciousness like clear bells of a cathedral pealing across the land. Instead of being unusually strong, different, or unrecognized like they had been before, they felt natural, intoned, and as if a Greater Wisdom had graced me with a specific vibrational shift. In other words, I felt different hearing them than I had before, as if everything in the world around me would now be seen from a different perspective. Yet, I still had the same feet, my back still sent painful electrical currents throughout innocent tissues, and my hands still looked like they were older than I felt. I listened intently, intuitively, hoping the words would lead to paragraphs about authenticity, love, and personal choice.

Not much more was intuited. Just words of opposites flowed around me like swarms of coupling flies.

> *Good or evil. Happy or sad. Depressed or joyful. Enthusiastic or lackadaisical. Stoic or moving forward. Light or dark. Psychological function or dysfunction. Your choice of response becomes your experience, not your reality. Your reality is of God.*

On they went; all the while I realized that my perception of myself had changed from one of no self-esteem to one of understanding myself as a woman who was on her own journey of self-discovery while gaining appreciation for her own talents, gifts, and innate being as she learned. No longer was I to think of myself as victim, but as one utilizing her personal power. No longer would I assume that things just randomly happen, but I would do my best to participate in the direction and way they happened to me, for me, through my own perspective and intentions. I also would change my attitude about others, seeing them also as journeymen on their own emotional paths whether they chose spiritual directions or not. Instead of hiding my intuition, I determined to use it daily while making important decisions as well as ordinary choices. I realized the Southern culture of my youth presented itself not as a directive, but as simply a form of culture I had the ability to accept or reject. Never again would I subjugate myself to the will of others just to be liked. Whatever my life presented to me in the future, I fully intended to participate in the choices of presentation, making sure I chose Light, chose God's love, and chose to feel love inside as me. Nothing else would do. I felt the strong, spiritual voice smile with me.

Somehow I got off of the floor of the King's Chamber, sashaying in my own happy, hobbling way to the exit. I looked down at all the stairs I had to maneuver before going into the narrow stone tunnel. I knew I could do it and do it without fatigue. It was my choice. When I got to the narrow tunnel, I paused momentarily, deciding to enter, to be able to breathe, and to be calm and steady as I crouched down into my duck-waddling imitation to get out into the clean, fresh, lung-baking Egyptian air. Again, it was my choice. For the first time, I had that power to make those determinations; I felt God's grace in my soul.

Securing my camera from the pile on the rocky shelf, I nodded to the officials with a smile. The fresh air felt good to me, but the sunshine felt better. I climbed down the rocky steps from the entranceway, happily touching the sandy ground again. As best I could, I shifted my feet from side to side, making my own footprints in the ancient sands. Nothing hovered above me—no walls, no narrow corridors, and no ceiling. Raising my arms fully above me, I looked upward into the blue, knowing the power of infinity somehow has to be part of choice. I felt forever fly through my bones, felt goodness as part of my life, and felt that my future somehow would be filled with my own choices of love, spirit, and grace. Whatever lay before me, I knew my reactions would be my own personal choice. I had that power now.

Once again, I looked back to the Great Pyramid looming into the firmament. I was still very much me, with the same painful back, the same body, and the same desire simply to find love and happiness in my life; I just had a new, more empowered and loving attitude.

Slowly, after meeting back up with Peter, I moved down the hill into the city of Cairo in order to return to my hotel. People packed into the blocks walking, I assumed, to and from work for the day. Five o'clock traffic evidently is a worldwide phenomenon. Sidewalks were packed with people going home after a long day's work, and the streets were filled with cars hugging each other's bumpers as their drivers traveled onward. For a moment, waves of panic threatened to move through me, for I truly did not wish to be on the street of Cairo alone; Peter had stopped to talk to a man he just met. Then I realized that even experiencing panic could be a choice. I determined not to experience it at that moment. For the most part, I did not, at least not intensely. What little anxiety I did feel had absolutely no effect on me whatsoever. On I walked into my future, continuing to persevere from my own fear causing darkness into the Light assisted by the powerful, all-sufficiency of God's grace. Tomorrow would be yet another day; I had empowering choices to make.

"Life is a series of natural and spontaneous changes. Don't resist them; that only creates sorrow. Let reality be reality. Let things flow naturally forward in whatever way they like."

LAO TZU

◆

CHAPTER ELEVEN

Passage

AS THE PLANE to Belgium ascended, I pressed my left hand to the window beside me while I looked down to the trees below, noting how the golds, crimsons, and oranges of fall blended together into swirls of nature's palette as the view of Atlanta got smaller and smaller. After the trip to Cairo, I hadn't felt the need to travel to different places in the world as a means of self-discovery. Actually, this trip was my first in four months. Instead of feeling excited about going back to Belgium, an unusual sense of foreboding seemed to be shadowing me, one I did not fully understand. Instead of feeling as if I were on a grand adventure, I dreaded the eight-hour flight. Yet, this time a very specific reason for returning for a couple of days overcame my sense of dread.

As usual, I bought a couple of granola bars and a banana on the long concourse at Hartsfield Atlanta International Airport, more to entertain myself than anything else. Along with the granola bars and the banana, pen, paper, and a rather mindless novel lay at my feet, all squished into a small canvas bag substituting as my purse. At the top of the bag I had stuffed the enormous book subsidized and initiated by the Etty Hillesum Foundation—*Etty: The Letters and Diaries of Etty Hillesum 1941–1945*—mainly so I could read it during the overnight flight to Belgium. As our aircraft soared above the clouds, I slid my seat-belted girth sideways in the narrow seat in order to reach into the canvas bag, pretending not to notice how my rear end slightly brushed the knee of the unknown gentleman sitting next to me on my right. I wanted to read more of Etty's thoughts. Even though I had read selections of the translation many times, deeper meanings always became more obvious.

Two weeks before, approximately one year following the Great Pyramid adventure, Peter had emailed me about a gathering of people from all over the world convening in Ghent, Belgium, to present papers about Etty Hillesum's diary. Called "The Etty Hillesum Congress," this conference was organized by the Etty Hillesum Research Centre [sic] of Ghent University in Ghent, Belgium. Twenty scholars from all over Europe were to present papers on the "Spirituality of Etty Hillesum." Although most of my intuitive need to travel had ended with the trip to the Great Pyramid at Giza, Etty's story called out to me because of her search for deeper meaning during the years of the Holocaust in her home in the Netherlands. Peter correctly assumed I would be interested.

Because the book was so heavy, I first positioned it on top of the tray table on the back of the seat in front of me. Not being comfortable with the distance of the book from my eyes, I placed the small airline pillow on my lap, centered the bottom edge of the book on the pillow, and rested the back of the book on the small tray. As I turned page after page, I quickly glimpsed phrases instead of sentences or paragraphs. It seemed as if Etty was rambling in her writing, looking for some sort of concrete foundation upon which to focus. The contrast between her life as it was—including the emotional dishevelment, relationship choices, and Holocaust—contrasted deeply with her sense of God, her only solid foundation. Occasionally, she wasn't even sure about that, or so it seemed to me. Because I so related to much of what she wrote, I wondered how the others at the conference would relate to her writing.

Looking out the window while noticing how the clouds covered the earth below me, I thought about how the earth was still there, yet obscured from my vision temporarily—just like my own future seemed to be. Just like my many years of spiritual awakening, the early years of the Holocaust were for her a profound time of personal liberation. From her home in Amsterdam, she wrote by hand almost daily during the years 1941 and 1942 in order to process her random thoughts on paper. Her relationships with her parents and colleagues, her two lovers, her health, and her emotions all found expressive voice in the tiny lettering of her sentences. Yet, the writing governed her emotions at deeper levels, as she also wrote of her feelings about Judaism, women, passion, health, and the disruption of Holland as the Nazi occupation took over the body and soul of Jewish culture. In the midst of all that horror, she sought the meaning of her existence, as well as her own spirituality as evidenced by her written conversations with God and about God.

That got my attention. In my own way, through my spiritual messages and journaling, I had been doing the same thing for not only a great portion of the time I visited Europe, but for several years previous. Since the hours I had spent in the King's Chamber of the Great Pyramid, all my spiritual writing, all my question and answer sessions, and all my written prayers evidently remained buried deep in the hot Egyptian sands of my own experience; I could not intuit one word.

With considerable effort, I secured the tray table to the seat in front of me while I gently shuffled my feet around my canvas bag in order to drag it out from under the seat in order to reach my yellow writing tablet and pen. Instead of asking a question as I used to do and then receiving an answer, I drew a huge question mark on my tablet large enough to cover the page from top to bottom. Over the question mark in letters made intense by retracing them time and time again, I wrote the words "what now." In Egypt, I had discovered my own depths, just like Hillesum had, and found them to be filled with love that came from some form of Divine grace of that creation called "me." But the feeling was so new; what in the world would I do with it? Everything only led to more questions for me these days. Maybe the entire six-year experience had been one of not doing, but of undoing? Of being? Of recognition of myself in a more profound way?

Since my divorce, so much had happened—so many mystical experiences, so much inner processing, and so much growth through solitary contemplation—not out there in the world of action, but in my self-perceptions. Contemplation became my intense purpose, just like Hillesum had experienced, driving me to travel to many places in the world just so I could intuit from the different locations what it felt like to feel holy, to feel free, to feel honor, and to feel spirituality. Most of all, I learned what it felt like to witness myself as love, and to witness God's love in everyone. The inner journey had become my life, not out of curiosity, but rather as a need to survive. My experiences were intense, but profound; mystical, but changing; frightening, but loving; ecstatic, but ordinary. Even with all the newfound wisdom, still I did not know what could be next. Was this the end of something, or was it a beginning? I had no idea, yet I had multitudes of questions.

Every page of Etty's diary intermingled with profound opposites, spiritual highs and daily lows. Reading those passages felt like I was conversing with the inner dialog of her soul; the deep thoughts felt familiar to me. I had not only written my own passages through the spiritual message experiences, but had lived their soul-felt wisdom as my own sacred story. Frankly, I wondered how her diary affected others in the world. Perhaps I could determine my own future by getting to know Hillesum more. Even though Peter would not be attending, I had made the perplexed decision to attend the convention by myself.

Endlessness flew past me just outside the tiny window, to the world of clouds below and sky above. The cerulean blue touched me, engulfed me, and enclosed me like a divine mother's loving hug. Rays of sunlight painted the clouds with an amber glow, which then turned into gentle wisps of ginger and auburn glows of sunset. For what seemed forever, I stared out that window, caught between here and there, past and present, now and future. On I watched, waiting for something—anything—to let me know the details of whatever it was that seemed forthcoming yet just out of conscious recognition. For several months I had been feeling as if change once again would assert itself into my life, though I did not have one clue as to what this change would be about. However, I knew for certain that it would happen. As our plane eased upward, I clutched the Hillesum book close to my heart, as if the energetic nuances behind her thoughts could penetrate mine.

"It must be a good book," the man sitting next to me mused. "You only read about three pages before you had to pause to think about it." He folded his newspaper back into just-delivered shape before shoving it into the little pocket in the seat before him that was already stuffed with his water bottles and the magazines no one reads.

"Sometimes what you think may be real is actually very real but for an entirely different reason," I answered back. Even though my answer did not match his question, it seemed to be quite enough for a small conversation between two strangers who really did not care to even know each other's names.

My seating companion turned toward me, looking just over his glasses as if he wanted to see something from a different point of view. "And this book let you come to that conclusion this fast? What is that book?"

"Oh, this is Etty Hillesum's diary," I explained. "You know, she left a diary and letters about the time in her life during the Holocaust?"

"Ah, yes," he answered, turning his eyes toward the front of the plane.

Frankly, I was not sure he knew about her diary at all. But, evidently the topic also gave him something to think about or perhaps gave him something not to think about. For the rest of the flight, we said nothing else to each other, than my "excuse me" when I climbed over him to walk to the end of the narrow center aisle to use the facilities.

Just outside of my window, a memory played above the clouds just like a sitcom on television. I saw myself—afraid, alone, and hopeful, pulling along a fifty-pound bag of clothing, computer, and purse in which I had tucked a map of Bruges—dutifully following someone I hardly knew. Hoping all would work out for the best, I crossed the arched stone bridge into a metaphysical adventure more profound than I could have ever imagined.

If I were honest with myself, I would have to admit that I longed for love that fateful day on the bench in Bruges when I first met Peter. Even though I had determined I had to do my inner work myself and that I had to delve into my own mysteries to find that soul longing to express herself as me, I knew I did need help just managing the day-to-day activities of life. For a while, Peter had sufficed as that help, a welcome bridge from dysfunction to function.

Just as Theseus had served as a rite of passage for Ariadne, Peter had assisted my rite of passage from dysfunction and fear into a more manageable lifestyle. His travel expertise had allowed me to safely journey to those destinations that called out to me from specific esoteric mysteries. I knew from the beginning that our relationship never was about love, not the kind of love where man and woman bond together in marriage and commitment. Peter and I were friends, spiritual companions at most. In fact, Peter and I had several conversations about my dreams of the man coming into my life; it was not Peter.

The first of those dreams started with me peeking into the window of a one-story brick library. *A rather thin man is sitting at a table studying something intently. His hair is salt-and-pepper grey, and his facial expression seems intent, as if he is really busy with his book, busy with his life.* In subsequent dreams, he looks up at me staring at the window, but goes back to his book reading. Several nights before this last fateful trip to Belgium, the man in my dream had gotten up, walked to the door of the library, and opened the door. I hadn't yet shared this with Peter, because we were not talking to each other as regularly as we were heading into different directions in life.

In the myth of the Minotaur, if Ariadne had not left the home of her father, if she had not bonded in some way with Theseus, if she had not been left by him on the island alone, she never would have been discovered by Dionysus, who provided her the chance for happiness ever after. It took all of these chaotic events to get her to the place of her desires.

Perhaps crossing that bridge with Peter years ago was the catalyst to get me to my own dreams, whatever they were. Sitting on the plane to Belgium yet again, all I wanted was the same thing I have always ever wanted: love. From infancy, I have craved profound spiritual love so deep one falls intently into its mystery. So far, I hadn't found it, at least not in human form. No relationship can ever substitute for the spiritual, and I'd had to learn to love myself first. At least the metaphysical experiences had guided me in this direction.

◆ ◆ ◆ ◆ ◆

After a flight that seemed to last forever, I joined the groggy, weary travelers in line at the customs desk.

"Next!" the customs official in charge of my line shouted, his hand gesturing above his head as if to create enough wind to blow askew the hair on his thirty year-old head.

Just as I always had the last five years of travel, I handed him my passport with confidence.

He flipped through the pages three times before his already exaggerated demeanor intensified. Any wind he'd created with the waving of his hand changed to gale-like force. I had become his enemy for some reason unbeknownst to me. He looked at me, down at the passport, then around the room as if he wanted to see who could be watching. The scowl on his face foretold the troubles yet to come.

"You have been in Belgium too much this year," he shouted, loud enough for not only me to hear, but the entire hall. All conversation between the people in four lines approximately twenty to thirty feet long screeched to a halt as the fearful silence swooped upon the room like a bird of prey. I had become fodder for some unforeseen need of his to prove a point.

"No, I don't think so," I managed to stammer. "I have been very careful to make sure I stayed within the limits of international travel laws." My knees gave way out of shock. However, I was able to maintain a steady posture because I had proof of my travel times in my canvas bag. It never dawned on me he wouldn't be interested in hearing my explanation.

"You just look at these dates," he exclaimed in a voice mean enough to stop a stampeding elephant. He waved the passport in an exaggerated motion above his head once more so that everyone in the entire hall could see it. "Just read the numbers here on the passport. You are breaking the law!"

I squinted but could not see the stamped marks on the passport because he was now waving it vigorously back and forth between us.

Visions of imprisonment in a foreign place with me hovering in a corner afraid to breathe, starving, and without anyone to call for help flew through my mind. Maybe because of my previous fear of aggressive men, my emotions caused me to overreact to the situation. Nonetheless, this official felt out of control. Somehow, this conversation needed to be turned around. I reached for the passport in order to read the dates that were causing him such trouble.

Abruptly, he withdrew it, shouting, "You cannot touch this. At this point, your passport is in my possession. The dates here are quite clear to me. You have broken the law. You do not need to be in Belgium anymore!"

The panic that had waned after Birkenau and all but disappeared after the trip to Egypt started once again, moving through me like a strike of lightning. Actually, from the way the man was behaving, I wasn't sure I wasn't going to be struck in some way. I tried once again to explain even without knowing the dates he mentioned.

"I have all my airline ticket receipts in my bag proving when I have been in the country the last two years. You'll be able to coordinate them with the passport dates." I reached into the canvas bag, which by this time felt like it carried stones instead of books, papers, and granola wrappings.

Again, he bellowed, "The dates are here, printed clearly! I do not need your artificial paperwork." Still he held up the passport for everyone to see. And undeniably they were indeed looking at me. "You are in violation. I am in charge, and I find you in violation."

I closed my eyes momentarily, partly to fight the tears that lapped on the shores of my face like overwrought waves of an angry sea. Frankly, I didn't know how to handle this man. I had looked at my passport many times before I left, checking the date of my last travel on the passport stamp. I also remembered that the date had not been stamped thoroughly. Part of the numbers had printed incompletely, making the numerals eight, six, and nine indistinguishable from each other. When coupled with the fact that in Belgium the day and date is backwards from the way it is in the United States, I had found it necessary to check the previous entrance dates by airline receipts for confirmation before I traveled. Perhaps he was either misinterpreting the date or had gotten the day and month mixed up. Yet, I knew to correct him would only lead to more anger on his part, which would only lead to more panic on my part. I had to change the energetic dynamics of this conversation fast.

Just as I had in the temple area of the Nile when the trinket merchants stood around me asking what I thought of war and aggression, I tapped into Spirit while my eyes were still closed. *"Tell me what I need to do,"* I asked silently. *"What do I need to do to calm this man down?"*

Be the mouse, the thoughts came to me from somewhere beyond simple consciousness. *Be the mouse; explain why you are here with meekness drenched with enthusiasm. Most of all, make him the hero and apologize.*

I opened my eyes and then focused upon this man who had evidently decided to make an example out of me. I took a deep breath to center myself. Although my tears were still rolling, I began to play my part of this little charade just as the wisdom I'd channeled suggested.

"I've tried so hard to obey the laws of international travel. Maybe I read the passport wrong," I added in my most remorseful voice, knowing full well I had not. "I'm just coming for a week's conference to listen to people give papers about Etty Hillesum, a Holocaust victim. Belgium is the perfect place for this. People here seem wise and quite understanding. I'm so sorry if I have done anything wrong. I will be more cautious from now on."

With that, I threw this man the only bones I had, hoping to calm what I interpreted as savageness. I put my former airline ticket receipts in my blue canvas bag, stuffing them on the side pocket just in case I needed them quickly. For added effect, I hung my head just a tad, saying nothing more. After all, if he had not previously wanted to hear me explaining the facts, I knew full well he would not hear anything other than what he wanted to hear. I gave him full pelt "I was wrong and you are right" to the best of my ability.

It worked.

He paused, looked around at each face of the travelers in front of him, and then glanced sideways to the other official on his left. This second official had stopped doing the passport checking procedure for a moment in order to listen to this particular tirade. I wondered then, and wonder still now, if he believed his companion or thought he was out of control just as I did. No matter, my apology worked.

"Well, you better not do this again," he chortled, handing me back my passport and sending me on my way.

Unfortunately, I did not get over the incident easily: I cried intermittently for two days. Something about this man's voice took me back to places in my memory I did not wish to visit. It wasn't just the fact that I evidently could not speak my own truth to this official who had an agenda to not hear me for his own purposes, an experience I also have had in the past; it was something else. Intermittently, something nagged my thoughts the entire first day of the conference.

During the second day of the conference, a speaker from Italy came to the front of about fifty or so participants present, rearranging her printed speech on the podium's angled top before she spoke. I turned a page in my notes while she got ready for the presentation of her paper, noting that each speaker, regardless of religion, felt that Hillesum was a great example of his or her specific religion. For instance, the Catholic presenter saw Hillesum's diary as parallel with the truths of his faith, as did the Protestant, Islam, Hindu, and, of course, Hebrew presenters. I wondered how this Italian would present her version of Hillesum's truths.

Unfortunately, I couldn't understand this speaker from Italy, not only because of her heavy accent, but also because I was sitting toward the back of the room. I always hear best from the front of a room, but the front chairs had been taken by the time I arrived. I reached into the same canvas bag I'd carried with me on the plane and pulled out my heavy book. Others were following along with the speaker as she quoted from the different diary passages of Etty. I thought perhaps I would pretend to do the same. After flipping quickly through a couple of pages, a passage caught my attention rather profoundly. On July 16, 1942, Etty Hillesum wrote in her diary, "Have You any other plans for me, oh God?"

This one line from Hillesum's writing had so much impact upon me that I have absolutely no recollection of anything else the speaker said or how the audience reacted to her well-researched paper. Evidently, this particular sentence carried my own truth before me like a road sign pointing the way. The words of the customs official flew into my face once more: "You do not need to be in Belgium anymore."

I stayed for the rest of the conference, amazed that one woman's inner thoughts could affect people from different countries so much. At one point Hillesum wrote that she thought not to destroy her old diaries, because she wanted to read about the woman that she once was. Hoping her writing would survive, she hastily threw them out of small slats in her transport car as she rode the train to Birkenau. Like Hillesum, I also had changed.

The person I was who had to hug the sides of the train station before entering the daylight had grown into a person who moved from one station to another without undue effort. The person who had so many fears left most of them in the Temple of Isis, clinging to the words of the 23rd Psalm that promised a table being prepared before her in the presence of enemies. I knew this to be true because I had just experienced it in the airport on the way to the conference. The woman in Birkenau who tried to protect the twins by hiding them behind her skirt when she got off of the train just inside the Gates of Death never visited me again in my dreams. In fact, all versions of this Holocaust dream that had plagued me were non-existent at this point.

During lunch that last day of the conference, food seemed grossly unimportant. Instead of dining, I chose to wander the streets in the Patersol area of Ghent. More than ever I felt like those ancient cobblestones had something to do with my own feeling of home. Yet, instead of feeling like I had been there before as I did that first day when walking upon them, I knew for certain my definition of home had expanded. Instead of home being a location, shelter, and stability, home resided inside the deeper crevices of my soul. From Spirit I came, Spirit is my presence, and to There I will return. This is the home I take with me every moment regardless of where I am. The ancient houses packed next to each other like tall thin ladies conjoined at the hips made me smile. Still, I knew for certain I had to leave them.

On the way back to the conference, I stood one last time on St. Michael's Bridge over the River Leie, just as I had that first trip to Ghent when I finally made it downtown. I watched the boats of tourists travel under the bridge and then back again. The river flowed beneath me, originating somewhere and ending somewhere else. For me, Belgium had been about the journey, not the location. Somewhere, somehow, I realized another familiar place in the world would welcome me one day. Like walking right out of a picture page in a book of ancient history, I knew my own pages would be turning yet again to a new story, filled with just as much wonder as this chapter of my life had been.

Five days later, I left Belgium, only returning once more about eight months later to gather what few belongings I wanted to take with me. Within a few days, I closed a very small bank account, changed the Belgian email address to my American address, and disposed of all the travel literature I had accumulated. My books, furniture, and the many mugs I had gathered as souvenirs those years when traveling I left with Peter to dispose of as he saw fit.

The last time I left Belgium, Peter did not drive me to the airport as he had so many times before. (Frankly, I don't even remember whether

I caught the train or scheduled a taxi service for transportation early that last morning in Belgium.) Our treasured friendship had served as a point of passage for me to get from where I thought I was psychologically and spiritually to I AM.

As the jet took off from the Belgium airport, one last time I said goodbye to the land that had nurtured my soul back into love again. I felt like I was stepping into a new world, although I had not one clue what this new world would be.

◆ ◆ ◆ ◆ ◆

Several months after I got back from Belgium, I wandered outside my house to sit on the back patio. Large stones decorated the area on the outside of the plain, cement slab. I had placed a carved statue of a woman in a seated yoga pose on top of one of the larger flat rocks. She seemed so content this particular night, just like I felt. I nestled into the lounge chair in order to bask in the early nighttime air along with her. My strength now came from God—my stone foundation, my fortress, and my love.

Lowering the recliner position so that my face angled to the tops of the trees in my wooded backyard, I stared at the stars dancing between the late spring leaves. First I would see one of them, and then it would be gone because a branch of leaves would blow in the breeze, hiding it. I smiled watching those stars dance among the leaves because it reminded me of a child's game of hide and seek. Still, only the brightest stars played that night, because the Atlanta skyline stays bright with artificial lights. I vowed one day I would live in a place where the stars can all shine brightly. They beckon me to float far beyond myself into realms unseen but felt, realized at spiritual levels, and loved entirely.

As night deepened into the mysteries, I stayed on that recliner under the August evening sky. Time became quite unimportant; instead, the moment stretched out beyond the simplicity of my own wandering thoughts. No longer would I be in Atlanta for only four months at a time before traveling somewhere, experiencing some new adventure where the earth taught me how to feel strong, how choices could be made for good or evil, or how confusing life can become when journeying to the center of the soul. No longer would it be necessary to journey to the most profound sites of abuse in the world just to discover the immense power of forgiveness. I pulled my legs up to my abdomen then stretched them out beyond me again, allowing a new thought to enter from a place I had never witnessed before, much less actualized. Truly, for everyone I knew presently and everyone I had known in my past, I wished happiness. In a way I had not understood before, I loved them as the souls they were.

My life, after all, had never consisted only of my experiences, whatever they have been or may be. Instead, my life was part of a Greater Presence. Just above me, the trees grew still, allowing the stars to linger within my sight for a moment. I did not see them, though. Instead, I began to feel them, to feel their pull, to feel their infinity, to feel their love.

Reaching out to my sides with arms extended and palms upward, I felt this love surge through me. I became part of the green leaves on the trees, yet still ever-present. I became part of the trees' trunks straight and tall, so proud to be alive. I felt roots going deep into Mother Earth, nurturing my very soul into unconditional spiritual unity while branches reached up to the heavenly light.

Although the sky was dark with night, I felt the peacefulness of blue sky surge right through me. I became the sky, I soared through the sky, and I loved the sky. Infinity no longer lingered in conceptualized thought, but became unlimited possibility. I looked to the stars glowing out of creation, twinkling light right through me. It was then I knew with every fiber of my being, every thread of my soul, every moment of my spiritual conception: Love exists out there in the trees, in the sky, in the stars. Love lives in the eyes of not only my fondest friends and family but in the deeper recesses of people I thought were my enemies. Love is not only the experiences I have but also the space between these events, these holy moments of every day, all day, each day. No longer would it be necessary anymore to look to others for love, to look to the spiritual places on the earth to show me how to feel love, or to look to religious practices to learn about love. All those were part of a spiritual dynamic, just teaching points along the journey to fruition.

Somewhere the angels were singing. Somewhere, the Seraphim already knew. Finally, I understood. I felt love throughout my soul. *Life couldn't be any sweeter,* I thought before adding, *I am LOVE.*

I drew my hands back to my chest over my heart, not to cover it but to integrate every cell in my body. For over sixty years I had done what others wanted me to do in order to be loved. I had become what others wanted me to be to feel loved. I had left a marriage because I did not feel loved. I had journeyed over the entire world discovering different aspects of love. Now I knew for sure. I knew for sure how I fit into the bigger picture. What I realized that night under the stars in such a profound way affected my entire outlook. It had been with me the entire time. All I had to do was open up to it. Love flooded my soul.

"I am Love," I whispered so softly only the angels could hear me. "I AM."

For a while I remained still. The leaves on the trees started to move again, as if to bring me back into the present. The feeling remained, however, swirling through me, around me, and as me. I had no idea what the future would bring. I had no idea how I would be living the rest of my wild, wonderful life. Yet I did know it would be authentic, just as God created me to be.

That night in my dreams, the eagle and I were one as I soared through the open sky.

Books Mentioned

Dean, Paula and Sherry Suib Cohen. *It Ain't All About the Cooking*. New York: Simon and Schuster Paperbacks, 2007.

Evans, Patricia. *Controlling People: How to Recognize, Understand, and Deal with People Who Try to Control You*. Massachusetts: Adams Media Corporation, 2002.

Evans, Patricia. *The Verbally Abusive Relationship: How to Recognize It and How to Respond*. Massachusetts: Adams Media Corporation, 1996.

Merriam-Webster Dictionary and Thesaurus. United States: Merriam-Webster, Incorporated, 2007.

Myss, Caroline. *Anatomy of the Spirit: The Seven Stages of Power and Healing*. New York: Three Rivers Press, 1996.

Rilke, Ranier Maria. *Letters to a Young Poet*. Translated with a Foreword by Stephen Mitchell. New York: Random House, 1984.

Sheldrake, Rupert. *The Presence of the Past: Morphic Resonance and the Habits of Nature*. London: Icon Books, Ltd, 2011.

Smelik, Klass A. D., ed and Arnold J. Pomerans, trans. *Etty: The Letters and Diaries of Etty Hillesum 1941-1943*. Michigan: William B. Eerdmans Publishing Company, 2002.

Weiss, Brian. *Many Lives, Many Masters*. New York: Simon and Schuster Inc., 1988.

About the Author

PADDY FIEVET spent the first fifty years of her life following Southern society's directives for a conventional life, embracing traditional church-going religion just as she had been told to do, and agreeing with almost everything anyone said. Although her connection to God remained strong, after decades of becoming the period at the end of society's sentence, she was barely surviving. To thrive, she turned to the Divine for direction, ready to give up everything she held near and dear in order to discover innate Love, joy, and purpose found within her own sacred story. Embracing her intuition as the voice of that Divine connection, she was led to travel the world to rediscover her authentic self at deeper, meaningful levels, eventually earning a PhD in Metaphysics. Through this transformational awakening, she realized that instead of just living, Life desires to express itself through each of us, a huge difference that embraces the qualities of allowing, trust, and instinctual faith. Her first two books, *When Life Cried Out* and *Making of a Mystic* are being published in 2014. She is currently writing her third book with another to follow shortly thereafter. Currently Paddy works as a modern mystic, speaker, storyteller, teacher, and writer as she assists others in discovering their own Sacred Story. She's happily married and loves living in North Carolina. Visit Paddy online at www. paddyfievet.com.